Take Charge of Your Health! Self-Assessment Workbook with Review and Practice Tests

for

Donatelle and Davis

Access To Health

Sixth Edition

Rebecca J. Donatelle
Oregon State University

Vickie Krenz

Allyn and Bacon
Boston London Toronto Sydney Tokyo Singapore

ISBN 0-205-30506-7

Printed in the United States of America

10 9 8 7 6 5 4 3 2   03 02 01 00 99

Contents

Preface

On the surface, the concept of taking charge of your health probably seems easy. But when put into practical terms, developing a personal and relevant plan of action can be difficult. It requires general health knowledge, the ability to critically assess yourself, and the discipline to set and follow through on personal goals. That's where this book can be of help to you. *Take Charge of Your Health* contains two distinct sections: a self-assessment workbook and a set of review and practice tests.

- The self-assessment guide, pages 1 to 191, can help you identify behavior patterns that affect your health status - both positively and negatively. Upon completion of each assessment, review the results and consider whether you need to make any adjustments in your health practices.

- The practice and review tests follow the self-assessment guide and are located on pages A-1 to A-75. This section includes two tests for each chapter that will assist you in the development of health knowledge. As you progress through *Access to Health,* use the tests to check your retention of information.

Materials within the self-assessment and test sections correspond directly with the chapters in *Access to Health.* Use these materials in whichever way is most appropriate for your purposes, such as in preparation for upcoming exams. For greatest effectiveness, the following three-step model is recommended.

Step 1: Prior to beginning a chapter, complete the self-assessment exercises that apply to the chapter information and review the results to identify where attention may need to be placed. This will also help you identify content areas that need to be focused on during the course of study or areas that you may wish to explore further.

Step 2: After completing the reading and study of a chapter, take the corresponding practice and review tests and score your results.

Step 3: Once you have finished the chapter, review your completed self-assessment exercises and identify your strengths and weaknesses. Set goals for making improvements where necessary and consider strategies for attaining these goals. Your Access to *Health* text, including the Health Resource Guide in the book, can serve as a helpful resource for goal setting.

The exercises in *Take Charge of Your Health* can be used throughout your course of study and beyond. By using the self-assessments and practice and review tests provided in this workbook, you will be better equipped to truly "Take Charge" of your health.

Health Improvement Project

Name: _____ Date: _____

Purpose: This health improvement project provides you with the opportunity to apply concepts covered in class toward improving any aspect of health. The project includes four steps:

Step 1   Assess your own health behaviors by completing Martin's Index of Health Behavior (1-2) and decide on a particular health behavior to be changed during the academic term.

Step 2   Complete the Health Improvement Contract (1-1a) to plan, guide, and evaluate your progress toward changing a specific habit that is detrimental to your health.

Step 3   Write an abstract of three separate journal articles that are pertinent to the behavior change. Your instructor can provide examples of current scholarly health journals that you might use for researching your area of interest. Each written abstract should include the following information:

   1. Author, date published, title of article, name of journal, volume numbers, and pages.

   2. Several paragraphs stating the main points of the article and conclusions reached if the article was a research report.

   3. An evaluation of how this material will be helpful in validating or following through with the proposed behavior change. You should ask the question "Of what value is this information to me now or later in life?"

Step 4   Keep a journal and write two journal entries per week describing your progress and pitfalls as you work toward your personal goal. Include barriers encountered, successes, emotional and physical reactions to the changes, reactions of others to the changes, and your comments and feelings about the project. For some changes, a daily entry would be appropriate. The more seriously you treat your journal writing, the more you will benefit from this project.

Step 5   Write an evaluation of your health improvement project by answering the questions on form 1-1b.

HEALTH IMPROVEMENT CONTRACT

Name: _____ Date: _____

Health habit or behavior I intend to change: _____
_____
_____

Goal to be reached (in specific terms): _____
_____
_____

Current self-assessed status (refer to self-assessment scale from 1-2
Martin's Index of Health Behavior):
_____
_____
_____

Benefits I anticipate as a result of the change:
(1) _____
(2) _____
(3) _____

Any benefits of **not** changing?
(1) _____
(2) _____
(3) _____

What will happen if I don't change? _____
_____
_____

Specific activities, behaviors, attitudes, or thoughts I will monitor and
chart during the 9-week period: _____
_____
_____
_____
_____
_____

Target date to reach goal: _____

Indicators of successful achievement of my health behavior change will be:_

_____

_____

How I will reward myself (daily, weekly, overall) for this change: _____

_____

_____

_____

_____

Names and phone numbers of HIP partners and times to meet to discuss

progress: _____

_____

_____

_____

Name: _____   Date: _____

Signature _____

Instructor's signature _____

3

Name: _____ Date: _____

1. Did you follow your plan? If so, did your timeline work? Were journal entries helpful? Were your support people valuable? If not, where did your plan break down? Was your goal unreasonable? What barriers hindered your progress?

Health Habit or Behavior: _____

2. How do you feel about your efforts and any changes made?

3. How will you maintain your changed behavior?

MARTIN'S INDEX OF HEALTH BEHAVIOR

Name: _____ Date: _____

Directions: For the following questions put a check in the blank by the choice that best describes your health behavior. There are no right or wrong answers. The best answer is the one that honestly describes you.

1. How many days per week do you eat breakfast?

    ___ a. 6-7   ___ c. 2-3
    ___ b. 4-5   ___ d. 0-1

2. Which choice most closely describes your daily eating pattern?

    ___ a. eating snack foods (potato chips, soda pop, etc.) whenever I am hungry
    ___ b. eating one balanced meal per day and eating snack foods at other times during the day
    ___ c. eating two balanced meals a day and eating snack foods at other times of the day
    ___ d. eating three balanced meals a day and eating snack foods at other times of the day
    ___ e. eating three balanced meals per day and not snacking

3. How many days per week do you eat a balanced diet that includes the minimum number of servings from the four food groups as listed below?
    2 servings of meat or protein substitutes
    2 servings of dairy products
    4 servings of breads and cereals
    4 servings of fruits and vegetables

    ___ a. 6-7   ___ c. 2-3
    ___ b. 4-5   ___ d. 0-1

4. How many servings per day of concentrated sources of sugar (soda pop, candy, cookies, etc.) do you eat?

    ___ a. 0 or less than 1   ___ c. 3-4
    ___ b. 1-2   ___ d. 5 or more

5. Considering your height and body build, how many pounds within your ideal weight do you fall?

    ___ a. within 10 pounds
    ___ b. within 20 pounds
    ___ c. within 30 pounds
    ___ d. more than 30 pounds from ideal

6. Which choice most closely describes your dieting behavior?

___ a. never being overweight, so never dieting

___ b. being more than 10 pounds overweight, but not dieting

___ c. when overweight, going on a fad diet to lose weight quickly

___ d. when overweight, attempting to lose weight gradually (1-2 pounds per week) by increasing exercise *or* decreasing food intake

___ e. when overweight, attempting to lose weight gradually (1-2 pounds per week) by increasing exercise *and* decreasing food intake

7. What is the average number of hours per night that you sleep?

___ a. more than 10   ___ d. 5-6

___ b. 9-10   ___ e. 0-4

___ c. 7-8

8. How often do you use seatbelts while driving or riding in a car?

___ a. always

___ b. never in town and always on the highway

___ c. sometimes in town and sometimes on the highway

___ d. never

9. How often do you drive or ride with someone under the influence of alcohol or drugs?

___ a. more than once per week

___ b. once per week

___ c. a few times per year

___ d. never

10. Which choice best describes your consumption of alcoholic beverages?

___ a. not drinking

___ b. drinking one drink or less per day

___ c. drinking two drinks or less per day

___ d. drinking two drinks or less on weekdays, more than two drinks per day on weekends

___ e. drinking more than two drinks per day on most days

11. Which choice best describes your drug use patterns (over the counter, prescription, and recreational drugs)?

___ a. using the drugs I want whenever I want

___ b. using the drugs I feel I need while following common sense

___ c. using only medically required drugs exactly as directed

___ d. rarely using drugs of any kind

12. How many cups of caffeinated beverages (coffee, tea, cola, etc.) do you drink per day?

   ___ a. none or less than 1   ___ c. 4-6

   ___ b. 1-3   ___ d. 7 or more

13. Which choice best describes your cigarette smoking behavior?

   ___ a. not smoking

   ___ b. smoking less than one pack per day

   ___ c. smoking 1-2 packs per day

   ___ d. smoking more than 2 packs per day

14. How many times per week do you exercise aerobically (biking, jogging, swimming, aerobics, etc.)?

   ___ a. less than 1   ___ d. 3-4

   ___ b. 1   ___ e. 5 or more

   ___ c. 2

15. How many times per week do you do other types of exercise (weight lifting, tennis, calisthenics, racquetball, basketball, etc.) besides aerobic activities?

   ___ a. less than 1   ___ d. 3-4

   ___ b. 1   ___ e. 5 or more

   ___ c. 2

16. How often do you brush your teeth?

   ___ a. after every meal

   ___ b. twice per day

   ___ c. once per day

   ___ d. less than once per day

17. How often do you have a dental check-up?

   ___ a. never or only when something is wrong

   ___ b. every 2-3 years

   ___ c. every year

   ___ d. every six months

18. How often do you have a medical check-up?

   ___ a. never or only when something is wrong

   ___ b. only for Pap tests or other checks

   ___ c. every 3-5 years

   ___ d. at least every 2 years

19. How often do you read the labels of foods and over-the-counter drugs before purchasing them?

___ a. always   ___ c. sometimes

___ b. usually   ___ d. rarely

20. How many times per week do you make a conscientious effort to manage your stress by utilizing progressive relaxation, exercise, religion, music, or other stress-reduction techniques?

___ a. 6-7   ___ c. 2-3

___ b. 4-5   ___ d. 0-1

21. Which choice most correctly describes your closest interpersonal relationship?

___ a. not having a friend

___ b. having a friend, but I am not able to share my real feelings with the person

___ c. having a friendship where I can sometimes share my real feelings, but sometimes can't

___ d. having a friendship where I can always share my real feelings

22. How many servings per day of foods high in saturated fats or cholesterol (whole milk, eggs, sausage, bacon, red meat, etc.) do you eat?

___ a. 0   ___ c. 3-4

___ b. 1-2   ___ d. 5 or more

23. How often do you limit your consumption of salt by doing things like not salting your foods at the table, using salt sparingly when preparing foods, and limiting your intake of salty foods?

___ a. always   ___ c. sometimes

___ b. usually   ___ d. rarely

24. How often do you practice breast self-examination (female) or testicular self-examination (male)?

___ a. every month

___ b. every 2-6 months

___ c. less frequently than every 6 months

___ d. never

25. Which choice best describes your contraceptive use?

    ___ a. not sexually active, so don't use contraceptives

    ___ b. attempting to get pregnant or am pregnant, so don't use contraceptives

    ___ c. sexually active and always use contraceptives

    ___ d. sexually active and usually use contraceptives

    ___ e. sexually active and sometimes use contraceptives

    ___ f. sexually active and rarely use contraceptives

Scoring:

For Items: 1, 3, 4, 5, 8, 12, 13, 16, 19, 20, 22, 23, 24
    a=3, b=2, c=1, d=0

For Items: 2, 9, 11, 17, 18, 21
    a=0, b=1, c=2, d=3

For Item: 6
    a=3, b=1, c=0, d=2, e=3

For Item: 7
    a=1, b=2, c=3, d=2, e=0

For Item: 10
    a=3, b=3, c=2, 2=1, e=0

For Items: 14 and 15
    a=0, b=1, c=2, d=3, e=3

For Item: 25
    a=3, b=3, c=3, d=2, e=1, f=0

Total scores can range from 0-75. Health behavior is generally *poor* if the total score is below 25; *average but needing change* if between 25 and 50; and *good* if over 50.

Source: Joan Peterson Martin, The Relationship of Self Concept to Health Behavior in Community College Students (unpublished thesis). University of Chicago, December 1985.

Life Orientation Test

Name: _____ Date: _____

Purpose: Do you see the cup as half full or half empty? Are you generally optimistic or pessimistic? Do you expect good things to happen or do you find the cloud around the silver lining? Optimism and pessimism are general expectations about what will happen to us--and how well we can influence what will happen to us--in the future. The Life Orientation Test may provide you with insight into whether you are basically optimistic or pessimistic in your outlook on life.

Directions: Indicate whether or not each of the items represents your feelings by writing a number in the blank space according to the following code. Then use the scoring key at the end of the test.

4 = strongly agree   1 = disagree
3 = agree   0 = strongly disagree
2 = neutral

____ 1. In uncertain times, I usually expect the best.

____ 2. It's easy for me to relax.

____ 3. If something can go wrong for me, it will.

____ 4. I always look on the bright side of things.

____ 5. I'm always optimistic about my future.

____ 6. I enjoy my friends a lot.

____ 7. It's important for me to keep busy.

____ 8. I hardly ever expect things to go my way.

____ 9. Things never work out the way I want them to.

____ 10. I don't get upset too easily.

____ 11. I'm a believer in the idea that "every cloud has a silver lining."

____ 12. I rarely count on good things happening to me.

Scoring: In order to arrive at your total score for the test, first reverse your score on items 3, 8, 9, and 12. That is, on those four items, 4 is changed to 0, 3 is changed to 1, 2 remains a 2, 1 is changed to 3, and 0 is changed to 4. Now add the numbers of items 1, 3, 4, 5, 8, 9, 11, and 12 (items 2, 6, 7, and 10 are "fillers" only, and your responses on them are not scored as part of the test. Your total score can vary from 0 to 32. Write your **total score here** ____.

Interpretation: Scheier and Carver (1985) provide the following norms for the test, based on administration to 357 undergraduate men and 267 undergraduate women. The average score for men was 21.03 (standard deviation = 4.56), and the average score for women was 21.41 (standard deviation = 5.22). The majority of undergraduates score between 16 and 26. Scores below 16 are quite pessimistic. Scores above 26 are quite optimistic.

Source: Michael F. Scheier and Charles S. Carver, 1985. Optimism, coping and health: Assessment and implications of generalized outcome expectancies. Health Psychology, 4, 219-247.

Multidimensional Health Locus of Control

Name: _____   Date: _____

Directions: Indicate your degree of agreement with each statement by placing a number in the blank before it. Use the following scale:

        5 = strongly agree   2 = disagree
        4 = agree   1 = strongly disagree
        3 = neither agree nor disagree

Subscale A: **Internal**

___ 1. If I get sick, it is my own behavior that determines how soon I get well.

___ 2. I am in control of my health.

___ 3. When I get sick, I am to blame.

___ 4. The main thing that affects my health is what I myself do.

___ 5. If I take care of myself, I can avoid illness.

___ 6. If I take the right actions, I can stay healthy.

Subscale B: **Powerful Others**

___ 1. Having regular contact with my physician is the best way for me to avoid illness.

___ 2. Whenever I don't feel well, I should consult a medically trained professional.

___ 3. My family has a lot to do with my becoming sick or staying healthy.

___ 4. Health professionals control my health.

___ 5. When I recover from an illness, it's usually because other people (e.g., doctors, nurses, family, and friends) have been taking good care of me.

___ 6. Regarding my health, I can only do what my doctor tells me to do.

Subscale C: **Chance**

___ 1. No matter what I do, if I am going to get sick, I will get sick.

___ 2. Most things that affect my health happen to me by accident.

___ 3. Luck plays a big part in determining how soon I will recover from an illness.

___ 4. My good health is largely a matter of good fortune.

___ 5. No matter what I do, I'm likely to get sick.

___ 6. If it's meant to be, I will stay healthy.

Scoring: To obtain your score for a subscale, add the numbers you chose in that subscale.

1. A score of 23-30 on any subscale means you have a strong inclination to that particular dimension. For example, a high C score would indicate you hold strong beliefs that your health is a matter of chance.

2. A score of 15-22 means you are moderate on that particular dimension. For example, a moderate B score would indicate you have moderate belief that your health is due to powerful others.

3. A score of 6-14 means you are low on that particular dimension. For example, a low A score means that you generally do not believe that you personally control your health

Interpretation: If you scored *high* on the internal health locus-of-control scale and low or moderate on the powerful others and chance scales, you are a person who feels that your health is basically under your control. If you scored *moderately* on the internal health locus-of-control, you are a person who feels that sometimes your health is under your control and sometimes it is not. For the moderately internal individual, the scores on the powerful others and chance scales would determine the relative weight on these other two dimensions.

If you scored *low* on the internal health locus-of-control scale, you are a person who feels that you do not have control over your own health. Your scores on the powerful others and chance scales would determine the relative influence of these other two dimensions. If you scored relatively high on the powerful others scale and moderate to low on the other two scales, you are a person who feels that powerful others (e.g., physicians) control your health. If you scored relatively high on the chance scale and moderate to low on the other two scales, you are a person who feels that chance, fate, or luck determines your health status.

Based on the Multidimensional Health Locus-of-Control Scales, you should have gained some insight into your perceptions of control over your health.

We neither have complete control nor lack of complete control over life outcomes. As we learn how to gain greater control over aspects of our environment, we will be able to make changes in stressful behaviors.

Name: _____   Date: _____

Directions: Before you can begin to change negative patterns of behavior, you must determine where you are right now. Asking yourself the following questions should help you realistically take stock of your situation and start the process toward change.

1. *What would I* most like to change about myself right now?

2. *What do I* believe about the impact of this behavior on my health right now?

Severity:

Susceptibility:

Benefit to be derived vs. cost to me:

Likelihood of success:

3. *Who am I trying to please* by changing this behavior? Who is influencing me to do it? Why?

4. *What* positive reinforcing, predisposing, and enabling factors will help me achieve my goals?

Reinforcing:

Predisposing:

Enabling:

5. *What* negative reinforcing, predisposing, and enabling factors will stand in the way of my achieving my goals?

Reinforcing:

Predisposing:

Enabling:

6. *Can I do anything* to reduce the impact or alter the negative factors?

7. *What actions will I take to get started?*

Develop Your Own Support System

Name: _____   Date: _____

    We all need different kinds of friends. Different friends are able to complement the different aspects of our personalities. For instance, we may have some friends with whom we are silly and other friends with whom we are more serious. One person cannot possibly fill all the needs we have in friends, so we must look for more.

    The following suggestions are designed to help you build or improve your social support system.

1. Look for different qualities in different people.
2. Accept and enjoy what others have to offer.
3. Accept that others have limitations.
4. Offer only what you are willing to give.
5. Realize that your time and your friendship are precious.

Keep a written record of the names and roles of your social support system below.

Person: How this person might help:

_____   _____

_____   _____

_____   _____

_____   _____

_____   _____

_____   _____

_____   _____

_____   _____

Health center phone number: _____

Self-Esteem Inventory - Part I

Name: _____   Date: _____

Purpose: The Self-Esteem Inventory will help you determine attitudes you have toward yourself. Such attitudes are an important part of emotional well-being.

Directions: Read each statement. Then decide if you strongly agree, agree disagree, or strongly disagree with the statement. Circle the number in the column that corresponds to your response.

	Strongly Agree	Agree	Disagree	Strongly Disagree
1. I feel that I'm a person of worth, at least on an equal plane with others.	4	3	2	1
2. I feel that I have a number of good qualities.	4	3	2	1
3. All in all, I am inclined to feel that I am a failure.	1	2	3	4
4. I am able to do things as well as most other people.	4	3	2	1
5. I feel I do not have as much to be proud of as others.	1	2	3	4
6. I take a positive attitude toward myself.	4	3	2	1
7. On the whole, I am satisfied with myself.	4	3	2	1
8. I wish I could have more respect for myself.	1	2	3	4
9. I certainly feel useless at times.	1	2	3	4
10. At times I think I am no good at all.	1	2	3	4

Scoring: Add *all* the numbers you circled. Then divide the total by 10.
Total _____ divided by 10 = _____

Interpretation:
    4.0 = Highest self-esteem level
3.5-3.9 = High self-esteem
3.0-3.4 = Above-average self-esteem
2.0-2.9 = Below-average self-esteem
  < 2.0 = Low self-esteem

Source: Peggy Blake, Robert Frye, and Michael Pejsach, Discover Your Health Behaviors. New York: Random House, 1987.

Self-Esteem Inventory - Part II Personal Application

Name: _____ Date: _____

Purpose: Becoming aware of positive qualities and attributes increases self- esteem.

List 10 of your positive qualities.

1. _____

2. _____

3. _____

4. _____

5. _____

6. _____

7. _____

8. _____

9. _____

10. _____

o If you were to die in the next hour, what good characteristics would people remember about you? Write a eulogy for yourself.

o Think about a person in your life whom you greatly respect. What causes you to respect that person? How are *you* similar or different? How could you emphasize qualities about yourself that are similar to those of the respected person? How could you change those aspects of you that are dissimilar?

o You affect other people's self-esteem. Think of someone with whom you regularly spend time. What do you do to improve his or her self-esteem?

Source: Peggy Blake, Robert Frye, and Michael Pejsach, Discover Your Health Behaviors. New York: Random House, 1987.

Need for Uniqueness Scale

Name: _____ Date: _____

Directions: The following statements concern your perceptions about yourself in a variety of situations. Your task is to indicate the strength of your agreement with each statement utilizing a scale in which 1 denotes strong disagreement, 5 denotes strong agreement, and 2, 3, and 4 represent intermediate judgments. In the blank preceding each statement, place your number from 1 to 5. There are no "right" or "wrong" answers, so select the number that most clearly reflects you on each statement.

___ 1. When I am in a group of strangers, I am not reluctant to express my opinion openly.

___ 2. I find that criticism affects my self-esteem.

___ 3. I sometimes hesitate to use my own ideas for fear they might be impractical.

___ 4. I think society should let reason lead it to new customs and throw aside old habits or mere traditions.

___ 5. People frequently succeed in changing my mind.

___ 6. I find it sometimes amusing to upset the dignity of teachers, judges, and "cultured" people.

___ 7. I like wearing a uniform because it makes me proud to be a member of the organization it represents.

___ 8. People have sometimes called me "stuck-up."

___ 9. Others' disagreements make me uncomfortable.

___ 10. I do not always need to live by the rules and standards of society.

___ 11. I am unable to express my feelings if they result in undesirable consequences.

___ 12. Being a success in one's career means making a contribution that no one else has made.

___ 13. It bothers me if people think I am being too unconventional.

___ 14. I always try to follow rules.

___ 15. If I disagree with a superior on his or her views, I usually do not keep it to myself.

___ 16. I speak up in meetings in order to oppose those whom I feel are wrong.

___ 17. Feeling "different" in a crowd of people makes me feel uncomfortable.

___ 18. If I must die, let it be an unusual death rather than an ordinary death in bed.

___ 19. I would rather be just like everyone else than be called a "freak."

___ 20. I must admit I find it hard to work under strict rules and regulations.

___ 21. I would rather be known for always trying new ideas than for employing well-trusted methods.

21

22. It is better always to agree with the opinions of others than to be considered a disagreeable person.

23. I do not like to say unusual things to people.

24. I tend to express my opinions publicly, regardless of what others say.

25. As a rule, I strongly defend my own opinions.

26. I do not like to go my own way.

27. When I am with a group of people, I agree with their ideas so that no arguments will arise.

28. I tend to keep quiet in the presence of persons of higher rank, experience, etc.

29. I have been quite independent and free from family rule.

30. Whenever I take part in group activities, I am somewhat of a non-conformist.

31. In most things in life, I believe in playing it safe rather than taking a gamble.

32. It is better to break rules than always to conform with an impersonal society.

Scoring: Reverse score on items 2, 3, 5, 7, 9, 11, 13, 14, 17, 19, 22, 23, 26, 27, 28, and 31. On these items, a 5=1, 4=2, 3=3, 2=4, and 1=5. Then add the score for all 32 items. The *higher* the score, the greater the *need for uniqueness*. The scale does not necessarily tell how different one actually is. Of 1400 students at the University of Kansas and Purdue University, a score of 100 was the 50th percentile.

Source: C.R. Snyder and H.L. Fromkin. 1980 Uniqueness: The human pursuit of difference. New York: Plenum Press, pp. 79-80.

Self-Actualization Inventory

Name: _____   Date: _____

Purpose: To make you aware of the characteristics of self-actualization. Also, to help you find out whether you are a self-actualizing person; that is, a person who is fulfilling his or her potentials, including esthetic, creative, and spiritual capacities.

Directions: Circle the number in the column on the right side that you feel honestly describes how you feel or behave.

Characteristics	Frequency			
	Very Often	Often	Some- times	Never
1. Judge others accurately	5	3	1	0
2. Detect falseness in others	5	3	1	0
3. Tolerate uncertainty	5	3	1	0
4. Accept your good and bad aspects	5	3	1	0
5. Accept others even though you disagree with them	5	3	1	0
6. Get creative ideas	5	3	1	0
7. Enjoy doing unplanned and unrehearsed things	15	10	4	0
8. Involved with problems of others	10	7	3	0
9. Able to be alone (by yourself)	10	7	3	0
10. Able to be honest self when with strangers	5	3	1	0
11. Resist local customs and traditions	5	3	1	0
12. Have your friends support you before making decisions	5	3	1	0
13. Able to make decisions	5	3	1	0
14. Get a lot of enjoyment from playing or socializing with others	5	3	1	0
15. Appreciate seeing a play or concert	5	3	1	0
16. Feel inspired after hearing or seeing outstanding artists/persons perform	5	3	1	0
17. Have empathy for how another person feels	5	3	1	0
18. Help others to grow and become better persons	5	3	1	0
19. Have deep and meaningful relationships with a few friends	5	3	1	0
20. Feel that a person should be hired on ability and competency	5	3	1	0
21. Do work that you enjoy	10	7	3	0
22. Feel that your work is important	5	3	1	0
23. Laugh at yourself	10	7	3	0
24. Look forward to new experiences	10	7	3	0
25. Enjoy peak and unusual experiences	15	12	4	0
26. Believe that honesty is the best policy	5	3	1	0
27. Believe that one should always tell the truth	5	3	1	0
28. Have dedication to life or social purpose	10	7	3	0

Total _____

Scoring: Add the numbers you circled. This is your self-actualization
score. Classify your score in the appropriate score range.

<u>Score Range</u>   <u>Current potential for self-actualization</u>

150-200   High self-actualization
112-149   Moderate self-actualization
 80-111   Approaching self-actualization
  0-79   Below average self-actualization

Source: Walter D. Sorochan. <u>Personal Health Appraisal</u>. New York: Wiley & Sons, Publishers, 1976, 37-40.

How Hardy Are You?

Name: _____   Date: _____

Purpose: Below are 12 items similar to those that appear in the hardiness questionnaire. Evaluating someone's hardiness requires more than this quick test. But this simple exercise should give you some idea of how hardy you are.

Directions: Write down how much you agree or disagree with the following statements, using this scale:

0 = strongly disagree
1 = mildly disagree
2 = mildly agree
3 = strongly agree

___ A. Trying my best at work makes a difference.

___ B. Trusting to fate is sometimes all I can do in a relationship.

___ C. I often wake up eager to start on the day's projects.

___ D. Thinking of myself as a free person leads to great frustration and difficulty.

___ E. I would be willing to sacrifice financial security in my work if something really challenging came along.

___ F. It bothers me when I have to deviate from the routine or schedule I've set for myself.

___ G. An average citizen can have an impact on politics.

___ H. Without the right breaks, it is hard to be successful in my field.

___ I. I know why I am doing what I'm doing at work.

___ J. Getting close to people puts me at risk of being obligated to them.

___ K. Encountering new situations is an important priority in my life.

___ L. I really don't mind when I have nothing to do.

Scoring: These questions measure control, commitment and challenge. For half the questions, a high score (like 3, "strongly agree") indicates hardiness; for the other half, a low score (disagreement) does.

To get your scores on control, commitment and challenge, first write in the number of your answer-0,1,2 to 3-above the letter of each question on the score sheet. Then add and subtract as shown. (To get your score on "control", for example, add your answers to question A and G; add your answers to B and H; and then subtract the second number from the first.)

Add your scores on commitment, control and challenge together to get a score for total hardiness.

A total score of **10-18** shows a hardy personality, **0-9** moderate hardiness. Below **0** low hardiness.

___ + ___ = ___   ___ + ___ = ___   ___ + ___ = ___
A   G   C   I   E   K

___ + ___ = ___   ___ + ___ = ___   ___ + ___ = ___
B   H   Control   D   J   Commitment   F   L   Challenge
          Score   Score   Score

_____ + _____ + _____ = _____
Control   Commitment   Challenge   Total Hardiness
                                                 Score

Source: Joan Luckman, Your Health. Englewood Cliffs, NJ: Prentice Hall, 1991.

Inventory of Negative Thoughts

Name: _____ Date: _____

Purpose: Cognitive theorists believe that people can make themselves depressed by thinking negative thoughts. The following inventory includes many negative thoughts that are commonly linked to depression. How many of them have you experienced in recent months? Do they strike you as accurate and appropriate to your situation? Or are you giving in to cognitive distortions that can lead to feelings of depression?

Directions: Using the code below, write in a number from 1 to 4 to indicate how frequently you have the thoughts contained in the list that follows. Pay particular attention to the content of the thought rather than the specific wording.

    1. Never   2. Seldom   3. Often   4. Very Often

____ 1. It seems such an effort to do anything.

____ 2. I feel pessimistic about the future.

____ 3. I have too many bad things in my life.

____ 4. I have very little to look forward to.

____ 5. I'm drained of energy, worn out.

____ 6. I'm not as successful as other people.

____ 7. Everything seems futile and pointless.

____ 8. I just want to curl up and go to sleep.

____ 9. There are things about me that I don't like.

____ 10. It's too much effort even to move.

____ 11. I'm absolutely exhausted.

____ 12. The future seems just one string of problems.

____ 13. My thoughts keep drifting away.

____ 14. I get no satisfaction from the things I do.

____ 15. I've made so many mistakes in the past.

____ 16. I've got to really concentrate just to keep my eyes open.

____ 17. Everything I do turns out badly.

____ 18. My whole body has slowed down.

____ 19. I regret some of the things I've done.

____ 20. I can't make the effort to liven up myself.

____ 21. I feel depressed with the way things are going.

____ 22. I haven't any real friends anymore.

____ 23. I do have a number of problems.

____ 24. There's no one I can feel really close to.

27

___ 25. I wish I were someone else.

___ 26. I'm annoyed at myself for being bad at making decisions.

___ 27. I don't make a good impression on other people.

___ 28. The future look hopeless.

___ 29. I don't get the same satisfaction out of things these days.

___ 30. I wish something would happen to make me feel better.

Source: From _The Psychological Treatment of Depression: A Guide to the Theory and Practice of Cognitive-Behavior Therapy_ by J. Mark G. Williams. Copyright (c) 1984 by J. Mark G. Williams.

Therapeutic Readiness Scale

Name: _____ Date: _____

Directions: Read each statement carefully and candidly indicate your degree of agreement using this scale:

0 = Disagreement   2 = Probable agreement
1 = Probable Disagreement   3 = Agreement

____ 1. Although there are clinics for people with mental troubles, I would not have much faith in them.

____ 2. If a good friend asked my advice about a mental health problem, I might recommend that he or she see a psychiatrist.

____ 3. I would feel uneasy going to a psychiatrist because of what some people would think.

____ 4. A person with a strong character can get over mental conflicts by him or herself, and would have little need of a psychiatrist.

____ 5. There are times when I have felt completely lost and would have welcomed professional advice for a personal or emotional problem.

____ 6. Considering the time and expense involved in psychotherapy, it would have doubtful value for a person like me.

____ 7. I would willingly confide intimate matters to an appropriate person if I thought it might help me or a member of my family.

____ 8. I would rather live with certain mental conflicts than go through the ordeal of getting psychiatric treatment.

____ 9. Emotional difficulties, like many things, tend to work out by themselves.

____ 10. There are certain problems that should not be discussed outside of one's immediate family.

____ 11. A person with a serious emotional disturbance would probably feel more secure in a good mental hospital.

____ 12. If I believed I was having a mental breakdown, my first inclination would be to get professional attention.

____ 13. Keeping one's mind on a job is a good solution for avoiding personal worries and concerns.

____ 14. Having been a psychiatric patient is a blot on a person's life.

____ 15. I would rather be advised by a close friend than by a psychologist, even for an emotional problem.

____ 16. A person with an emotional problem is not likely to solve it alone; he is likely to solve it with professional help.

____ 17. I resent a person--professionally trained or not--who wants to know about my personal difficulties.

___ 18. I would want to get psychiatric attention if I was worried or upset for a long period of time.

___ 19. The idea of talking about problems with a psychologist strikes me as a poor way to get rid of emotional conflicts.

___ 20. Having been mentally ill carries with it a burden of shame.

___ 21. There are experiences in my life I would not discuss with anyone.

___ 22. It is probably best not to know everything about oneself.

___ 23. If I were experiencing a serious emotional crisis at this point in my life, I would be confident that I could find relief in psychotherapy.

___ 24. There is something admirable in the attitude of a person who is willing to cope with his or her conflict and fears without resorting to professional help.

___ 25. At some future time I might want to have psychological counseling.

___ 26. A person should work out his or her own problems; getting psychological counseling would be a last resort.

___ 27. Had I received treatment in a mental hospital, I would not feel that it had to be "covered up."

___ 28. If I thought I needed psychiatric help, I would get it no matter who knew about it.

___ 29. It is difficult to talk about personal affairs with highly educated people such as doctors, teachers, and clergymen.

Scoring: Reverse score (i.e., 0=3, 1=2, 2=1, and 3=0) for the following items: 1, 3, 4, 6, 8, 9, 10, 13, 14, 15, 17, 19, 20, 21, 22, 24, 26, 29. Add one's total score for all 29 items.

Interpretation: Low scores (up to 49) have a negative attitude toward seeking professional help. If they had problems that could benefit from professional help, they would still be reluctant to contact and interact with a counselor. Seeking therapy may be viewed as a social stigma and/or personal weakness. Medium scorers (50-63) view professional help as potentially useful but may be unsure about personally utilizing therapy. High scorers (64-87) have a positive attitude toward therapy, which actually leads to more effective therapy.

Source: E. Fischer and J. Turner, 1970. Attitudes toward seeking professional help: Development and research utility of an attitude scale. Journal of Consulting and Clinical Psychology, 35, 82-83. Copyright (c) 1970, The American Psychological Association. Reprinted by permission.

Assertiveness Scale

Name: _____   Date: _____

Purpose: This inventory is designed to give you an indication of your own degree of assertiveness.

Directions: Respond to each statement by circling the letter that best represents how you would generally respond in the given situation. If the situation does not apply to you, respond according to what you think would best characterize your behavior. Keep in mind that your responses should be your honest opinion of what you actually do or would do in these situations, not what you wish you could do.

Response Scale:	A	B	C	D	E
	Never	Rarely	Sometimes	Often	Always

1. In conversation I find it difficult to maintain eye contact.
   Never   A   B   C   D   E   Always

2. When I meet new people in situations, I initiate introductions and start conversations.
   Never   A   B   C   D   E   Always

3. My close friends dominate decisions about how we spend our leisure time together.
   Never   A   B   C   D   E   Always

4. If I am angry with friends/parents/roommates, I find it difficult to directly communicate my feelings to them.
   Never   A   B   C   D   E   Always

5. I ignore it when someone cuts in line in front of me.
   Never   A   B   C   D   E   Always

6. When a friend or roommate is overdue in returning something valuable, I mention it.
   Never   A   B   C   D   E   Always

7. If someone were tapping my chair in class or constantly talking during a movie, I would ask them to stop.
   Never   A   B   C   D   E   Always

8. I feel comfortable asking reasonable favors of other people.
   Never   A   B   C   D   E   Always

9. When family or friends, I find it difficult to break into or even initiate a conversation.
   Never   A   B   C   D   E   Always

10. If someone's cigarette smoke were bothering me in a public building I would politely ask them to stop.
    Never   A   B   C   D   E   Always

11. In regard to necessary chores, I insist that a roommate or partner take on a fair share.
    Never   A   B   C   D   E   Always

Response Scale:		A	B	C	D	E
		Never	Rarely	Sometimes	Often	Always

12. I avoid asking questions in class fearing that they just won't sound right.

Never   A   B   C   D   E   Always

13. If my instructor made, in my opinion, an unfair request, I would express my feelings to him or her.

14. I will buy things I really don't need if a salesman applies pressure.

Never   A   B   C   D   E   Always

15. If my dinner in a restaurant were not to my liking, I would demand that it be corrected.

Never   A   B   C   D   E   Always

16. I feel uncomfortable when someone give me a compliment.

Never   A   B   C   D   E   Always

17. I would freely offer information or my opinion in group discussions, even if I didn't know the other people very well.

Never   A   B   C   D   E   Always

18. I have difficulty communicating with an attractive person of the opposite sex.

Never   A   B   C   D   E   Always

19. I feel uncomfortable about returning a defective piece of merchandise.

Never   A   B   C   D   E   Always

20. I would be reluctant to invite someone of the opposite sex out on a date.

Never   A   B   C   D   E   Always

21. I would feel uncomfortable explaining to a friend/boss/instructor a better way, in my opinion, of completing a specific task.

Never   A   B   C   D   E   Always

Scoring: Use the following table to determine the number of points to assign to each of your responses. To determine your total score, add all the numbers that match the letter (A,B,C,D, or E) you circled for each statement.

Statement	A	B	C	D	E
1.	4	3	2	1	0
2.	0	1	2	3	4
3.	4	3	2	1	0
4.	4	3	2	1	0
5.	4	3	2	1	0
6.	0	1	2	3	4
7.	0	1	2	3	4
8.	0	1	2	3	4

Statement	A	B	C	D	E
9.	4	3	2	1	0
10.	0	1	2	3	4
11.	0	1	2	3	4
12.	4	3	2	1	0
13.	0	1	2	3	4
14.	4	3	2	1	0
15.	0	1	2	3	4
16.	0	1	2	3	4
17.	0	1	2	3	4
18.	4	3	2	1	0
19.	4	3	2	1	0
20.	4	3	2	1	0
21.	4	3	2	1	0

Total Score _____ This is your assertiveness score. Classify your score in the appropriate level.

66-84	Very Assertive
44-65	Somewhat Assertive
22-43	Somewhat Unassertive
0-21	Very Unassertive

Interpretation: Assertiveness is different from both passiveness and aggressiveness. It is not, as some people might think, halfway between these; it is quite different. Passiveness refers to acquiescing to another person's demands regardless of the consequences to yourself. Aggressiveness means attempting to force your desires on another person in order to satisfy your own needs, regardless of the other person's rights. Assertiveness is characterized by a degree of confidence in your pursuits combined with respect for your fellow human beings-respect that you would expect in a reciprocating manner. With each of the situations listed, an aggressive statement or assertive statement could be made. Keep in mind that assertiveness is determined not only be the words stated, but also in the tone of voice and body language. In addition, the individual on the receiving end of a statement may perceive the circumstances of statement differently and therefore view what was intended to be assertive as an aggressive act.

Source: Sandra Kammerman et al, Wellness RSVP. Menlo Park, CA: Benjamin Cummings, 1993. 47-49.

How Do You Handle Conflict?

Name: _____ Date: _____

Purpose: It can be stated with confidence that people will face conflict throughout their lives. Dealing with conflict effectively is an important factor in human dynamics. There are different ways of dealing with conflict. This exercise will help you identify the methods you use.

Directions: The following statements describe possible responses to various conflict situations. Read each statement carefully, and circle the number on the scale below each statement that most closely describes your behavior.

Response Scale:	1	2	3	4	5
	Never	Rarely	Sometimes	Often	Always

---

1. When strong conflict occurs, I prefer to leave the situation.
   Never 1 2 3 4 5 Always

2. I feel very comfortable about taking a conflict between a friend and me to a third person.
   Never 1 2 3 4 5 Always

3. I try to find a compromise when a conflict occurs.
   Never 1 2 3 4 5 Always

4. I find conflict exciting and challenging.
   Never 1 2 3 4 5 Always

5. I tend to concentrate on the problem and the issues in a conflict rather than the other person.
   Never 1 2 3 4 5 Always

6. When conflict occurs, I act as though there is no real problem and try to "get along."
   Never 1 2 3 4 5 Always

7. I prefer to have a third person help solve a conflict between a friend and me.
   Never 1 2 3 4 5 Always

8. I'm willing to give a little if the other person in a dispute is also willing to give on some things.
   Never 1 2 3 4 5 Always

9. It's important that I win, even if the problem or issue in a disagreement is not really important to me.
   Never 1 2 3 4 5 Always

10. I search for a solution to a conflict that both the other person and I can find acceptable.
    Never 1 2 3 4 5 Always

Response Scale:	1	2	3	4	5
	Never	Rarely	Sometimes	Often	Always

11. I would quit a job if many conflicts occurred daily.
    Never   1   2   3   4   5   Always

12. It's easier to have an outsider settle a dispute than to argue it out alone with another person.
    Never   1   2   3   4   5   Always

13. I like to find what each person wants most strongly, then work for a point in the middle.
    Never   1   2   3   4   5   Always

14. I hate to lose or not get my own way.
    Never   1   2   3   4   5   Always

15. I like to look at lots of possibilities and options before trying to find a solution to a conflict.
    Never   1   2   3   4   5   Always

16. When conflict occurs, I prefer to get out of the situation rather than work to resolve the conflict.
    Never   1   2   3   4   5   Always

17. I like to take disagreements to someone who has authority and have that person make a ruling.
    Never   1   2   3   4   5   Always

18. I believe resolving conflict requires that each person give up something.
    Never   1   2   3   4   5   Always

19. When someone tries to get me to back down or give in during a conflict, that makes me hold my position more strongly.
    Never   1   2   3   4   5   Always

20. When I especially need to have my plan accepted or when an issue is very important to me, I tell the person with whom I am in conflict.
    Never   1   2   3   4   5   Always

21. I prefer to walk away from conflict if there is strong personal disagreement.
    Never   1   2   3   4   5   Always

22. I prefer to have a counselor decide for two people in conflict, not just ask the two people to listen to each other.
    Never   1   2   3   4   5   Always

23. I believe working out a middle-of-the-road agreement is best, even if both people are still somewhat unhappy about not getting their own way completely.
    Never   1   2   3   4   5   Always

24. When I work to resolve a conflict, I work to win.
    Never   1   2   3   4   5   Always

25. I consider the other person's preference as well as my own and work to find a solution both of us can live with.
Never   1   2   3   4   5   Always

26. I prefer to let conflicts "work themselves out."
Never   1   2   3   4   5   Always

27. I believe it is important to get the opinion of a friend when I am in conflict with someone.
Never   1   2   3   4   5   Always

28. It's okay to give up some things if the other person gives up something too.
Never   1   2   3   4   5   Always

29. I believe setting a conflict with another person is not different from competing in sports--the goal is to win.
Never   1   2   3   4   5   Always

30. I believe a conflict is really a problem, not a contest; therefore, the goal is to find a solution both people can live with, not to "beat" the other person.
Never   1   2   3   4   5   Always

Scoring: The numbers listed below refer to the statements that you have just responded to. Write down the number you circled on the scale for each statement.

1 _____	2 _____	3 _____	4 _____	5 _____
6 _____	7 _____	8 _____	9 _____	10 _____
11 _____	12 _____	13 _____	14 _____	15 _____
16 _____	17 _____	18 _____	19 _____	20 _____
21 _____	22 _____	23 _____	24 _____	25 _____
26 _____	27 _____	28 _____	29 _____	30 _____

Total Scores,
each column:

A _____	B _____	C _____	D _____	E _____
Withdrawing-Avoiding	Going to a Third Person	Compromise	Win-Lose	Win-Win or Problem-Solving

List the letters and total scores from the highest down to the lowest.

Letter	Total Score	
_____	_____	*Highest*
_____	_____	
_____	_____	
_____	_____	
_____	_____	*Lowest*

Interpretation: The total score indicate which ways to handling conflict you use most. If two or more scores are close together (for example, compromise 30 and withdrawing-avoiding 28), you tend to use those methods about the same amount of time.

If your total score is   *You tend to use this method*

26-30 .... a great deal
21-25 .... often
16-20 .... sometimes
11-15 .... occasionally
6-10 .... infrequently

A. *Withdrawing-Avoiding*--handling conflict by getting away from it or ignoring it. This includes giving in quickly to avoid unpleasantness, pretending there is no conflict, moving out of the situation by quitting, breaking the relationship, or physically moving. Withdrawing may be helpful if the problem is not important to you, or if it is not a good time to discuss the disagreement. Withdrawing usually mans the other person wins.

B. *Going to a Third Person*--having a third person listen to both sides of a conflict and then help settle it. A third person can be useful if he or she helps the two people in conflict see each other's points of view. Many times, however, third persons are not fair. The success of this method depends on an unbiased third person and on whether the two people in conflict will follow what the third person recommends.

C. *Compromise*--finding a solution that allows each person to win something. Both persons may be somewhat disappointed, and yet each has the satisfaction of getting part of what he or she wanted. Most conflicts have more than two solutions, and many possibilities should be discussed before a compromise is made.

D. *Win-Lose*--holding out for your point of view or working to get the other person to give in. This is a high-risk method because you tend to win completely or lose completely. If the other person insists on trying to win totally, you have little choice but to use win-lose, unless you can get the other person to change methods.

E. *Win-Win or Problem-Solving*--looking at conflict as a problem and search-ing for a solution or plan that both persons feel good about. This method may end in a compromise, but usually not until after many solutions are discussed. The spotlight is on the problem, not on the personalities of the people in conflict. If personalities are the problem, then they are discussed openly, along with how each person needs to behave differently to resolve or reduce the conflict.

Source: Sandra Kammerma et al. Wellness RSVP. Menlo Park, CA: Benjamin Cummings, 1993. 51-54.

Constructive Fighting

Name: _____ Date: _____

Purpose: People who are closely involved, whether as a family, good friends, or partners, often find it difficult to resolve disagreements. One person may try to ignore a problem until it becomes very obvious and is forced into the open. Then when the issue is discussed the people involved are often dissatisfied with the outcome and the feelings they are left with. However, there are constructive methods of fighting to solve problems. This may seem too technical or mechanical, yet people find some guidelines for constructive fighting are practical, and the outcome of constructive fighting often enhances the relationship. This inventory will give you an opportunity to check your fight style.

Directions: Reach each questions carefully and respond by writing a YES or NO in the blank to the right. Respond in terms of a present relationship or a significant one from the past.

1. When your anger surfaces, do you take time to look at where it is coming from? _____

2. Whenever you argue, do you make "I" statements to explain how the other person's behavior makes you feel? _____

3. Do you say directly what change you would like to see in the current situation? _____

4. Are you sensitive to the hints your partner sends out when he/she is not happy with a situation? _____

5. Do you know what you and your partner expect of your relationship? _____

6. Do you threaten infidelity, divorce, violence, or telling others of your disagreement? _____

7. Are you dependent on your partner to fulfill many of your needs? _____

8. Are you aware of tensions that naturally occur when major lifestyle changes are made? _____

9. Do you feel that "winning" an argument is important to your self-image? _____

10. Do you keep score of who "wins" arguments? _____

11. Do you regard compromising as losing? _____

12. Are you afraid of being rejected by your partner? _____

13. Do you bring up problem areas as they arise instead of storing grudges to release all at once? _____

14. Do you belittle your partner in an attempt to control him/her? _____

15. Do you set aside a time and place where both you and your partner can discuss a problem without distractions? _____

16. Do you confine your discussions about problems to the current issue and not bring up past issues? _____

17. Are there recurring themes behind your disagreements? _____

18. If you are not sure of your partner's message, do you repeat it in your own words and ask if you understand correctly? _____

19. Do you feel you learn something from your disagreements? _____

20. Are you uneasy with the changes that may result from an argument? _____

Scoring: The questions above actually list many suggestions for constructive fighting. The correct answers are as follows:

1. YES. When you feel anger rising, it is helpful to stop to think about what is causing the anger. You need to realize that you yourself created the anger. Then ask yourself why you feel this way; it may be a result of unfair demands or expectations.

2. YES. You do not have the right to make assumptions about your partner's feelings and thoughts. Therefore, it is important to learn to begin statements with "I feel..." to let your partner know your feelings. Statements that begin "You..." tend to make assumptions and put your partner on the defensive.

3. YES. Learn to say directly what changes in the current situation you would like to see. After your partner has given his/her viewpoint, you can explore which options are fair or possible. Try to be positive in your statements, saying what you "do want" instead of focusing on the negative and what you "do not want."

4. YES. If you can understand your partner's nonverbal communication, you can ask what he/she is feeling. Your partner may want your help or support but may feel uncomfortable telling you so.

5. YES. If you have not recently discussed your expectations of your relationship, you may have conflicting ideas. Review them together to decide if any need to be change. Do not expect your partner to change just for you.

6. NO. Threats will not solve the conflict. Remember: threats are most effective if seldom used. Use them only if you feel the action is absolutely necessary and you are willing to carry it through.

7. NO. Any overdependence on your partner can cause conflict. Your partner may feel he/she is giving more than receiving. Take a look at your needs and reevaluate how to meet them.

8. YES. Many lifestyle changes naturally result in more tension and stress. Be aware of those situations and avoid blaming your partner for the stress.

9. NO. If you feel you must "win" an argument to keep your self-image, think about where your real happiness in the relationship comes from. Solving the problem that caused the conflict is the most important factor.

10. NO. Do not keep score of who "wins." Again the real issue is that the conflict is resolved. Keeping score tends to make. people want to "get even." Stable relationships involve cooperation.

11. NO. Again, the real issue is that the conflict is resolved. A compromise is usually best since there is no "loser" whose feelings are hurt.

12. NO. If communication is open in your relationship, your partner will not reject you because you do not always agree. In fact, couples often find conflict resolution serves to strengthen a relationship.

39

13. YES. It is easier to find a compromise for problem issues if they are discussed and resolved one at a time as they arise. If one partner holds grudges for a period of time, it may cause conflicts in other areas.

14. NO Attempting to belittle your partner is likely to put him/her on the defensive. In addition, the real concern should be reaching a compromise together.

15. YES. When a conflict needs to be resolved, one partner may want to make an appointment with the other. Discussion should not take place while either partner is tired, rushed, or under the influence of alcohol or drugs. Both partners need to be able to devote their full attention to the issue. If one person has an important presentation to make or paper to write, the discussion may need to be delayed for a reasonable length of time.

16. YES. Discussions should be limited to the current problem since it is better to deal with one issue at at time. If an unresolved issue is brought up, agree to discuss it at a later time.

17. NO. If the same arguments or variations on the same theme keep recurring, perhaps you need to look at your process for conflict resolution. Ask yourself if any positive changes have been made since the last time you discussed the issue.

18. YES. This is a basic rule of good communication. Restate what you heard your partner say but in your own words. This helps to clear up misunderstandings before they become problems.

19. YES. When fighting is constructive, both partners will learn something about themselves and their partner. This new information can then be applied to similar situations that arise in the future. Thus, no conflict would result.

20. NO. Both partners should feel   20. NO. Both partners should feel fairly comfortable with the changes agreed upon, although feel completely comfortable if they are changing habits developed over several years. Both partners need encouragement and positive strokes when making changes.

Now that you have evaluated your fight style, try to practice these suggestions the next time you feel angry or disagree with someone. Remember, these basic guidelines can be applied to disagreements with anyone--partner, mate, co-worker, or family member. However, if you cannot solve the problem, seek professional help. Friends and family may be able to help some, but a potentially long-term relationship is too important to trust to well-meaning friends. Seek professional help together. Once you resolve the conflict, put the problem behind you and have some fun!

Source: Robert F. Valois and Sandra Kammerman. Your Sexuality: A Self Assessment, 2nd Ed. New York: McGraw Hill, 1992. 113-116.

Assessing and Managing Stress
Part I: Stress Danger Signals

Name: _____   Date: _____

Purpose: The danger signals listed below focus on the medical and physical symptoms common to tension stress. Your physician can make the best determination of your medical condition, of course, but these guidelines can provide a rough measure of your stress level.

Directions: Check the signals you have.

___ 1. General irritability, hyperexcitation, or depression.

___ 2. Pounding of the heart.

___ 3. Dryness of mouth and throat.

___ 4. Impulsive behavior, emotional instability.

___ 5. Overpowering urge to cry or run or hide.

___ 6. Inability to concentrate, flight of thoughts, disorientation.

___ 7. Feelings of unreality, weakness, dizziness.

___ 8. Fatigue.

___ 9. Floating anxiety, being afraid and not knowing why.

___ 10. Emotional tension and alertness: "keyed up."

___ 11. Trembling, nervous.

___ 12. Tendency to be easily startled by small sounds.

___ 13. High pitched, nervous laughter.

___ 14. Stuttering, other speech difficulties.

___ 15. Bruxism, or grinding of teeth.

___ 16. Insomnia.

___ 17. Hypermotility, an increased tendency to move about without any reason.

___ 18. Sweating.

___ 19. Frequent need to urinate.

___ 20. Diarrhea, indigestion, queasiness in the stomach, and sometime vomiting.

___ 21. Migraine headaches.

___ 22. Pain in the neck and lower back.

___ 23. Loss of appetite or excessive appetite.

___ 24. Increased smoking.

___ 25. Increased use of prescribed drugs.

___ 26. Alcohol and drug abuse.

___ 27. Nightmares

___ 28. Accident proneness.

41

Interpretation: The more signs that are present, the stronger the likelihood that there is a serious problem.

Part II: Monitoring Events and Reactions

Directions: Monitor specific events that trigger stress by keeping a stress journal to record not only events but emotional, physical, and behavioral reactions. The following is just one format for recording this information:

Time of day	Reactions (physical and emotional)	Stressor (situation, event)
Monday		
Tuesday		
Wednesday		
Thursday		
Friday		
Saturday		
Sunday		

Part III: Stress Management

After identifying stressful events, you may choose to attend a college or community-sponsored stress management workshop, or construct your own stress management plans. In developing a stress-management plan, consider the following:

o   Time management/establishing priorities.
o   Improvement in nutrition and eating habits.
o   Aerobic exercise.
o   Cognitive measure (for example, autogenics, visualization, and affirmations).
o   Relaxation techniques--for example, progressive relaxation, massage and music. (See 5-3.)
o   Pleasure.

A Time Management Questionnaire for College Students

Name: _____ Date: _____

Response Scale:	Never 0	Sometimes +1	Often +2	Almost Always +3

Planning

1. I keep in writing my short-term and long-term professional and personal goals.
   Never   0   +1   +2   +3   Almost always

2. I update in writing my professional and personal goals.
   Never   0   +1   +2   +3   Almost always

3. At the start of a semester I record all dates and due dates for exams, term papers, etc., in my planning calendar.
   Never   0   +1   +2   +3   Almost always

4. I write out my daily activities on a to-do list.
   Never   0   +1   +2   +3   Almost always

5. I prioritize the items on my to-do list and make sure that the priority items are done.
   Never   0   +1   +2   +3   Almost always

6. I schedule my most important work to occur during my "most alert" or "peak energy" hours.
   Never   0   +1   +2   +3   Almost always

My Desk and/or Study Area

7. My desk top is clean and contains only the project on which I'm currently working.
   Never   0   +1   +2   +3   Almost always

8. I get a positive feeling when I approach my desk.
   Never   0   +1   +2   +3   Almost always

9. I have a well-organized place for everything (books, notebooks, etc.).
   Never   0   +1   +2   +3   Almost always

10. I put everything in its place.
    Never   0   +1   +2   +3   Almost always

11. I can easily find items in my work area when I look for them.
    Never   0   +1   +2   +3   Almost always

12. My work space is well-lit, quiet, and conducive to good work.
    Never   0   +1   +2   +3   Almost always

13. I use a formal sign-out system for keeping track of books and other items that I lend to others.
    Never   0   +1   +2   +3   Almost always

Obtaining Results

14. I plan ahead and set reasonable deadlines for myself concerning
    studying, term projects, etc.
    Never   0   +1   +2   +3   Almost always

15. I begin and finish projects on time and meet my deadlines.
    Never   0   +1   +2   +3   Almost always

16. I concentrate on one task at a time.
    Never   0   +1   +2   +3   Almost always

17. I perform time-consuming projects in short steps or stages.
    Never   0   +1   +2   +3   Almost always

18. When going to meetings or appointments, I always have something with me
    to read to take advantage of "waiting" time.
    Never   0   +1   +2   +3   Almost always·

Time Savers Involving Myself and Others

19. I try to arrange nonacademic activities and meetings during my "least
    alert" times (For most students, these times are late in the afternoon
    and late in the evening.)
    Never   0   +1   +2   +3   Almost always

20. I politely resist requests from my friends to socialize or have coffee
    during my scheduled study time and especially during my "most alert"
    time.
    Never   0   +1   +2   +3   Almost always

21. When doing a project with another student, I set appointments so that
    we can review a number of items at one time.
    Never   0   +1   +2   +3   Almost always

22. When having coffee or socializing with friends during a study break, I
    suggest *at the start* of the break that we agree on a time to get back
    to studying, and I stick to our agreement.
    Never   0   +1   +2   +3   Almost always

23. I am politely assertive about cutting off long-winded telephone callers
    and/or other instances where people just want to "shoot the breeze."
    Never   0   +1   +2   +3   Almost always

Scoring: To score the Time Management Questionnaire, add your points
together and compare yourself with the scale below.

Interpretation:
50-69   You already manage your time very well.
35-49   You are on your way to being an effective time manager. However,
         you should increase the frequency with which you follow various
         time-saving strategies.
20-34   There is definite room for improvement in your time management
         skills. You need to take formal steps to implement some of the
         recommendations in this chapter in order to put more time into
         your life.
 0-19   You're disorganized, overwhelmed, and spending far too much time
         on low-priority activities and time wasters. Take immediate steps
         to implement some of the recommendations in this chapter.

Uptight?

Name: _____ Date: _____

Purpose: This exercise will enable you to determine the degree to which your habits and attitudes encourage stress and cause you to become tense and uptight. When you recognize stress-producing behaviors in yourself, you can find ways to change those behaviors and thereby relieve stress.

Directions: For each of the following statements circle the appropriate number (1-4) according to how often the statement is true for you.

1 = None or a little of the time
2 = Some of the time
3 = Good part of the time
4 = Most or all of the time.

1. I prefer things to be done my way.	1	2	3	4
2. I am critical of people who don't live up to my standards or expectations.	1	2	3	4
3. I stick to my principles, no matter what.	1	2	3	4
4. I am upset by changes in the environment and in the behavior of people.	1	2	3	4
5. I am meticulous and fussy about my possessions.	1	2	3	4
6. I get upset if I don't finish a task.	1	2	3	4
7. I insist on full value for everything I purchase.	1	2	3	4
8. I like everything I do to be perfect.	1	2	3	4
9. I follow an exact routine for everyday tasks.	1	2	3	4
10. I do things precisely to the last detail.	1	2	3	4
11. I get tense when my day's schedule is upset.	1	2	3	4
12. I plan my time so that I won't be late.	1	2	3	4
13. It bothers me when my surroundings are not clean.	1	2	3	4
14. I make lists for my activities.	1	2	3	4
15. I think that I worry about minor aches and pains.	1	2	3	4
16. I like to be prepared for any emergency.	1	2	3	4
17. I am strict about fulfilling every one of my obligations.	1	2	3	4
18. I think that I expect worthy moral standards in others.	1	2	3	4

45

19. I am badly shaken when someone takes advantage of me.	1	2	3	4
20. I get upset when people do not replace things exactly as I left them.	1	2	3	4
21. I keep used or old things because they might still be useful.	1	2	3	4
22. I think that I am sexually inhibited.	1	2	3	4
23. I find myself working rather than relaxing.	1	2	3	4
24. I prefer being a private person.	1	2	3	4
25. I like to budget myself carefully and I live on a cash-and-carry basis.	1	2	3	4

Total Score

Scoring:

25-45   Not compulsive or uptight

46-55   Mildly O-C (obsessive-compulsive). Your compulsiveness is working for you, and you are successfully adaptive.

56-70   Moderately O-C. You are adaptive but uptightness has crept into your personality function, and you experience uncomfortable days of high tension.

71-100   Severely O-C. You are adaptive but quite uptight, insecure, and driving hard. You have many days of nervous tension that should be eased off. The closer you are to the rating of 100, the nearer you come to playing brinkmanship at the ragged edge that borders on exhaustion of your adaptive reserve and a slump into depression.

However, a few compulsive idiosyncrasies do not necessarily mean an O-C personality. They are often laughed off. "That's just my screwball way." Inconsequential in their impact, they merely color the normal tones of a functioning personality. A caveat then--don't judge the whole person by a few harmless quirks that one barely notices.

Source: Leonard Cammer, M.D. Freedom from Compulsion. Copyright (c) 1976 by Harold I. and Robert Cammer, Trustees FBO Beatrice Cammer. Reprinted by permission of Simon & Schuster, a division of Paramount Publications.

Introduction to Relaxation Techniques

Name: _____ Date: _____

Directions: Try one or several of the following relaxation techniques. **Take** your pulse before and after these exercises.

1. Guided Imagery

Guided imagery is another way to employ your imagination to create relaxation. You should read the following passage into a tape recorder and then experience it. If a tape recorder is not available, perhaps a friend or family member could read it to you.

Mountain Path

Close your eyes...Imagine yourself leaving the area where you live... Leave the daily hassles and the fast pace behind...Imagine yourself going across a valley and moving closer and closer to a mountain range...Imagine yourself in a mountain range...You are going up a winding road...Find a place on the winding road to stop..Find a path to walk up...Start walking up the path...Find a comfortable place to stop on the path...At this place take some time to examine all the tension and stress in your life...Give the tension and stress shapes and colors...Look at them very carefully and after you have done this, put them down on the side of the path...Continue walking up the path until you come to the top of a hill...What do you see?...Find an inviting, comfortable place and go there...Be aware of your surrounding...What is your special place like?...Be aware of the sights, smells and sounds... Be aware of how you are feeling...Get settled and gradually start to relax...You are now feeling totally relaxed...Experience being relaxed totally and completely...Pause for three to five minutes...Look around at your special place once more...*Remember this is your special place to relax, and you can come here anytime you want to*...Come back to the room and tell yourself that this imagery is something you have created, and you can use it whenever you want to feel relaxed.

2. Autogenic Phrases For Relaxation

Repeat each of the following phrases to yourself four to eight times as you focus on the body parts and functions identified in the phrases.

1. My right arm is heavy and relaxed.
   My right arm is heavy and relaxed and warm.

2. My left arm is heavy and relaxed.
   My left arm is heavy and relaxed and warm.

3. My right leg is heavy and relaxed.
   My right leg is heavy and relaxed and warm.

4. My left leg is heavy and relaxed.
   My left leg is heavy and relaxed and warm.

5. My heart beats slow and regular.

6. My body breathes easy and relaxed.

7. My abdomen is warm.

8. My forehead is cool.

9. My mind is at peace.

10. Repeat your own affirmation four to eight times.

3. Music

Play soft music and do breathing exercises provided in text. You can order a tape with a combination of music and relaxation exercises from:

    Relaxation Exercise
    8364 Hickman Road
    Des Moines, Iowa 50322

Source: Davis, McKay, and Eshelman. <u>The Relaxation and Stress Reduction Workbook</u>. Oakland, CA: New Harbinger Publications, 1981.

Social Readjustment Rating Scale

Name: _____   Date: _____

Directions:

Life Event	Mean Value	Score
1. Death of Spouse	100	_____
2. Divorce	73	_____
3. Marital separation from mate	65	_____
4. Detention in jail or other institution	63	_____
5. Death of a close family member	63	_____
6. Major personal injury or illness	53	_____
7. Marriage	50	_____
8. Being fired from work	47	_____
9. Marital reconciliation with mate	45	_____
10. Retirement from work	45	_____
11. Major change in the health or behavior of a family member	44	_____
12. Pregnancy	40	_____
13. Sexual difficulties	39	_____
14. Gaining a new family member (e.g., through birth, adoption, oldster moving in, etc.)	39	_____
15. Major business readjustment (e.g., merger, reorganization, bankruptcy, etc.)	39	_____
16. Major change in financial state (e.g., a lot worse off or a lot better off than usual)	38	_____
17. Death of a close friend	37	_____
18. Changing to a different line of work	36	_____
19. Major change in the number of arguments with spouse (e.g., either a lot more or a lot less than usual regarding child rearing, personal habits, etc.)	35	_____
20. Taking out a mortgage or loan for a major purchase (e.g., for a home, business, etc.)	31	_____
21. Foreclosure on a mortgage or loan	30	_____
22. Major change in responsibilities at work (e.g., promotion, demotion, lateral transfer)	29	_____
23. Son or daughter leaving home (e.g., marriage, attending college, etc.)	29	_____
24. Trouble with in-laws	29	_____

Life Event	Mean Value	Score
25. Outstanding personal achievement	28	_____
26. Wife beginning or ceasing work outside the home	26	_____
27. Beginning or ceasing formal schooling	26	_____
28. Major change in living conditions (e.g., building a new home, remodeling, deterioration of home or neighborhood)	25	_____
29. Revision of personal habits (e.g., dress, manners, associations, etc.)	24	_____
30. Troubles with the boss	23	_____
31. Major change in working hours or conditions	20	_____
32. Change in residence	20	_____
33. Changing to a new school	20	_____
34. Major change in usual type and/or amount of recreation	19	_____
35. Major change in church activities (e.g., a lot more or a lot less than usual)	19	_____
36. Major change in social activities (e.g., club, dancing, movies, visiting, etc.)	18	_____
37. Taking out a mortgage or loan for a lesser purchase (e.g., for a car, TV, freezer, etc.)	17	_____
38. Major change in sleeping habits (e.g., a lot more or a lot less sleep, or change in part of day when asleep)	16	_____
39. Major change in number of family get-togethers (e.g., a lot more or a lot less than usual)	15	_____
40. Major change in eating habits (e.g., a lot more or a lot less food intake, or very different meal hours or surroundings)	15	_____
41. Vacation	13	_____
42. Christmas	12	_____
43. Minor violations of the law (e.g., traffic tickets, jaywalking, disturbing the peace, etc.)	11	_____
Your Score	Total	_____

Interpretation: Of those people with 300 or more Life Change Units for the past year, almost 80% get sick in the near future; with 150 to 299 Life Change Units, about 50% get sick in the near future; and with less than 150 Life Change Units, only about 30% get sick in the near future.

Source: T.H. Holmes and R.H. Rabe, 1967 Social Readjustment Rating Scale. Journal of Psychosomatic Research, 11. Pergamon Press, Ltd. 213-218.

How Stress Resistant Are You?

Name: _____   Date: _____

Directions: Treating a score of "1" as something that is almost always true and "5" as something that is virtually never true about your stress reactions, circle the appropriate response for each of the following questions:

1. I eat a least one hot, balanced meal a day.
   Always   1   2   3   4   5   Never

2. I get seven to eight hours of sleep at least four nights a week.
   Always   1   2   3   4   5   Never

3. I give and receive affection regularly.
   Always   1   2   3   4   5   Never

4. I have at least one relative within 50 miles of home on whom I can rely.
   Always   1   2   3   4   5   Never

5. I exercise until perspired at least twice weekly.
   Always   1   2   3   4   5   Never

6. I limit myself to less than half a pack of cigarettes a day.
   Always   1   2   3   4   5   Never

7. I take fewer than five alcoholic drinks a week.
   Always   1   2   3   4   5   Never

8. I am the appropriate weight for my height and build.
   Always   1   2   3   4   5   Never

9. My income covers my basic expenses.
   Always   1   2   3   4   5   Never

10. I get strength from my religious beliefs.
    Always   1   2   3   4   5   Never

11. I regularly attend social activities.
    Always   1   2   3   4   5   Never

12. I have a network of close friends and acquaintances.
    Always   1   2   3   4   5   Never

13. I have one or more friends to confide in about personal matters.
    Always   1   2   3   4   5   Never

14. I am in good health (including eyesight, hearing, teeth).
    Always   1   2   3   4   5   Never

15. I am able to speak openly about my feelings when angry or worried.
    Always   1   2   3   4   5   Never

16. I discuss domestic problems--chores and money, for example--with the members of my household.
    Always   1   2   3   4   5   Never

17. I have fun at least once a week.
    Always   1   2   3   4   5   Never

51

18. I can organize my time effectively.
    Always   1   2   3   4   5   Never

19. I drink fewer than three cups of coffee (or other caffeine-rich beverages) a day.
    Always   1   2   3   4   5   Never

20. I take some quiet time for myself during the day.
    Always   1   2   3   4   5   Never

Scoring: Add up all the points you have circled

Interpretation:
20-45   You probably have excellent resistance to stress.
46-55   You are somewhat vulnerable to stress.
56-100   You are seriously vulnerable to stress.

Source: Test developed by psychologists Lyle H. Miller and Alma Dell Smith. Reproduced in C.L. Mee Jr., et al. Managing Stress from Morning to Night. Alexandria, VA: Time-Life Books, 1987. p 27.

What Is Your Intimacy Quotient?

Name: _____ Date: _____

Purpose: This exercise is designed to measure your capacity for intimacy—how well you have fared in (and what you have learned from) your interpersonal relationships from infancy through adulthood. In a general way, it helps measure your sense of security and self-acceptance, which gives you the courage to risk the embarrassment of proffering love or friendship or respect and getting no response. This exercise can provide insight and can alert you to weaknesses that may be reducing your performance in everything from business, to meeting and interacting with potential mates, to ordering food in a restaurant.

Directions: Read each question carefully. If your response is yes or mostly yes, place a plus (+) on the line preceding the question. If your response is no or mostly no, place a minus (-) on the line. If you honestly cannot decide, place a zero on the line; try to enter as few zeros as possible. Even if a particular questions doesn't apply to you, try to imagine yourself in the situation described, and answer accordingly.

Do not look for any significance in the number of the frequency of plus or minus answers. Simply be honest when answering the questions.

____ 1. Do you have more than your share of colds?

____ 2. Do you believe that emotions have very little to do with physical ills?

____ 3. Do you often have indigestion?

____ 4. Do you frequently worry about your health?

____ 5. Would a nutritionist be appalled by your diet?

____ 6. Do you usually watch sports rather than participate in them?

____ 7. Do you often feel depressed or in a bad mood?

____ 8. Are you irritable when things go wrong?

____ 9. Were you happier in the past than you are right now?

____ 10. Do you believe it possible that a person's character can be read or his future foretold by means of astrology, I Ching, tarot cards, or some other means?

____ 11. Do you worry about the future?

____ 12. Do you try to hold in your anger as long as possible and then sometimes explode in a rage?

____ 13. Do people you care about often make you feel jealous?

____ 14. If your intimate partner were unfaithful one time, would you be unable to forgive and forget?

____ 15. Do you have difficulty making important decisions?

____ 16. Would you abandon a goal rather than take risks to reach it?

____ 17. When you go on a vacation, do you take some work along?

____ 18. Do you usually wear clothes that are dark or neutral in color?

____ 19. Do you usually do what you feel like doing, regardless of social pressures or criticism?

____ 20. Does a beautiful speaking voice turn you on?

____ 21. Do you always take an interest in where you are and what's happening around you?

____ 22. Do you find most odors interesting rather than offensive?

____ 23. Do you enjoy trying new and different foods?

____ 24. Do you like to touch and be touched?

____ 25. Are you easily amused?

____ 26. Do you often do things spontaneously or impulsively?

____ 27. Can you sit still through a long committee meeting or lecture without twiddling your thumbs or wriggling in your chair?

____ 28. Can you usually fall asleep and stay asleep without the use of sleeping pills or tranquilizers?

____ 29. Are you a moderate drinker rather than either a heavy drinker or a teetotaler?

____ 30. Do you smoke or not at all or very little?

____ 31. Can you put yourself in another person's place and experience his emotions?

____ 32. Are you seriously concerned about social problems even when they don't affect your personally?

____ 33. Do you think most people can be trusted?

____ 34. Can you talk to a celebrity or a stranger as easily as you talk to your neighbors?

____ 35. Do you get along well with sales clerks, waiters, service station attendants, and cab drivers?

____ 36. Can you easily discuss sex in mixed company without feeling uncomfortable?

____ 37. Can you express appreciation for a gift or a favor without feeling uncomfortable?

____ 38. When you feel affection for someone, can you express it physically as well as verbally?

____ 39. Do you sometimes feel that you have extrasensory perception?

____ 40. Do you like yourself?

____ 41. Do you like others of your own sex?

____ 42. Do you enjoy an evening alone?

____ 43. Do you vary your schedule to avoid doing the same things at the same times each day?

____ 44. Is love more important to you than money or status?

_____ 45. Do you place a higher premium on kindness than on truthfulness?

_____ 46. Do you think it is possible to be too rational?

_____ 47. Have you attended or would you like to attend a sensitivity or encounter-group session?

_____ 48. Do you discourage friends from dropping in unannounced?

_____ 49. Would you feel it a sign of weakness to seek help for a sexual problem?

_____ 50. Are you upset when a homosexual seems attracted to you?

_____ 51. Do you have difficulty communicating with someone of the opposite sex?

_____ 52. Do you believe that men who write poetry are less masculine than men who drive trucks?

_____ 53. Do most women prefer men with well-developed muscles to men with well-developed emotions?

_____ 54. Are you generally indifferent to the kind of place in which you live?

_____ 55. Do you consider it a waste of money to buy flowers for yourself or for others?

_____ 56. When you see an art object you like, do you pass it up if the cost would mean cutting back on your food budget?

_____ 57. Do you think it pretentious and extravagant to have an elegant dinner when alone or with members of your immediate family?

_____ 58. Are you often bored?

_____ 59. Do Sundays depress you?

_____ 60. Do you frequently feel nervous?

_____ 61. Do you dislike the work you do to earn a living?

_____ 62. Do you think a carefree hippie lifestyle would have no delights for you?

_____ 63. Do you watch TV selectively rather than simply to kill time?

_____ 64. Have you read any good books recently?

_____ 65. Do you often daydream?

_____ 66. Do you like to fondle pets?

_____ 67. Do you like many different forms and styles of art?

_____ 68. Do you enjoy watching an attractive person of the opposite sex?

_____ 69. Can you describe how your date or mate looked the last time you went out together?

_____ 70. Do you find it easy to talk to new acquaintances?

_____ 71. Do you communicate with others through touch as well as through words?

_____ 72. Do you enjoy pleasing members of your family?

_____ 73. Do you avoid joining clubs or organizations?

_____ 74. Do you worry more about how you present yourself to perspective dates than about how you treat them?

_____ 75. Are your afraid that if people knew you too well they wouldn't like you?

_____ 76. Do you fall in love at first sight?

_____ 77. Do you always fall in love with someone who reminds you of your parent of the opposite sex?

_____ 78. Do you think love is all you presently need to be happy?

_____ 79. Do you feel a sense of rejection if a person you love tries to preserve his or her independence?

_____ 80. Can you accept your loved one's anger and still believe in his or her love?

_____ 81. Can you express your innermost thoughts and feelings to the person you love?

_____ 82. Do you talk over disagreements with your partner rather than silently worry about them?

_____ 83. Can you easily accept the fact that your partner has loved others before you and not worry about how you compare with them?

_____ 84. Can you accept a partner's disinterest in sex without feeling rejected?

_____ 85. Can you accept occasional sessions of unsatisfactory sex without blaming yourself or your partner?

_____ 86. Should unmarried adolescents be denied contraceptives?

_____ 87. Do you believe that even for adults in private, there are some sexual acts that should remain illegal?

_____ 88. Do you think that hippie communes and Israeli kibbutzim have nothing useful to reach the average American?

_____ 89. Should a couple put up with an unhappy marriage for the sake of their children?

_____ 90. Do you think that mate swappers necessarily have unhappy marriages?

_____ 91. Should older men and women be content not to have sex?

_____ 92. Do you believe that pornography contributes to sex crimes?

_____ 93. Is sexual abstinence beneficial to a person's health, strength, wisdom or character?

_____ 94. Can a truly loving wife or husband sometimes be sexually unreceptive?

_____ 95. Can intercourse during a woman's menstrual period be as appealing or as appropriate as at any other time?

___ 96. Should a woman concentrate on her own sensual pleasure during intercourse rather than pretend enjoyment to increase her partner's pleasure?

___ 97. Can a man's effort to bring his partner to orgasm reduce his own pleasure?

___ 98. Should fun and sensual pleasure be the principal goals in sexual relation?

___ 99. Is pressure to perform well a common cause of sexual incapacity?

___ 100. Is sexual intercourse for you an uninhibited romp rather than a demonstration of your sexual ability?

Scoring: Questions   1–18, count your minuses.   _____

            Questions   19–47, count your pluses.   _____

            Questions   48–62, count your minuses.   _____

            Questions   63–72, count your pluses.   _____

            Questions   73–79, count your minuses.   _____

            Questions, 80–85, count your pluses.   _____

            Questions, 86–93, count your minuses.   _____

            Questions, 94–100, count your pluses.   _____

                                    Total: _____

Subtract from this total *half* the number of zero answers to obtain your corrected total.

Interpretation: If your corrected total score is under 30, you have a shell like a tortoise and tend to draw your head in at the first sign of psychological danger. Probably life handed you some bad blows when you were too young to fight back, so you've erected strong defenses against the kind of intimacy that could leave you vulnerable to ego injury.

If you scored between 30 and 60, you are about average, which shows you have potential. You have erected some strong defenses, but you have matured enough, and have had enough good experiences, that you are willing to take a few chances with other human beings, confident that you will survive regardless.

Any score over 60 means you possess the self-confidence and sense of security not only to run the risks of intimacy but to enjoy it. This could be a little discomforting to another person who does not have your capacity or potential for close interpersonal relationships, but you are definitely ahead in the game, and you can make the right person extremely happy just by being yourself.

If your score approaches 100, you are either an intimate superperson, or you are worried too much about giving the right answers, which put you back in the under-30 category.

Source: Excerpted from <u>Go to Health</u>. copyright (c) 1973 by Communications Research Machines, Inc. Used with permission of Delacorte Press.

Types of Love

Name: _____ Date: _____

Directions: Read these descriptions carefully. How have you either given or received each of these types of love? Write down the occasions when you have been the source or recipient of each type of love, or write down the first names of people you have been involved with for each type of love. Can these types of love be combined?

Type of Love	Given To	Received From
Romantic Love	_____	_____
	_____	_____
	_____	_____
Possessive Love	_____	_____
	_____	_____
	_____	_____
Best Friends Love	_____	_____
	_____	_____
	_____	_____
Pragmatic Love	_____	_____
	_____	_____
	_____	_____
Altruistic Love	_____	_____
	_____	_____
	_____	_____
Game-Playing Love	_____	_____
	_____	_____
	_____	_____

Are You and Your Partner Suited for a Life Together?

Name: _____ Date: _____

Purpose: Most people carry an image in their hearts of the "perfect" marriage--marriage as they would wish it to be. But it can be hard to articulate. It is not always possible to state explicitly what it is you want...dream...wish...especially if you are not really sure yourself. And sometimes, it spoils everything when you have to ask for it.

Directions: Below you will find an inventory divided into ten areas. In the blanks provided to the right of each statement, you and your partner should answer either AGREE or DISAGREE or NEUTRAL to each statement.

	You	Partner

COMMUNICATION

1. Let's share our experiences; ask me what I've been doing and tell me what you've been doing. _____ _____

2. I'd like to be able to express my feelings without fear of criticism. _____ _____

3. You shouldn't talk so much. _____ _____

4. You shouldn't assume what I need without finding out first if you're right. _____ _____

5. You shouldn't moralize. _____ _____

6. Never lie to me. _____ _____

7. I'd like you to guess what I need without having to tell you. _____ _____

8. I wish you would learn to listen to me. _____ _____

9. You can yell sometimes. _____ _____

10. I don't like you to interrupt me. _____ _____

DECISIONS

1. I'd like to be the one who makes the important decisions. _____ _____

2. Let's talk over everything and always make joint decisions. _____ _____

3. I am ready to lie, bribe, and blackmail just to get my way. _____ _____

4. Let's agree in advance who's to make decisions in each area of our lives together. _____ _____

5. Let's try to persuade each other quietly and rationally. _____ _____

6. When we disagree on major issues let's turn to somebody more experienced for help. _____ _____

59

7. We should try to give in without trying to "get back" at each other. _____ _____

8. When we disagree, we should flip a coin in order to reach a decision. _____ _____

9. I want you to have the responsibility for making our decisions. _____ _____

10. In order to stay together, we should agree on everything. _____ _____

RELATIVES

1. I'd like to spend more time with my family. _____ _____

2. I would like our parents to help us out financially. _____ _____

3. I don't like you to criticize my family. _____ _____

4. I'd like to live near my parents. _____ _____

5. You should be nicer to my parents. _____ _____

6. We should spend our holidays with my family. _____ _____

7. You consult your parents too frequently. _____ _____

8. Don't compare me to your mother/father. _____ _____

9. I'd like your parents not to interfere in our lives. _____ _____

10. We should consult our parents on important issues. _____ _____

ROLES

1. We should divide chores equally between us. _____ _____

2. My career should come first. _____ _____

3. You should plan our social life. _____ _____

4. You should be the one to invite friends over. _____ _____

5. You should be responsible for the children's education. _____ _____

6. I'll be responsible for the yard and garden work. _____ _____

7. You should be responsible for household repairs. _____ _____

8. My job is to earn a living for the family. _____ _____

9. I'll be responsible for decorating our home. _____ _____

10. We'll share the cooking between us. _____ _____

CONFLICTS

1. We should never quarrel. _____ _____
2. You should be the first to make up. _____ _____
3. You should learn to control your emotions. _____ _____
4. I don't like you to run away in the middle of a fight. _____ _____
5. We should always make up before we go to bed. _____ _____
6. During a quarrel, we should be allowed to curse. _____ _____
7. When we argue, we shouldn't bring up grievances from the past. _____ _____
8. It's all right to cry during a quarrel. _____ _____
9. It's all right to yell and let off steam when we argue. _____ _____
10. We should always keep our anger under control. _____ _____

ENTERTAINMENT

1. We should spend all our free time together. _____ _____
2. We must invite friends over at least once a week. _____ _____
3. We should get out of the house quite often and go to a movie, play, concert, or just out to dinner. _____ _____
4. Once a year we should go on a special vacation together. _____ _____
5. I'd like to have time on my own at least once a week. _____ _____
6. We should take time every day to talk things over and be together. _____ _____
7. You shouldn't spend so much time sleeping when we are together. _____ _____
8. I need to have enough time alone to spend on my hobbies. _____ _____
9. We should have a large circle of friends. _____ _____
10. I want to spend as much time as possible at home. _____ _____

AFFECTION

1. You should often tell me you love me. _____ _____
2. I would like you to hug and caress me a lot. _____ _____
3. It's OK for us to show affection in public. _____ _____

4. I'd like you to give me a gift from time to time, not just on birthdays or anniversaries. _____ _____

5. You should tell me more often that I'm attractive. _____ _____

6. You should always remember my birthday/our anniversary. _____ _____

7. From time to time, I'd like to act out romantic fantasies together. _____ _____

8. I like it when you dance only with me at parties. _____ _____

9. I like you to baby me from time to time. _____ _____

10. I'd like you to take me in your arms and comfort me when I'm sad. _____ _____

MONEY

1. We should have separate bank accounts. _____ _____

2. We should plan all our household expenses together. _____ _____

3. You should be responsible for paying monthly bills. _____ _____

4. I'll decide what our expenses should be. _____ _____

5. I don't want to have to report to you every time I spend money. _____ _____

6. We should each have some money for our personal use, to spend any way we choose. _____ _____

7. We should put every spare penny into a savings account. _____ _____

8. We should keep a monthly record of expenses. _____ _____

9. We should make only cash purchases and not buy credit. _____ _____

10. We should spend our money as we please, enjoying today and not worrying about tomorrow. _____ _____

SEX

1. You should initiate sex. _____ _____

2. You should be able to guess what makes me feel good. _____ _____

3. We should have sex more often. _____ _____

4. We should have sex only when I show signs that I really want it. _____ _____

5. Our sex life should be varied. _____ _____

6. You should not feel rejected or try to make me feel guilty when I'm not in the mood to make love. _____ _____

7. You should never desire anyone else. _____ _____

8. You should feel free to have an affair. _____ _____

9. You should tell me if you have an affair. _____ _____

10. You should be responsible for birth control. _____ _____

PARENTHOOD

Note: If you do not have--or plan to have--children answer "as if" you do, to questions 5-10.

1. We should have only "planned" children. _____ _____

2. We should postpone having children until we have established our careers and are prepared financially. _____ _____

3. It's a mother's duty to stay home to bring up the children. _____ _____

4. We will have no children. _____ _____

5. We should always keep a united front and never argue in front of our children. _____ _____

6. Our children's needs should always come before our own. _____ _____

7. Our children should be punished when they are bad. _____ _____

8. Our children should grow up free from any restrictions. _____ _____

9. Our children should have everything we could not have as children. _____ _____

10. Whatever happens, we should stay together for the children's sake until they are grown. _____ _____

Scoring: Now compare your answers. For each "compatible" answer, score 1 point. There are several ways to arrive at a compatible score, so a discussion period aimed at determining compatibility is very important.

For example: You have a compatible answer if you both gave the same answer to a statement such as "Let's talk over everything and always make joint decisions."

However, you also have a compatible answer if one of you answers "Disagree" to such a statement as "I'd like to be the one to make the important decisions" (this person does not want to make the decisions). Therefore, if the other partner answered "Agree" to the same statement, the one person's objection is compatible with the other's agreement with the statement.

A third example is where both of you have answered "Neutral" to an item; your choice is compatible since the issue is not important to either of you. Even if one of you answered "Neutral" and the other answered either "Agree" or "Disagree," communication about the issue involved may determine whether your attitudes are in conflict. One of you may even change your original choice, if the issue--after discussion--fades (or increases) in importance. Being able to arrive at an answer through this discussion indicates compatibility.

After discussing your answers with your partner, total your "compatibility" answers for each questionnaire. List them here:

Communication	____
Decisions	____
Relatives	____
Roles	____
Conflicts	____
Entertainment	____
Affection	____
Money	____
Sex	____
Parenthood	____
TOTAL	____

Analysis:

Score	Compatibility Prognosis
Below 10	You had better part on friendly terms right now (if you haven't already done so while answering the questionnaires). You are not suited for a life together.
11 to 50	Each one of you is a distinct individual, with different ambitions and goals. However, this does not mean that you cannot live happily together if you do not mistake interference for intimacy. Keep your distinct worlds.
51 to 90	You are well matched but should re-examine the issues you disagree on. Try to reach a common denominator.
91 and up	You suit each other perfectly and stand a good chance for a long and happy life together.

Source: Robert F. Valois and Sandra Kammerman. Your Sexuality: A Self- Assessment, 2nd Ed. New York McGraw-Hill, 1992: 212-217.

Getting to Know Your Own Level of Trust

Name: _____ Date: _____

Directions: Reach each of the following statements and decide whether it is true of your relationship with your partner. Indicate how strongly you agree or disagree by choosing the appropriate number from the scale below and placing it in the space provided in the left-hand margin.

1 = strongly disagree   5 = mildly agree

2 = moderately disagree   6 = moderately agree

3 = mildly disagree   7 = strongly agree

4 = neutral

Initial Score   *Final Score*

___ 1. I know how my partner is going to act. May partner can always be counted on to act as I expect. ___

___ 2. I have found that my partner is a thoroughly dependable person, especially when it comes to things that are important. ___

___ 3. My partner's behavior tends to be quite variable. I can't always be sure what my partner will surprise me with next. ___

___ 4. Though times may change and the future in uncertain, I have faith that my partner will always be ready and willing to offer me strength, come what may. ___

___ 5. Based on past experience, I cannot with complete confidence, rely on my partner to keep promises made to me. ___

___ 6. It is sometimes difficult for me to be absolutely certain that my partner will always continue to care for me; the future holds too many uncertainties and too many things can change in our relationship as time goes on. ___

___ 7. My partner is a very honest person and, even if my partner were to make unbelievable statements, people should feel confident that what they are hearing is the truth. ___

___ 8. My partner is not very predictable. People can't always be certain how my partner is going to act from one day to another. ___

___ 9. My partner has proven to be a faithful person. No matter who my partner was married to, she or he would never be unfaithful, even if there was absolutely no chance of being caught. ___

___ 10. I am never concerned that unpredictable conflicts and serious tensions may damage our relationship because I know we can weather any storm. ___

___ 11. I am very familiar with the patterns of behavior my partner has established, and he or she will behave in certain ways. ___

___ 12. If I have never faced a particular issue with my partner before, I occasionally worry that he or she won't take my feelings into account. ___

___ 13. Even in familiar circumstances, I am not totally certain my partner will act in the same way twice. ___

65

Initial Score   *Final Score*

____ 14. I feel completely secure in facing unknown new situations
        because I know my partner will never let me down.   ____
____ 15. My partner is not necessarily someone others always
        consider reliable. I can think of some times when my   ____
        partner could not be counted on.
____ 16. I occasionally find myself feeling uncomfortable with the
        emotional investment I have made in our relationship   ____
        because I find it hard to completely set aside my doubts
        about what lies ahead.
____ 17. My partner has not always proven to be trustworthy in the
        past, and there are times when I am hesitant to let my   ____
        partner engage in activities that make me feel vulnerable.
____ 18. My partner behaves in a consistent manner.   ____

Scoring: This is how to score yourself: For questions 3, 5, 6, 8, 12, 13,
15, 16 and 17, reverse numbers. That is, if you put down a 1, change it to
a 7, and write this in the space provided in the right-hand margin. In the
same way, if you scored a 2 change it to a 6, 3 to a 5, 5 to a 3, 6 to a 2,
and 7 to a 1. A neutral score of 4 remains unchanged.

When you have reversed the scoring for the items listed above, take the
scores for the remaining items and write them in the right-hand margin just
as they are. Add all the scores in the right-hand margin to obtain your
final trust score.

If you are interested, you can add up the scores for the following
questions to arrive at a score for each subscale of trust: Predictability,
add 1, 3, 8, 11, 13, and 18. Dependability, add 2, 5, 7, 9, 15, and 17.
Faith, add 4, 6, 10, 12, 14, and 16.

How Jealous Are You?

Name: _____ Date: _____

Purpose: One feeling that often causes conflict between two people is jealousy, perhaps because men and women often experience and express jealousy in different ways. If partners are unable to communicate openly about an issue, a conflict may result. The following exercise is designed to help bring to light your experiences with jealousy so that you may better understand yourself and your partner. If you currently do not have partner, simply respond to the questions in terms of your last relationship or a hoped-for future one.

Directions: Read each statement carefully, then respond YES or NO in the blank following the statement.

1. You have found at times that you actually like feeling jealous. ____

2. Your spells of jealousy seem to follow a pattern,one after another.____

3. Sometimes you get so jealous that you lose your appetite or you overeat. ____

4. When you hear about, or think about, your partner's former lovers, you are jealous. ____

5. You avoid close relationships with people other than your partner because such situations may cause your partner to be jealous. ____

6. You are very jealous of your partner's friends, yet you tell people you are not the jealous type. ____

7. You are apt to display fits of jealousy with no apparent cause. ____

8. You are often jealous of your partner's friends even when you know your partner has no romantic feelings toward them. ____

9. At social gatherings you are aware of every move your partner makes. ____

10. Jealousy has led you to spy on your partner. ____

11. You want to know where your partner is at all times. ____

12. It would definitely be a crisis if you discovered your partner had one sexual encounter with another person. ____

13. The feeling of loneliness is common to you. ____

14. You have though of taking revenge on a person you felt was a rival. ____

15. You feel that jealousy is proof of your love for your partner. ____

16. You are jealous of your partner's hobbies. ____

Scoring: If you have responded YES to *more than five of these statements*, you are allowing jealousy to control your life. To continue in this way to leave yourself open to considerable pain and anguish. When jealousy arises, talk about it and reaffirm your commitment to your partner. You need to listen to each other.

Source: Robert F. Valois and Sandra Kammerman. <u>Your Sexuality: A Self-Assessment, 2nd Ed.</u> New York: McGraw-Hill, 1992,:111-112.

Needs In Close Relationships

Name: _____ Date: _____

Check one: I want my boy friend to ...   I want my girl friend to ...
           I want my husband to ...   I want my wife to ...

Directions: Choose from the list below the affectional needs you feel the strongest.

___ 1. Allow me more freedom.

___ 2. Display more affection for me.

___ 3. Have more respect for my judgment.

___ 4. Feel more attached to me.

___ 5. Treat me in a warmer and friendlier manner.

___ 6. Be more interested in my activities.

___ 7. Take me out more.

___ 8. Engage more in activities with me.

___ 9. Allow me to make more decisions.

___ 10. Display more love for me.

___ 11. Feel more strongly that I am a significant aspect of his/her life.

___ 12. Have more respect for my ability to think for myself.

___ 13. Share more of his/her recreational time with me.

___ 14. Expect less accomplishment from me.

___ 15. Be more interested in me.

___ 16. Be warmer and closer in his/her behavior toward me.

___ 17. Feel more strongly that I am an important member of the family.

___ 18. Have more confidence in my ability to learn things.

___ 19. Spend more time with me.

___ 20. Give me more freedom to choose my own friends.

___ 21. Be more interested in the things I'm interested in.

___ 22. Spend more time alone with me.

___ 23. Put fewer limits on what I do.

___ 24. Give me more praise for my accomplishments.

___ 25. Be more confident that I will succeed in life.

___ 26. Give me more attention.

___ 27. Feel more love for me.

___ 28. Be more interested in being with me around the house.

___ 29. Feel more confident about my ability to think critically.

69

_____ 30. Allow me to think for myself.

_____ 31. Feel closer to me as a person.

_____ 32. Feel more strongly that I am significant person.

_____ 33. Have more respect for my ability to solve problems.

_____ 34. Take me out more/go on more trips with me.

_____ 35. Criticize me less for my conduct and manners.

_____ 36. Feel more strongly that I am an important person.

_____ 37. Feel more confident about my ability to succeed at difficult tasks.

_____ 38. Spend more of his/her free time with me.

_____ 39. Supervise my activities less.

_____ 40. Feel more affection for me.

_____ 41. Be more confident that I can be trusted with responsibilities.

_____ 42. Spend more time showing me how to do certain things.

_____ 43. Insist less on respect from me.

_____ 44. Feel more warmth for me.

_____ 45. Display more romantic love and/or sexual passion with me.

Describe your needs in a close relationship.

Muehlenhard-Quackenbush Sexual Attitude Scale

Name: _____ Date: _____

Purpose: This exercise is designed for you and your partner or friend to examine some of their attitudes about male and female sexuality.

Directions: Reach each of the statements below carefully and respond using the scale provided.

A = Agree Strongly	B = Agree Mildly	C = Disagree Mildly	D = Disagree Strongly

	You	Partner/ Friend
1. It's worse for a woman to sleep around than it is for a man.	____	____
2. It's best for a guy to lose his virginity before he's out of his teens.	____	____
3. It's okay for a woman to have more than one sexual relationship at a time.	____	____
4. It is just as important for a man to be a virgin when he marries as it is for a woman.	____	____
5. I approve of a 16-year-old girl having sex just as much as a 16-year-old boy having sex.	____	____
6. I kind of admire a girl who has had sex with a lot of guys.	____	____
7. I kind of feel sorry for a 21-year-old woman who is still a virgin.	____	____
8. A woman having casual sex is just as acceptable to me as a man having casual sex.	____	____
9. It's ok for a man to have sex with a woman he is not in love with.	____	____
10. I kind of admire a guy who has had sex with a lot of girls.	____	____
11. A woman who initiates sex is too aggressive.	____	____
12. It's ok for a man to have more than one sexual relationship at a time.	____	____
13. I question the character of a woman who has had a lot of sexual partners.	____	____
14. I admire a man who is a virgin when he gets married.	____	____
15. A man should be more sexually experienced than his wife.	____	____
16. A girl who has sex on the first date is easy.	____	____
17. I kind of feel sorry for a 21-year-old man who is still a virgin.	____	____

	You	Partner/ Friend
18. I question the character of a guy who has had a lot of sexual partners.	____	____
19. Women are naturally more monogamous (inclined to stick to one partner) than are men.	____	____
20. A man should be sexually experienced when he gets married.	____	____
21. A guy who has sex on the first date is easy.	____	____
22. It's ok for a woman to have sex with a man she is not in love with.	____	____
23. A woman should be sexually experienced when she gets married.	____	____
24. It's best for a girl to lose her virginity before she's out of her teens.	____	____
25. I admire a women who is a virgin when she gets married.	____	____
26. A man who initiates sex is too aggressive.	____	____

Scoring: Convert your A's to zeros, your B's to 1's, your C's to 2's, your D's to 3's. Computing your total involves some simple mathematics:

#4 + #5 + #8 + (3 - #1) + (3 - #15) + (3 - #19) + (#24 - #2) + (#3 - #12) + (#6 - #10) + (#7 - #17) + (#22 - #9) + (#26 - #11) + (#18 - #13) + (#14 - #25) + (21 - #16) + (#23 - #20) = YOUR TOTAL

Interpretation: The actual name of the scale is the Sexual Double Standard Scale. A person having identical sexual standards for women and men should score zero. A score greater than zero reflects more restrictive sexual standards for women than for men; the highest possible score is 48. A score less than zero reflects more restrictive sexual standards for men than for women; the lowest possible score is -30.

From a sample of college students at a large southwestern university, researchers found a mean score for women to be 11.99 (N=461) and a mean score for men to be 13.15 (N=255).

Source: Charlene L. Muehlenhard and Debra M. Quackenbush The Sexual Double Standard Scale, Department of Psychology and Women's Studies University of Kansas. Reprinted with permission.

Sexual Arousal Scale (Men)

Name: _____   Date: _____

Purpose: Arousal is the magic key to sexuality and is a powerful persuader. We've included two versions of the Arousal Scale since men and women seem to be turned on by very different types of stimuli. If you have someone special in your life, the two of you may want to take the tests together and compare levels of arousal. Then look over the specific things that you each find stimulating.

Directions: In the arousal scale for men below, you'll find a list of 40 items or images that you may find sexually stimulating. Read each description and choose the number from the scale below that represents your level of arousal. Write your response next to each item, then turn the page to find your score.

Doesn't Turn Me On 1	A Little Turn-on for Me 2	A Pretty Good Turn-on for Me 3	Turns Me On a Great Deal 4

____ 1. A passionate couple in public

____ 2. The smell of perfume

____ 3. Romantic music

____ 4. The feel of lingerie

____ 5. An extremely intelligent woman

____ 6. Driving fast

____ 7. Wet bodies

____ 8. A woman in leather clothing

____ 9. A woman without a bra running across the street

____ 10. Tan lines

____ 11. A see-through blouse

____ 12. A crowded elevator

____ 13. The feel of a cashmere sweater

____ 14. Long hair

____ 15. Large breasts

____ 21. Pearls around a woman's neck

____ 22. A woman driving a powerful car

____ 23. Freckles on a woman's chest

____ 24. Pointed toenails

____ 25. Small, firm breasts

____ 26. A pregnant woman

____ 27. A very tall woman

____ 28. A woman driving a motorcycle

____ 29. Very high heels

____ 30. A pleasingly plump woman

____ 31. Tall boots

____ 32. A nubile adolescent girl

____ 33. Erotic talk

____ 34. The nape of a woman's neck

____ 35. Long legs

___ 16. Tight jeans and T-shirts   ___ 36. A woman executive

___ 17. An aggressive woman   ___ 37. A pantyhose commercial on
                                                  television

___ 18. A woman in a tight skirt   ___ 38. A woman in sunglasses

___ 19. A silk blouse   ___ 39. An athletic woman

___ 20. A woman in velvet   ___ 40. Following a woman up stairs

Scoring: To find your score on the Arousal Scale, simply add up all your numerical responses and write the total below.

Total Score ___

Interpretation: The Norms Tables will show you where you score in terms of arousal intensity and frequency. The *average scorer* is indicating healthy feelings of arousal in his or her day-to-day life. Most of us score here. The *high scorer* is easily turned on and probably finds sexual undertones in many varied situations. Men who score high indicate strong requirements for body contact, but our research also reveals that these men express high levels of sexual satisfaction. Women who score in this range show low levels of inhibition, but also indicate they have an external locus of control, meaning that they rely on outside influences for their sexual motivations. The *low scorer* is turned on by few things on the scale. It could be that the specific qualities that serve as turn-ons for low scorers may not have been included, or the few high-ranking items chosen by a low scorer may be even more arousing than the scale indicates.

Problems can arise if high and low scorers are partners in a sexual relationship: One can't understand why the other is always so turned on; the second can't see (or accept) why the first is not. When partners have very different levels of arousal, a discussion of these differences may not be enough. The sex differences in the types of characteristics that trigger arousal also need to be understood--and accepted--by both. Arousal may be in the mind of the beholder, but meaningful communication can be the glue that holds the beholders together.

NORMS TABLE - MEN

Very Low	Low	Average	High	Very High
64 and below	65-74	75-76	88-100	101 and above

Sexual Arousal Scale (Women)

Name: _____   Date: _____

Purpose: Arousal is the magic key to sexuality and is a powerful persuader. We've included two versions of the Arousal Scale since men and women seem to be turned on by very different types of stimuli. If you have someone special in your life, the two of you may want to take the tests together and compare levels of arousal. Then look over the specific things that you each find stimulating.

Directions: In the Arousal Scale for women, below, you'll find a list of 40 items or images that you may find sexually stimulating. Read each description and choose the number from the scale below that represents your level of arousal. Write your response to each item, then turn the page to find your score.

Doesn't Turn Me On 1	A Little Turn-on for Me 2	A Pretty Good Turn-on for Me 3	Turns Me On a Great Deal 4

____ 1. An erotic romantic photograph

____ 2. The smell of fresh sweat

____ 3. Sounds of lovemaking from next door

____ 4. A men's underwear commercial on television

____ 5. Eye contact

____ 6. Dancing

____ 7. Watching a space launch

____ 8. A man in dark sunglasses

____ 9. Spending his money

____ 10. A good sense of humor

____ 11. A celebrity or movie star

____ 12. A male jogger in tight shorts

____ 13. A sexy passage in a romantic novel

____ 14. A vampire story

____ 15. An erotic conversation

____ 21. A bubble bath

____ 22. Well-manicured hands on a man

____ 23. A man wearing a wedding band

____ 24. Having a man give me flowers

____ 25. A beautiful woman

____ 26. A thoughtful and supportive man

____ 27. A man enjoying children

____ 28. Undressing in front of a full-length mirror

____ 29. A warm summer night

____ 30. A man with a foreign accent

____ 31. A man in a tuxedo

____ 32. An attractive doctor

____ 33. A man with muscles

____ 34. A moustache or beard

____ 35. A really smart man

_____ 16. A male stripper

_____ 17. A man in tight jeans

_____ 18. Flirtation

_____ 19. Drinking champagne

_____ 20. Knowing that I look good

_____ 36. The smell of a man's cologne

_____ 37. Wearing lingerie

_____ 38. An athletic man

_____ 39. A man in uniform

_____ 40. A man with a hairy chest

Scoring: To find your score on the Arousal Scale, simply add up all your numerical responses and write the total below.

Total Score _____

Interpretation: The Norms Tables will show you where you score in terms of arousal intensity and frequency. The *average scorer* is indicating healthy feelings of arousal in his or her day-to-day life. Most of us score here. The *high scorer* is easily turned on and probably finds sexual undertones in many varied situations. Men who score high indicate strong requirements for body contact, but our research also reveals that these men express high levels of sexual satisfaction. Women who score in this range show low levels of inhibition, but also indicate they have an external locus of control, meaning that they rely on outside influences for their sexual motivations. The *low scorer* is turned on by few things on the scale. It could be that the specific qualities that serve as turn-ons for low scorers may not have been included, or the few high-ranking items chosen by a low scorer may be even more arousing than the scale indicates.

Problems can aries if high and low scorers are partners in a sexual relationship: One can't understand why the other is always so turned on; the second can't see (or accept) why the first is not. When partners have very different levels of arousal, a discussion of these differences may not be enough. The sex differences in the types of characteristics that trigger arousal also need to be understood--and accepted--by both. Arousal may be in the mind of the beholder, but meaningful communication can be the glue that holds the beholders together.

NORMS TABLE - WOMEN

Very Low	Low	Average	High	Very High
62 and below	63-73	74-92	93-102	103 and above

Source: From <u>The Love Exam</u> Copyright (c) 1984 by Rita Aero and Elliot Weiner, Ph.D. Published by Quill Books. All rights reserved. Used with permission.

Index of Sexual Satisfaction

Name: _____   Date: _____

Directions: For each of the following statements, assign a number reflecting your current or past sexual relationships as follows:

1 = Rarely or none of the time
2 = A little of the time
3 = Some of the time
4 = A good part of the time
5 = Most or all of the time

___ 1. I feel that my partner enjoys our sex life.

___ 2. My sex life is very exciting.

___ 3. Sex is fun for my partner and me.

___ 4. I feel that my partner sees little in me except for the sex I can give.

___ 5. I feel that sex is dirty and disgusting.

___ 6. My sex life is monotonous.

___ 7. When we have sex it is too rushed and hurriedly completed.

___ 8. I feel that my sex life is lacking quality.

___ 9. My partner is very sexually exciting.

___ 10. I enjoy the sex techniques that my partner likes or uses.

___ 11. I feel that my partner wants too much sex from me.

___ 12. I think that sex is wonderful.

___ 13. My partner dwells on sex too much.

___ 14. I feel that sex is something that has to be endured in our relationship.

___ 15. My partner is too rough or brutal when we have sex.

___ 16. My partner observes good personal hygiene.

___ 17. I feel that sex is a normal function of our relationship.

___ 18. My partner does not want sex when I do.

___ 19. I feel that our sex life really adds a lot to our relationship.

___ 20. I would like to have sexual contact with someone other than my partner.

___ 21. It is easy for me to get sexually excited by my partner.

___ 22. I feel that my partner is sexually pleased with me.

___ 23. My partner is very sensitive to my sexual needs and desires.

___ 24. I feel that I should have sex more often.

___ 25. I feel that my sex life is boring.

Scoring: Use the following key to score your answers:
- Score number answered for questions 4, 5, 6, 7, 8, 11, 13, 14, 15, 18, 20, 24, and 25.
- Score reverse of number answered (see below) for questions 1, 2, 3, 9, 10, 12, 16, 17, 19, 21, 22, and 23.
- To score the reverse of number answered:
  if you answered "1," score 5
  if you answered "2," score 4
  if you answered "3," score 3
  if you answered "4," score 2
  if you answered "5," score 1

Interpretation:

0-29   You have little dissatisfaction with your sex life and enjoy a mutually enjoyable and stimulating sex life, probably in a long-lasting relationship.

30-100   You are somewhat to very dissatisfied with your sex life and may be involved in a disintegrating relationship.

Source: Rita Aero and Elliot Weiner The Mind Test New York: William Morrow & Co., 1981.

Love and Sex

Name: _____ Date: _____

Directions: Complete the following sentence by writing down your immediate thoughts. Do not think too much about your response.

1. Love is _____.

2. My greatest fear of love is _____.

3. To me, love without sex is _____.

4. To me, love with sex is _____.

5. To me, sex without love is _____.

6. I need love because _____.

7. I feel most loved when _____.

8. One lovable quality about me is _____
   _____.

9. I could increase my ability to love others by _____.

10. I express my love for others primarily by _____.

11. To me love means _____.

12. If nobody loved me, _____.

13. For me the greatest risk in loving is _____.

14. When I'm with those I love, I _____
    _____.

15. When I'm separated from my loved ones, I _____
    _____.

Parents? Inventory

Name: _____   Date: _____

Purpose: Because two people are needed to conceive a child, two people should determine whether and when to conceive. The advent of more reliable birth control makes such planning possible. If you are considering having a child, this exercise will help you examine the expectations that you and your partner have of parenthood. Even if you feel parenthood is far off in the future, this will help you determine your current expectations.

Directions: You and your partner should independently write a sentence or two in answer to each question. Then go through what you have written and indicate, by a check in the proper column, whether each of these predictions would make you pleased, unhappy, or neither if it came true. Pick out which of the areas covered in the questions are most important to you in your decision. (If you do not have a partner, ask a friend to complete the inventory. This will give you a perspective of differences of opinion that can be involved and the complexity of the issue.)

Assessment

	Pleased	Unhappy	Neither
1. How will having a child affect my partner's and/or my career and/or education?	_____	_____	_____
2. How will a child affect our financial situation now and later?	_____	_____	_____
3. How will the child affect our relationship with each other?	_____	_____	_____
4. How will the child affect our relationship with family and friends?	_____	_____	_____
5. How will the child affect our freedom, privacy, and spontaneity?	_____	_____	_____
6. How will my partner and I deal with the pregnancy and birth?	_____	_____	_____
7. How will each of us deal with supervising, training, and being with a young child (birth to 8 years)?	_____	_____	_____
8. How will we deal with supervising, training and being with an older child or teenager?	_____	_____	_____
9. How will we deal with possible problems of health and personality our child could have?	_____	_____	_____
10. How do we feel about bringing up a child in today's world (i.e., what kinds of problems and solutions are there for the child's future world)?	_____	_____	_____

Scoring: Compare answers with your partner. Discussing realistic predictions of parenthood can quell some fears (or bring others to mind) and be a starting point for making a decision.

Personal Application: The following worksheet will help you think through the impact a child will have on your life. In the first column list needs you have that a child might help satisfy--for example, the need for love, for attention, and for alleviation of boredom. Then, in the second column, list other ways these same needs could be met.

NEEDS A CHILD COULD SATISFY	OTHER WAYS THESE NEEDS COULD BE MET
_____	_____
_____	_____
_____	_____
_____	_____

NEEDS A CHILD COULD SATISFY	OTHER WAYS THESE NEEDS COULD BE MET
_____	_____
_____	_____
_____	_____
_____	_____

List reasons for choosing to have a child. These can range from very personal reasons to reasons having to do with external factors.

1. _____
2. _____
3. _____
4. _____
5. _____
6. _____
7. _____

List disadvantages of having children.

1. _____
2. _____
3. _____
4. _____

Source: Blake et al, _Self-Assessment and Behavior Change Manual._ New York: Random House, 1984. 84-86.

By Choice, Not by Chance

Name: _____   Date: _____

Directions: Indicate whether you think each of the following statements is true (T) or false (F).

____ 1. The purpose of birth control methods is to allow people the right to determine when they wish to enter parenthood.

____ 2. Preventing an unwanted pregnancy is an equal responsibility of both partners.

____ 3. A pregnancy will not result from any single act of intercourse.

____ 4. Natural methods of birth control present no problems of side effects but are less reliable than other methods.

____ 5. Douching is not a good method of birth control because sperm enter the uterus within seconds after intercourse.

____ 6. Withdrawal as a birth control method is about 75 percent effective.

____ 7. A female can have intercourse during her period without fear of pregnancy.

____ 8. Foam and a condom, used together, are about as effective as the pill.

____ 9. A very important factor in favor of the sponge, condom, and foam is their ready availability.

____ 10. A unique characteristic of the condom is that in addition to being an effective birth control method, it also provides a barrier to the spread of venereal disease.

____ 11. People are sterilized so that they cannot engage in sexual intercourse.

____ 12. A woman can verify the presence of her IUD by feeling the string at her cervix.

____ 13. The IUD may cause side effects because it is a foreign body.

____ 14. The contraceptive pill provides protection against venereal disease.

____ 15. The success of any birth control method is affected by the motivation of the people using it.

Scoring: Statements 1, 2, 4-6, 8-10, 12, 13, and 15 are true; 3, 7, 11, and 14 are false. The goal should be a perfect score.

Source: Adapted in part from Growing Awareness, 2nd ed. Rochester, NY; Planned Parenthood, 1979.

Personal Contraceptive Assessment

Name: _____   Date: _____

Directions: For each of the following contraceptive methods note the effectiveness, advantages, disadvantages, how comfortable you and your partner would feel using the approach, and the likelihood you would use it consistently without error. Use this information to help in your decision making.

Method	Effec-tiveness	Advan-tages	Disad-vantages	Comfort	Would Use Accurately & Consistently
Contraceptive Pill					
Spermicidal Foam					
Condom & Spermicide					
Diaphragm & Spermicide					
Vaginal Insert					
Sponge					
Rhythm					
Abstinence					
Sterilization					

Source: John LaPlace, Health, Englewood Cliffs, NJ; Prentice Hall, 1987.

Nutrition Quiz

Name: _____   Date: _____

Directions: Which of the following statements are true?

___   1. Large amounts of gelatin strengthen fingernails.

___   2. Toast has fewer calories than bread.

___   3. Food grown on depleted soils is nutritionally inferior.

___   4. Commercially canned and frozen foods are nearly worthless nutritionally.

___   5. Athletes need more protein in their diets than does the general population.

___   6. Feed a cold and starve a fever.

___   7. Taking extra vitamins and minerals will pep you up if you are fatigued.

___   8. Eating certain food combinations (such as fish and milk or cucumbers and milk) is dangerous.

___   9. Cheese causes constipation.

___ 10. Celery and fish are brain foods.

___ 11. Prunes, bran, and fresh fruits are "sure cures" for constipation.

___ 12. Yogurt is a nutritionally superior "wonder food" that will make you healthy.

___ 13. Vitamin supplements are necessary if you are to be well nourished.

___ 14. Oysters and black olives are aphrodisiacs (love potions).

___ 15. Any food craving indicates that the body needs the nutrients in that food.

___ 16. Obesity is usually caused by glandular disorders.

___ 17. "Health foods" are nutritionally superior to regular brands.

___ 18. Megadoses of vitamin C help to prevent colds.

Answers: All the statements are false.

1. Many factors influence fingernail formation including disease, environment, hormones, and nutrition. Gelatin is not one of them.

2. Toasting browns and dehydrates the exterior of the bread but does not reduce its caloric value.

3. Poor soil produces poor yields. Quantity is affected, not quality. For example, depleted soil produces fewer and smaller beans, but each bean is still nutritionally complete.

4. Some methods of food preparation--including home preparation--reduce the nutrient value of certain foods. But commercial methods of processing foods are designed to preserve their nutrient values.

5. Athletes may need more calories because of increased activity, but they do not need more protein.

6. The only valid guideline with colds and fever is to increase fluid   intake. With a fever, more calories are burned as a result of increased metabolic rate, but the person often eats less because of malaise and nausea.

7. Vitamins and minerals are not pep pills. They contain no calories (energy), nor are they stimulants. If fatigue persists, see a physician.

8. There are no known poisonous food combinations providing, of course, that neither food is contaminated or spoiled.

9. Generally, over 90 percent of the carbohydrate, protein, and fat in cheese is absorbed; constipation is not produced.

10. No one particular food builds any one body tissue.

11. There are several causes of constipation. If constipation is atonic, roughage may be helpful, but if it is spastic or obstructive, roughage is undesirable and the person is placed on a low-fiber diet.

12. Yogurt is a cultured milk product. It has the same nutritive value as the milk from which it was made. There are no "wonder foods."

13. A well-balanced diet provides all necessary vitamins. Hypervitaminosis can result from high amounts of ingested fat -soluble vitamins.

14. There are no known aphrodisiacs for humans.

15. Craving is a learned preference for a food rather than an indication that the body "needs" that food.

16. At the present time, it is thought that only 5 percent of obesity cases are caused by metabolic or glandular problems. The remaining 95 percent of cases are regulatory, which means too much food and too little exercise.

17. Foods claiming to be "natural" or "organic" are not superior to general foods available at the supermarket. Foods should be selected for their nutritional value, not their advertising value.

18. Many controlled and double-blind studies have been run. So far there is no statistical evidence that high doses of vitamin C help to prevent the common cold.

Source: Rosalind Reed and Thomas A. Lang, Health Behaviors, 2nd ed. St. Paul, MN: West Publishing Co., 1986.

Rating Your Diet

Name: _____ Date: _____

Purpose: The 40 questions which follow will help you focus on the key features of your diet. The (+) or (-) numbers under each set of answers instantly pat you on the back for good habits or alert you to problems you may not have realized you have.

The Grand Total rates your overall diet, on a scale from "Great" to "Arghh!"

The quiz focuses on fat, cholesterol, sodium, sugar, fiber, and vitamins A and C. It doesn't attempt to cover everything in your diet. Also, it doesn't try to measure precisely how much of these key nutrients you eat.

What the quiz will do is give you a rough sketch of your current eating habits and, implicitly, suggest what you can do to improve them.

Finally, please don't despair over a less-than-perfect score. A healthy diet isn't built overnight.

Directions:
o Next to each answer is a number with a + or - sign in front of it. Circle the number that is directly next to the answer you choose. That's your score for the question. (If you use a pencil, you can erase your answers and give the quiz to someone else.)

o Circle only one number for each question, unless the instructions tell you to "average two or more scores if necessary."

o How to average: In answering question 18, for example, if you drink club soda (+3) and coffee (-1) on a typical day, add the two scores (which gives you +2) and then divide by 2. That gives you a score of +1 for the question. If averaging gives you a fraction, round it to the nearest whole number.

o If a question doesn't apply to you, skip it.

o Pay attention to serving sizes. For example, a serving of vegetables is 1/2 cup. If you usually eat one cup of vegetables at a time, count it as two servings.

o Add up all your + scores and your - scores.

o Subtract your - scores from your + scores.
  That's your GRAND TOTAL.

1. How many times per week do you eat unprocessed red meat (steak, roast beef, lamb, or pork chops, burgers, etc.)?
   (a) never   +3   (d) 4-5   -1
   (b) 1 or less   +2   (e) 6 or more   -3
   (c) 2-3   0

2. After cooking, how large is the serving of red meat you usually eat? *(To convert from raw to cooked, reduce by 25 percent. For example, 4 oz. of raw meat shrinks to 3 oz. after cooking. There are 16 oz. in a pound.)*
   (a) 8 oz. or more   -3   (d) 3 oz. or less   0
   (b) 6-7 oz.   -2   (e) don't eat red meat   +3
   (c) 4-5 oz.   -1

3. Do you trim the visible fat when you cook or eat red meat?
   (a) yes   +1
   (b) no   -3
   (c) don't eat red meat 0

4. How many times per week do you eat processed meats (hot dogs, bacon, sausage, bologna, luncheon meats, etc.)? *(OMIT products that contain one gram of fat or less per serving.)*
   (a) none   +3   (d) 3-4   -1
   (b) less than 1   +2   (e) 5 or more -3
   (c) 1-2   0

5. What kind of ground meat or poultry do you usually eat?
   (a) regular ground beef -3   (d) ground turkey   +1
   (b) lean ground beef   -2   (e) Healthy Choice   +2
   (c) ground round   0   (f) don't eat ground meat +3

6. What type of bread do you usually eat?
   (a) whole wheat or other whole grain   +3
   (b) rye   +2
   (c) pumpernickel   +2
   (d) white, "wheat" French or Italian   -1

7. How many times per week do you eat deep-fried foods (fish, chicken, vegetables, potatoes, etc.)?
   (a) none   +3   (c) 3-4   -1
   (b) 1-2   0   (d) 5 or more -3

8. How many servings of nonfried vegetables do you usually eat per day? *(One serving = 1/2 cup. INCLUDE potatoes.)*
   (a) none   -3   (d) 3   +2
   (b) 1   0   (e) 4 or more +3
   (c) 2   +1

9. How many servings of cruciferous vegetables do you usually eat per week? *(ONLY count kale, broccoli, cauliflower, cabbage, Brussels sprouts, greens, bok choy, kohlrabi, turnip, and rutabaga. One serving = 1/2 cup.)*
   (a) none   -3   (c) 4-6   +2
   (b) 1-3   +1   (d) 7 or more +3

10. How many servings of vitamin-A-rich fruits or vegetables do you usually eat per week? *(ONLY count carrots, pumpkin, sweet potatoes, cantaloupe, spinach, winter squash, greens, and apricots. One serving = 1/2 cup.)*
    (a) none   -3   (c) 4-6   +2
    (b) 1-3   +1   (d) 7 or more +3

11. How many times per week do you eat at a fastfood restaurant? *(INCLUDE burgers, fried fish or chicken, croissant or biscuit sandwiches, topped potatoes, and other main dishes. OMIT meals of just plain baked potato, broiled chicken, or salad.)*
    (a) never   +3   (d) 2   -1
    (b) less than 1 +1   (e) 3   -2
    (c) 1   0   (f) 4 or more -3

12. How many servings of grains rich in complex carbohydrates do you eat per day? *(One serving = 1 slice of bread, 1 large pancake, 1 cup whole grain cold cereal, or 1/2 cup cooked cereal, rice, pasta, bulgur, wheat berries, kasha, or millet. OMIT heavily-sweetened cold cereals.)*
    (a) none   -3   (d) 6-8   +2
    (b) 1-3   0   (e) 9 or more +3
    (c) 4-5   +1

13. How many times per week do you eat fish or shellfish? *(OMIT deep-fried items, tuna packed in oil, shrimp, squid, and mayonnaise--laden tuna salad--a little mayo is okay.)*
    (a) never   -2   (c) 3-4   +2
    (b) 1-2   +1   (d) 5 or more +3

14. How many times per week do you eat cheese? *(INCLUDE pizza, cheese-burgers, veal or eggplant parmigiana, cream cheese, etc. OMIT low-fat or fat-free cheeses.)*
    (a) 1 or less   +3   (c) 4-5   -1
    (b) 2-3   +2   (d) 6 or more -3

15. How many servings of fresh fruit do you eat per day?
    (a) none   -3   (d) 3   +2
    (b) 1   0   (e) 4 or more +3
    (c) 2   +1

16. Do you remove the skin before eating poultry?
    (a) Yes   +3
    (b) No   -3
    (c) don't eat poultry 0

17. What do you usually put on your bread or toast? *(AVERAGE two or more scores if necessary.)*
    (a) butter or cream cheese   -3   (d) jam or honey   0
    (b) margarine or peanut butter -2   (e) fruit butter   +1
    (c) diet margarine   -1   (f) nothing   +3

18. Which of these beverages do you drink on a typical day? *(AVERAGE two or more scores if necessary.)*
    (a) water or club soda   +3   (d) coffee or tea   -3
    (b) fruit juice   +1   (e) soda, fruit "drink",
    (c) diet soda   -1   or fruit "ade"   -3

19. Which flavorings do you most frequently add to your foods? *(AVERAGE two or more scores if necessary.)*
    (a) garlic or lemon juice +3   (d) margarine   -2
    (b) herbs or spices   +3   (e) butter   -3
    (c) salt or soy sauce   -2   (f) nothing   +3

20. What do you eat most frequently as a snack? *(AVERAGE two or more scores if necessary.)*
    (a) fruits or vegetables   +3   (e) granola bar   -2
    (b) sweetened yogurt   +2   (f) candy bar or pastry -3
    (c) nuts   -1   (g) nothing   0
    (d) cookies or fried chips -2

21. What is your most typical breakfast? *(SUBTRACT an extra 3 points if you also eat bacon or sausage.)*
    (a) croissant, danish, or doughnut   -3
    (b) eggs   -3
    (c) pancakes or waffles   -2
    (d) cereal or toast   +3
    (e) low-fat yogurt or cottage cheese +3
    (f) don't eat breakfast   0

22. What do you usually eat for dessert?
    (a) pie, pastry, or cake   -3
    (b) ice cream   -3
    (c) fat-free cookies or cakes   -1
    (d) frozen yogurt or ice milk   +1
    (e) nonfat ice cream or sorbet   +1
    (f) fruit   +3
    (g) don't eat dessert   +3

23. How many times per week do you eat beans, split peas, or lentils?
    (a) none   -2   (c) 2   +2
    (b) 1   +1   (d) 3 or more +3

24. What kind of milk do you drink?
    (a) whole   -3   (d) 1/2% or skim   +3
    (b) 2% low-fat -1   (e) none   0
    (c) 1% low-fat +2

25. What dressings or toppings do you usually add to your salads? *(ADD two or more scores if necessary.)*
    (a) nothing, lemon or vinegar   +3
    (b) fat-free dressing   +2
    (c) low-or reduced-calorie dressing   +1
    (d) regular dressing   -1
    (e) croutons or bacon bits   -1
    (f) cole slaw, pasta salad, or potato salad -1

26. What sandwich filling do you eat most frequently? *(AVERAGE two or more scores if necessary.)*
    (a) luncheon meat   -3   (d) low-fat luncheon meat   +1
    (b) cheese or roast beef -1   (e) tuna, salmon, chicken, or turkey +3
    (c) peanut butter   0   (f) don't eat sandwiches   0

27. What do you usually spread on your sandwiches? *(AVERAGE two or more scores if necessary.)*
    (a) mayonnaise   -2
    (b) light mayonnaise   -1
    (c) catsup, mustard, or fat-free mayonnaise -0
    (d) nothing   +2

28. How many egg yolks do you eat per week? *(ADD 1 yolk for every slice of quiche you eat.)*
    (a) 2 or less   +3   (c) 5-6   -1
    (b) 3-4   0   (d) 7 or more -3

29. How many times per week do you eat canned or dried soups? *(OMIT low-sodium, low-fat soups.)*
    (a) none   +3   (c) 3-4   -2
    (b) 1-2   0   (d) 5 or more   -3

30. How many servings of a rich source of calcium do you eat per day? *(One serving = 2/3 cup milk or yogurt, 1 oz. cheese, 1 1/2 oz. sardines, 3 1/2 oz. salmon, 5 oz. tofu made with calcium sulfate, 1 cup greens or broccoli, or 200 mg of a calcium supplement.)*
    (a) none   -3   (c) 2   +2
    (b) 1   +1   (d) 3 or more   +3

31. What do you usually order on your pizza? *(Vegetable toppings include green pepper, mushrooms, onions, and other vegetables. SUBTRACT 1 point from your score if you order extra cheese.)*
    (a) no cheese with vegetables   +3
    (b) cheese with vegetables   +1
    (c) cheese   0
    (d) cheese with meat toppings   -3
    (e) don't eat pizza   +2

32. What kind of cookies do you usually eat?
    (a) graham crackers or ginger snaps   +1
    (b) oatmeal   -1
    (c) sandwich cookies (like Oreos)   -2
    (d) chocolate coated, chocolate chip, or peanut butter   -3
    (e) don't eat cookies   +3

33. What kind of frozen dessert do you usually eat? *(SUBTRACT 1 point from your score for each topping you use--whipped cream, hot fudge, nuts, etc.)*
    (a) gourmet ice cream   -3
    (b) regular ice cream   -1
    (c) sorbet, sherbet, or ices   +1
    (d) frozen yogurt, fat-free ice cream, or ice milk   +1
    (e) don't eat frozen desserts   +3

34. What kind of cake or pastry do you usually eat?
    (a) cheesecake, pie, or any microwave cake   -3
    (b) cake with frosting or filling   -2
    (c) cake without frosting   -1
    (d) unfrosted muffin, banana bread, or carrot cake   0
    (e) angelfood or fat-free cake   +1
    (f) don't eat cakes or pastries   +3

35. How many times per week does your dinner contain grains, vegetables, or beans, but little or no animal protein (meat, poultry, fish, eggs, milk, or cheese)?
    (a) none   -1   (c) 3-4   +2
    (b) 1-2   +1   (d) 5 or more   +3

36. Which of the following salty snacks do you typically eat? *(AVERAGE two or more scores if necessary.)*
    (a) potato chips, corn chips, or packaged popcorn   -3
    (b) reduced-fat potato or tortilla chips   -2
    (c) salted pretzels   -1
    (d) unsalted pretzels or baked corn or tortilla chips   +1
    (e) homemade air-popped popcorn   +3
    (f) don't eat salty snacks   +3

37. What do you usually use to saute vegetables or other foods? *(Vegetable oil includes safflower, corn, canola, olive, sunflower, and soybean.)*
    (a) butter or lard   -3
    (b) more than one tablespoon of margarine or vegetable oil   -1
    (c) no more than one tablespoon of margarine or vegetable oil   0
    (d) no more than one tablespoon of olive oil   +1
    (e) water or broth   +2

38. What kind of cereal do you usually eat?
    (a) whole grain (like oatmeal or Shredded Wheat)   +3
    (b) low fiber (like Cream of Wheat or Corn Flakes)   0
    (c) sugary low-fiber (like Frosted Flakes)   -1
    (d) granola   -2

39. With what do you make tuna salad, pasta salad, chicken salad, etc.?
    (a) mayonnaise   -2   (d) low-fat yogurt   +2
    (b) light mayonnaise   -1   (e) nonfat yogurt   +3
    (c) nonfat mayonnaise   0

40. What do you typically put on your pasta? *(ADD one point if you also add sauteed vegetables. AVERAGE two or more scores if necessary.)*
    (a) tomato sauce   +3
    (b) tomato sauce with a little Parmesan   +3
    (c) white clam sauce   +1
    (d) meat sauce or meat balls   -2
    (e) Alfredo, pesto, or other creamy sauce -3

Scoring:
+59 to + 116 GREAT! You're a nutrition superstar. Give yourself a big (nonbutter) pat on the back. Continue the good work.

0 to +58 GOOD Pin your Quiz on the nearest wall. Look at areas for improvement.

58 to -1 FAIR Hang in there. Keep a diary of the foods you eat and make daily changes whenever possible.

-117 to -59 ARGHH! Empty your refrigerator and cupboard. It's time to start over.

Source: CSPI Nutrition Quiz, Nutrition Health Action Letter, March 1992, P.O. Box 96611, Washington, D.C. 20090-6611.

Daily Food Diary

Name: _____   Date: _____

Directions: Keep a record of your daily food intake for one week. Carry
this recording sheet with you and note the foods you eat as you eat them.
Later, conduct a basic analysis of the nutritional value of your diet. Take
note of strengths and weaknesses and use this information to make
appropriate changes in your diet.

Food & Source	Portion Size	Calories	Food Group	Nutrients

Day 1

Day 2

Day 3

Day 4

Day 5

Day 6

Day 7

Your Eating Habits and Extra Calories

Name: _____ Date: _____

Directions: Think about your eating patterns and habits: What, how much, when, where and why do you eat. For each of these questions, check the answers that best describe your eating patterns and habits.

WHAT do I usually eat?

__ A varied and balanced diet that includes only moderate amounts of fat, and alcoholic beverages.

__ Deep-fat fried and breaded foods.

__ "Extras," such as salad dressings, potato toppings, spreads, sauces and gravies.

__ Sweets and rich desserts such as candies, cakes, pies.

__ Snack foods high in fat and sodium, such as chips and other "munchies."

__ Cocktails, wine and beer.

HOW MUCH do I usually eat?

__ A single, small serving.

__ A large serving.

__ Two servings or more.

WHEN do I usually eat?

__ At mealtime only.

__ While preparing meals or clearing the table.

__ While watching TV or participating in other activities.

__ At coffee break.

__ Anytime.

WHERE do I usually eat?

__ At the kitchen or dining room table.

__ At restaurants or fast food places.

__ In front of the TV or while reading.

__ Wherever I happen to be when I'm "hungry."

WHY do I usually eat?

__ It's time to eat.

__ I'm "starved."

__ Foods look tempting.

__ Everyone else is eating.

__ Food will get thrown away if I don't eat it.

__ I'm bored or frustrated.

Analysis: Look at the boxes you checked for "what" and "how much" you eat. Do they provide any clues to where your extra calories are coming from? Your answers to "when, where, and why" you eat are important too. They often affect **what** and **how much** you eat.

Can you identify some habits that may be due for a change? Try to think of ways to modify "problem" habits. If, for example, you often nibble while doing other things, make an effort to plan your meals and snacks ahead of time. For eating at home, make a rule to eat only while sitting at the kitchen or dining room table. If candy bars from the vending machine at your office coffee break are a problem, substitute a low-calorie snack brought from home. If you often eat because you're bored or frustrated think of other activities to get your mind off food-jog, call a friend, or walk the dog.

Why Do You Eat? Inventory

Name: _____ Date: _____

Directions: Here are some statements made by people to describe what they get out of eating. How *often* do you feel this way about eating? Circle one number for each statement. *Important*: Answer every question.

Response Scale:	5	4	3	2	1
	Always	Frequently	Occasionally	Seldom	Never

A. I eat to keep myself from slowing down.
   Always   5   4   3   2   1   Never

B. Handling food is part of the enjoyment of eating.
   Always   5   4   3   2   1   Never

C. Eating is pleasant and relaxing.
   Always   5   4   3   2   1   Never

D. When I feel angry about something, I eat.
   Always   5   4   3   2   1   Never

E. When I run out of my favorite foods I find it almost unbearable until I can get more.
   Always   5   4   3   2   1   Never

F. I eat automatically without even being aware of it.
   Always   5   4   3   2   1   Never

G. I eat to stimulate me, perk myself up.
   Always   5   4   3   2   1   Never

H. Part of the enjoyment of eating comes from the steps I take to prepare the food.
   Always   5   4   3   2   1   Never

I. I find eating pleasurable.
   Always   5   4   3   2   1   Never

J. When I feel uncomfortable or upset about something, I eat.
   Always   5   4   3   2   1   Never

K. I am very much aware of the fact when I am not eating.
   Always   5   4   3   2   1   Never

L. I eat without realizing what I am doing.
   Always   5   4   3   2   1   Never

M. I eat to give me a "lift."
   Always   5   4   3   2   1   Never

O. I want food most when I am comfortable and relaxed.
   Always   5   4   3   2   1   Never

P. When I feel "blue" or want to take my mind off cares and worries, I eat.
   Always   5   4   3   2   1   Never

Q. I get a real gnawing hunger for food when I haven's eaten for a while.
   Always   5   4   3   2   1   Never

R. I've found food in my mouth and didn't remember putting it there.
   Always   5   4   3   2   1   Never

Scoring:
1. Enter the numbers you have circled to the test questions in the following spaces, putting the number you circled to question A over line A, to question B over line B, and so on.
2. Total the three scores on each line to get your totals. For example, the sum of your scores over lines A, G, and M gives you your score on "Stimulation"; lines B, H, and N give you the score on "Handling," and so on.

                                                        Totals

___ + ___ + ___ = _____
 A   G   M   Stimulation

___ + ___ + ___ = _____
 B   H   N   Handling

___ + ___ + ___ = _____
 C   I   O   Pleasurable relaxation

___ + ___ + ___ = _____
 D   J   P   Crutch: tension reduction

___ + ___ + ___ = _____
 E   K   Q   Craving: psychological addiction

___ + ___ + ___ = _____
 F   L   R   Habit

Scores can vary from 3 to 15. Any score 11 and above is high; any score 7 and below is low.

Interpretation: The six factors measured by this instrument describe one or another way of experiencing or managing certain kinds of feelings. Three of these feeling states represent the positive feelings people get from eating: (1) a sense of increased energy or *stimulation*; (2) the satisfaction of *handling* or manipulating things; and (3) the enhancing of *pleasurable feelings* by reducing the state of tension or feelings of anxiety, anger, and shame, for example. The fifth is a complex pattern of increasing and decreasing "craving" for eating that represents a *psychological addiction* to food. The sixth, *habit*, is eating that occurs in an absence of feeling--purely automatic eating.

A score of 11 or above on any factor indicates that this factor is an important source of satisfaction for you. The higher your score (15 is the highest), the more important a particular factor is in your eating and the more useful the discussion of that factor can be in your attempt to cut down on eating.

If you do not score high on any of the six factors, chances are that you are not an excessive eater. If so, cutting down calories should be easy.

If you score high on several categories, you apparently get several kinds of satisfaction from eating and will have to find several solutions. Certain combinations of scores may indicate that reducing food intake will be especially difficult. Those who score high on both factor 4 and factor 5, "reduction of negative feelings and craving," may have a hard time cutting down on caloric intake. However, there are ways to do it; many excessive eaters represented by this combination have been able to cut down on caloric intake.

Others who score high on factors 4 and 5 may find it useful to change their patterns of eating and cut down at the same time. They can try to eat foods that are lower in calories such as carrots, fresh fruits, Ry-Crisp, or to substitute exercise and other physical activities for eating. After several months of trying this solution, they may find it easier to develop a habit pattern of low-calorie intake.

You must make a decision to cut down caloric intake either by (1) substituting appropriate volumes of less fattening foods for the high-calorie foods currently in your diet; or (2) reducing or eliminating excess calorie food (like junk food) from your diet without the substitution of low-calorie foods.

Source: Walter Sorochan, Promoting Your Health. New York: John Wiley & Sons, 1981, pp. 175-79. Adapted from Smoker's Self-Testing Kit, PHS Publication No. 1904, 1969, developed by Daniel Horn, Director of the National Clearinghouse for Smoking and Health of the Public Health Service and members of the Clearinghouse staff.

The Diet Readiness Test

Name: _____ Date: _____

Directions: To find out how well your attitudes equip you for a weight loss program, answer the questions that follow. For each question, circle the answer that best describes your attitude. As you complete each section, tally your score and note where it fits on the scale below.

Goals, Attitudes, and Readiness

1. Compared to previous attempts, how motivated are you to lose weight this time?

1	2	3	4	5
not at all motivated	slightly motivated	somewhat motivated	quite motivated	extremely motivated

2. How certain are you that you will stay committed to a weight loss program for the time it will take to reach your goal?

1	2	3	4	5
not at all certain	slightly certain	somewhat certain	quite certain	extremely certain

3. Considering all the outside factors in your life at this time--stress at work, family obligations, etc.--to what extent can you tolerate the effort required to stick to a diet?

1	2	3	4	5
cannot tolerate	can tolerate somewhat	uncertain	can tolerate well	can tolerate easily

4. Think honestly about how much weight you hope to lose and how quickly you hope to lose it. Figuring a weight loss of 1-2 pounds per week, how reliable is your expectation?

1	2	3	4	5
very unrealistic	somewhat unrealistic	moderately unrealistic	somewhat realistic	very realistic

5. While dieting, do you fantasize about eating a lot of your favorite foods?

1	2	3	4	5
always	frequently	occasionally	rarely	never

6. While dieting, do you feel deprived, angry, and/or upset?

1	2	3	4	5
always	frequently	occasionally	rarely	never

Scoring:

   6-16: This may not be a good time for you to start a diet. Inadequate motivation and commitment and unrealistic goals could block your progress. Think about what contributes to your unreadiness and consider changing these factors before undertaking a diet.

   17-23: You are close to being ready to begin a weight loss program, but you should think about ways to boost your readiness.

   24-30: The path is clear: you can decide how to lose weight in a safe, effective way.

7. When food comes up in conversation or in something you read, do you want to eat, even if you're not hungry?

1	2	3	4	5
never	rarely	occasionally	frequently	always

8. How often do you eat because of physical hunger?

1	2	3	4	5
always	frequently	occasionally	rarely	never

9. Do you have trouble controlling your eating when your favorite foods are around the house?

1	2	3	4	5
never	rarely	occasionally	frequently	always

Scoring:

3-6: You might occasionally eat more than you should, but this does not appear to be due to high responsiveness to environmental cues. Controlling the internal cues that make you eat may be especially helpful.

7-9: You may have a moderate tendency to eat just because food is available. Dieting may be easier for you if you try to resist external cues and eat only when you're physically hungry.

10-15: Some or much of your eating may be in response to fantasizing about food or exposing yourself to temptations to eat. Think of ways to minimize your exposure to temptations so you eat only in response to physical hunger.

Control Over Eating

If the following situations occurred while you were on a diet, would you be likely to eat more or less immediately afterward and for the rest of the day?

10. Although you planned on skipping lunch, a friend talks you into going for a midday meal.

1	2	3	4	5
would eat	would eat	would make	would eat	would eat
much less	somewhat less	no difference	somewhat more	much more

11. You break your diet by eating a fattening "forbidden" food.

1	2	3	4	5
would eat	would eat	would make	would eat	would eat
much less	somewhat less	no difference	somewhat more	much more

12. You have been following your diet faithfully and decide to test yourself by eating something you consider a treat.

1	2	3	4	5
would eat	would eat	would make	would eat	would eat
much less	somewhat less	no difference	somewhat more	much more

Scoring:

3-7 You recover rapidly from mistakes. However, if you frequently alternate between out-of-control eating and strict dieting, you may have a serious eating problem and should get professional help.

8-11: You do not seem to let unplanned eating disrupt your program. Yours is a flexible balanced approach.

9-15: You may be prone to overeat after an event causes you to break your control or throws you off the track. Your reaction to these problem-causing events can be improved.

Binge Eating and Purging

13. Aside from holiday feasts, have you ever eaten a large amount of food rapidly and felt afterward that this eating incident was excessive and out of control?

2	0
yes	no

14. If you answered yes to question 13, how often have you engaged in this behavior during the last year?

1	2	3	4	5	6
less than once a month	about once a month	a few times a month	about once a week	about three times a week	daily

15. Have you purged (used laxatives, diuretics, or induced vomiting) to control your weight?

5	0
yes	no

16. If you answered yes to question 15, how often have you engaged in this behavior during the last year?

1	2	3	4	5	6
less than once a month	about once a month	a few times a month	about once a week	about three times a week	daily

Scoring:
  0: Binge eating and purging do not seem to be problems for you.
  2-11: Pay attention to these eating patterns. Should they arise more frequently, get professional help.
  12-19: You show signs of having a potentially serious eating problem. See a counselor experienced in evaluating eating disorders right away.

Emotional Eating

17. Do you eat more than you would like to when you have negative feelings such as anxiety, depression, anger, or loneliness?

1	2	3	4	5
never	rarely	occasionally	frequently	always

18. Do you have trouble controlling your eating when you have positive feelings--do you celebrate feeling good by eating?

1	2	3	4	5
never	rarely	occasionally	frequently	always

19. When you have unpleasant interaction with others in your life, or after a difficult day at work, do you eat more than you'd like?

1	2	3	4	5
never	rarely	occasionally	frequently	always

Scoring:

3-8: You do not appear to let your emotions affect your eating.

9-11: You sometimes eat in response to emotional highs and lows. Monitor this behavior to learn when and why it occurs and be prepared to find alternative activities.

12-15: Emotional ups and downs often stimulate your eating. Try to deal with the feelings that trigger the eating and find other ways to express them.

Exercise Patterns and Attitudes

20. How often do you exercise?

1	2	3	4	5
			somewhat	
never	rarely	occasionally	frequently	frequently

21. How confident are you that you can exercise regularly?

1	2	3	4	5
not at all	slightly	somewhat	highly	completely
confident	confident	confident	confident	confident

22. When you think about exercise, do you develop a positive or negative picture in your mind?

1	2	3	4	5
completely	somewhat		somewhat	completely
negative	negative	neutral	positive	positive

23. How certain are you that you can work regular exercise into your daily schedule?

1	2	3	4	5
not at all	slightly	somewhat	quite	extremely
certain	certain	certain	certain	certain

Scoring:

4-10: You're probably not exercising as regularly as you should. Determine whether attitude about exercise or your lifestyle is blocking your way, then change what you must and put on those walking shoes!

11-16: You need to feel more positive about exercise so you can do it more often. Think of ways to be more active that are fun and fit your lifestyle.

17-20: It looks like the path is fairly clear: Now think of ways to get and stay motivated.

Source: Adapted from June 1989 issue of Psychology Today.

Do You Have An Eating Disorder?

Name: _____ Date: _____

Directions: Answer yes or no to the following questions.

____ 1. Are you intensely afraid of becoming fat?

____ 2. Do you feel fat even though others say you are thin and emaciated?

____ 3. Do you like to shop for food and cook for others but prefer not to eat the meals you make?

____ 4. Do you have eating rituals (e.g., cutting food into tiny bites, eating only certain foods in a particular order or at a particular time of day)?

____ 5. Have you lost 25 percent or more of your minimum body weight through diets and fasts?

____ 6. When you feel hungry, do you usually refrain from eating?

____ 7. If you are a female of childbearing age, have you stopped menstruating?

____ 8. Do you often experience cold hands and feet, dry skin, or cracked fingernails?

____ 9. Do you have a covering of fuzzy hair over your body?

____ 10. Do you often feel depressed, angry, guilty, or inadequate?

____ 11. When people express concern about your low weight, do you deny that anything is wrong?

____ 12. Do you often exercise strenuously or for long periods of time even when you feel tired or sick?

____ 13. Have you ever eaten a large amount of food and then fasted, forced yourself to vomit, or used laxatives, diuretics, or enemas to purge yourself?

____ 14. Are you frequently on a rigid diet?

____ 15. Do you regularly experience stomachaches or constipation?

____ 16. Do you eat large quantities of food in a short period of time, usually high-calorie foods that can be easily digested (e.g., bread, pasta, cake, cookies, ice-cream, or mashed potatoes)?

____ 17. Do you eat in secret, hide food, or lie about your eating?

____ 18. Have you ever stolen food or money to buy food so that you could start or continue a binge?

____ 19. Do you feel guilty and remorseful about your eating behavior?

____ 20. Do you start eating even when you are not hungry?

____ 21. Is it hard for you to stop eating even when you want to?

____ 22. Do you eat to escape problems, to relax, or to have fun?

____ 23. After finishing a meal, do you worry about making it to the next meal without getting hungry in between?

___ 24. Have others expressed concern about your obsession with food?

___ 25. Do you worry that your eating behavior is abnormal?

___ 26. Do you fall asleep after eating?

___ 27. Do you regularly fast, use laxatives or diet pill, induce vomiting, or exercise excessively to avoid gaining weight?

___ 28. Does your weight fluctuate 10 pounds or more between alternate periods of bingeing and purging?

___ 29. Are your neck glands swollen?

___ 30. Do you have scars on the backs of your hands from forced vomiting?

Scoring: Five or more "yes" answers within any of the following three groups of questions strongly suggest the presence of an eating disorder: questions 1-15, anorexia nervosa; questions 14-26, compulsive eating; questions 12-30, bulimia. Which behaviors are most problematic for you? What can you do to ensure that you minimize the damage you may have already caused to your body and psyche, and to prevent any further damage?

Source: Adapted from Barbara Yoder, <u>The Recovery Resource Book</u>. New York: Simon and Schuster, 1990 p. 159.

Fitness Tests

Name: _____   Date: _____

A. General Test: Resting Pulse Rate

Your pulse rate is the number of times per minute your heart beats. Normally, an adult's pulse is 60 to 100 beats per minute. Because of its greater ability to pump blood, the heart of an athlete may beat only 40 to 50 times per minute. Place the tips of two fingers (*not* your thumb) on the inside of your wrist just below your thumb. Referring to a watch with a second hand, count the number of pulses you feel in 15 seconds. Multiply that number by 4 to find your pulse rate in beats per minute.

B. Endurance Test: Lung Capacity

As the name implies, a lung capacity test measure how much oxygen you take in and, thus, to some degree, how much oxygen gets to your muscles. To take this test, inhale deeply. Next exhale all the air you can into a plastic bag. Choke off the top of the bag to force the air to the bottom and draw a line at the top of the air-filled portion. Then open the bag and fill it with water to the line. Then open the bag and fill it with water to the line. Measure the water to determine your lung capacity.

C. Endurance Test: Exercise Capacity

One of the best tests of your exercise capacity--the 3-minute step test--is also quite easy to perform. Simply step on to and off a 1-foot high block, bench, platform or other surface 24 times per minute for three minutes. Then, immediately check your pulse rate (see above).

D. Flexibility Test

Flexibility tests measure how far your muscles can stretch comfortably. As a test of your current flexibility, try the following:
   1. While standing, reach behind your head with your right arm. Can you reach your left shoulder blade without any discomfort? Switch arms. Can you reach your right shoulder blade easily?
   2. Lie on your back. Can you extend your right leg straight up while your left leg rests flat on the floor? Can you extend your left leg straight up while your right leg rests flat on the floor? Can you bend your knees and bring both knees to your chest?
   3. Lie on your stomach. Keeping your knees together, reach back and grab your ankles. Can you touch your heels to your buttocks comfortably?

E. Strength Test

Tests of muscular strength measure the power in large or small muscle groups. See how many bent-knee sit-ups you can do in one minute.

Source: Joan Luckman, Your Health! Englewood Cliffs, NJ: Prentice Hall, 1990. p.87.

Developing a New Mind Set About Exercise

Name: _____ Date: _____

Sometimes when we develop a new habit, we are often plagued with self-doubts and thoughts of failure. During the early stages of your newly started exercise program, you can become your own worst enemy. Examine the following list of excuses. Do any of these look familiar to you? Take a minute to prepare your own list of self-defeating thoughts about exercise. Prepare a list of positive thoughts, too.

Learn to use the list wisely. When self-defeating thoughts enter your mind, counteract them immediately with your positive ones. Write your positive thoughts on a card that you carry in your wallet or purse and refer to the list when you are about to avoid your scheduled exercise session. List both long-term benefits of your program, such as more energy, weight loss, improved appearance, disease prevention, emotional release, and other benefits.

Negative Thoughts About Exercise

---

1. I'm too busy to exercise today. I'm working too hard anyway and need a break.

2. I'm too tired to exercise today, and if I do work out, I won't have enough energy to do the other things I must do.

3. I missed my workout today. I might as well forget all this fitness stuff. I don't have the self-control to keep at it.

4. None of my friends are fit or trim and they don't worry about it. I'm not going to either.

5. I'm already, "over the hill." I should let myself go and enjoy life more.

Negative Exercise Thought

1. _____
   _____
   _____

2. _____
   _____
   _____

3. _____
   _____
   _____

4. _____
   _____
   _____

Positive Thoughts About Exercise

1. I can find time to exercise today. I just have to think about my routine and plan carefully.

2. I may feel tired today, but I'll do a light exercise routine instead of the heavy one I usually do. If I keep working out on a regular basis, I'll build my stamina so I won't feel so tired during the day.

3. Just because I missed one exercise session doesn't mean I should give up. I'm not going to let this small setback ruin everything I've accomplished all week.

4. What my friends do about exercising has nothing to do with my exercise habits. I'll make additional friends who do exercise.

5. I can get in shape and stay there. All I have to do is stick to my schedule. Knowing I can control my behavior is something I can enjoy every day.

Positive Exercise Thought

1. _____
   _____
   _____

2. _____
   _____
   _____

3. _____
   _____
   _____

4. _____
   _____
   _____

Source: Jerrold S. Greenberg/George B. Dintiman, Exploring Health. Englewood Cliffs, NJ: Prentice Hall, p. 225.

Your Exercise Contract

Name: _____ Date: _____

Directions: Make a written agreement with yourself about exercise. Set specific goals in Section 1 for increasing your energy and specific goals in Section 2 for increasing activity. Start slowly. Even a 100 calorie expenditure per day produces a weight loss of ten to twelve pounds in one year.

Remember to motivate yourself through a reward system in Section 3. List specific daily and weekly rewards for meeting your exercise goals. Self-payments may range from eating special foods to treating yourself to a night out. Choose rewards that are not destructive to your overall fitness program.

During this week _____ 19_____, I hereby agree to work as hard as possible at achieving the following:

1. Physical activity goals for increasing my energy use during occupational time:

    A. I will park my car or leave public transportation and walk ___ additional minutes per day.

    B. I will spend ___ minutes daily standing instead of sitting while I work.

    C. I will walk up ___ flights of stairs each work day.

    D. I will walk around my work area ___ minutes every day.

    E. I will spend ___ minutes during each coffee break standing instead of sitting.

    F. I will spend ___ minutes during each lunch break walking outside in the open air.

2. Physical activity goals for increasing my energy use during recreational time:

    A. I will spend ___ minutes daily doing stretching activities to increase my flexibility.

    B. I will spend ___ minutes at least three times per week doing aerobic activities to improve my endurance.

    C. I will spend ___ minutes at least three times per week doing strength activities.

    D. I will spend ___ minutes Saturday and Sunday in active recreational activities.

3. My rewards and consequences:

    A. I will reward myself daily with one of the following pleasures when I achieve my daily goals in increased activity:

1. _____   4. _____

2. _____   5. _____

3. _____   6. _____

107

B. When I do *not* make my daily goals I agree to do the following:

1. _____   2. _____

C. I will reward myself every week with one of the following pleasures
   when I achieve my weekly exercise goals:

1. _____   4. _____

2. _____   5. _____

3. _____   6. _____

D. When I do *not* make my weekly goals I agree to do the following:

1. _____   2. _____

I now agree to the above contract and with the goals and consequences. I
also agree to follow this contract until my goals are reached.

Signed _____   Date _____

Witnessed _____

Source: Jerrold S. Greenberg/George B. Dintiman, Exploring Health. Englewood Cliffs, NJ: Prentice Hall, p. 225.

How Much Do I Move?

Name: _____   Date: _____

Directions: We often have an unrealistic perception of how much **we actively** move. Be as honest as possible when assessing the amount that you move during the average day. If it is different on weekends, fill out for days during the week and weekend separately.

1. Types of movement. Check off those in which you participate.

Walking	____	Hiking	____
Climbing	____	Jogging/Running	____
Lifting weights	____	Team sports	____
Tennis	____	Dancing	____
Lovemaking	____	Bicycling	____
Swimming	____	Aerobics	____
Step climbing	____	Yoga	____
Jumping rope	____	Skiing	____
Physical labor	____	Ice skating	____
Other	____		

2. Time spent moving or exercising:

   Daily _____ minutes   Weekend _____

   Weekly _____ Min./Hrs.

   Monthly _____ Min./Hrs.

3. Record the amount of time spent exercising during the month. _____

4. Do you spend as much time moving as you would like? _____

5. If not, in what types of activity would you like to participate?

   _____

   _____

   _____

6. What small change will you make toward improving your degree of movement?

   _____

   _____

7. What are you going to do today to implement the small change? _____

   _____

   _____

8. What will you do tomorrow? _____

_____

_____

9. What will you do this weekend? _____

_____

_____

10. What will you do this month? _____

_____

_____

11. What reward will you give yourself for meeting your objective? _____

_____

_____

Addictive Personalities

Name: _____ Date: _____

Directions: Place a check mark alongside each of the following statements with which you agree:

____ 1. I am easily bored.

____ 2. I vomit often.

____ 3. I often got into trouble with the principal in grade school.

____ 4. I sweat easily.

____ 5. I believe in the second coming of Christ.

____ 6. I enjoy reading crime news.

____ 7. I have had periods when I couldn't remember what I'd done.

____ 8. I enjoy a game more when I can bet on it.

____ 9. I enjoy big noisy parties.

____ 10. I stole things as a child.

Scoring: Addicts and potential addicts tend to agree with these statements more often than others.* In addition, addicts tend to:

o Be impulsive.

o Be risk takers.

o Be outgoing and sociable (but superficial in interpersonal relationships).

o Have high-energy and high-activity levels.

o Often feel empty and meaningless.

o Usually make a good first impression.

o See themselves as leading unsuccessful lives.

o Often look for excitement and stimulation.

o Have problems with authority.

Don Oldenburg, "The Addictive Personality," The Washington Post. June 30, 1982: B5.

Are You in Control?

Name: _____   Date: _____

Directions: Check the degree to which you use the items in the categories at the left.

| | Frequency of Use | | | |
Category of Substance	Never	Occasional	Frequent	Extreme
I. Beverages containing caffeine	_____	_____	_____	_____
II. Over-the-counter drugs	_____	_____	_____	_____
III. Prescription drugs	_____	_____	_____	_____
IV. Illegal drugs	_____	_____	_____	_____

Scoring:

I. Caffeine-containing beverages (coffee, tea, colas). The abuse of these beverages can produce restlessness, irritability, and interference with sleep. Caution should be exercised during pregnancy in particular. Habituation may occur.

II. Over-the-counter drugs (sleeping aids, digestive aids, vitamin supplements, laxatives, painkillers, etc.). As nonprescription items these drugs can be purchased at the discretion of the user. Therefore they are easily and frequently abused. Abuse can cause impairment of bodily functions, and habituation may occur.

III. Prescription drugs (amphetamines, barbiturates, tranquilizers). Though these are legal drugs prescribed by physicians for medical reasons, they are among the most frequently abused drugs. They are all capable of producing drug dependence.

IV. Illegal drugs (heroin, cocaine, LSD, PCP, marijuana). These drugs have virtually no medical use in the United States, and each is capable of some adverse side effect, ranging from mild to fatal. It is possible that all may produce dependence, and most have been proven to do so.

Source: John LaPlace, Health. Englewood Cliffs, NJ: Prentice Hall, 1987. p. 335.

Are You a Compulsive Shopper?

Name: _____ Date: _____

1. Do you "take off for the stores" when you've experienced a setback or a disappointment, or when you feel angry or scared?

2. Are your spending habits emotionally disturbing to you and have they created chaos in your life?

3. Do your shopping habits create conflict between you and someone close to you (spouse, lover, parents, children)?

4. Do you buy items with your credit cards that you wouldn't buy if you had to pay cash?

5. When you shop, do you feel a rush of euphoria mixed with feelings of anxiety?

6. Do you feel you're performing a dangerous, reckless, or forbidden act when you shop?

7. When you return home after shopping, do you feel guilty, ashamed, embarrassed, or confused?

8. Are many of your purchases seldom or never worn or used?

9. Do you like to your family or friends about what you buy and how much you spend?

10. Would you feel "lost" without your credit cards?

11. Do you think about money excessively--how much you have, how much you owe, how much you wish you had--and then go out and shop again?

12. Do you spend a lot of time juggling accounts and bills to accommodate your shopping debts?

Interpretation: If you answered "yes" to more than four of these questions, chances are you're an out-of-control compulsive shopper. Ponder the questions to which you answered "yes." Are you concerned that your shopping behavior is causing problems for you? What can you do to change the direction in which you are headed?

Source: Janet Damon, Shopaholics. Los Angeles, CA: Price Stern Sloan, 1988.

How to Tell Whether Someone You Know is Chemically Dependent

Name: _____ Date: _____

Directions: For each of the following questions, provide a yes or no answer.

____ 1. Is the person drinking (or using any other drug) more now than he or she did in the past?

____ 2. Are you afraid to be around the person when he or she is drinking or using drugs because of the possibility of verbal or physical abuse?

____ 3. Has the person ever forgotten or denied things that happened during a drinking or drug episode?

____ 4. Do you worry about the person's drinking or drug use?

____ 5. Does the person refuse to talk about his or her drinking or drug use--or even to discuss the possibility that he or she might have a problem with it?

____ 6. Has the person broken promises to control or stop his or her drinking or drug use?

____ 7. Has the person ever lied about his or her drinking or using, or tried to hide it from you?

____ 8. Have you ever been embarrassed by the person's drinking or drug use?

____ 9. Have you ever lied to anyone else about the person's drinking or drug use?

____ 10. Have you ever made excuses for the way the person behaved while drinking or using?

____ 11. Are most of the person's friends heavy drinkers or drug users?

____ 12. Does the person make excuses for, or try to justify, his or her drinking or using?

____ 13. Do you feel guilty about the person's drinking or drug use?

____ 14. Are holidays and social functions unpleasant for you because of the person's drinking or drug use?

____ 15. Do you feel anxious or tense around the person because of his or her drinking or drug use?

____ 16. Have you ever helped the person to "cover up" for a drinking or using episode by calling his or her employer or by telling others that he or she is feeling "sick"?

____ 17. Does the person deny that he or she has a drinking problem because he or she only drinks beer (or wine)? Or deny that he or she has a drug problem because use is "limited" to marijuana, or diet pills, or some other supposedly harmless substance?

____ 18. Does the person's behavior change noticeably when he or she is drinking or using? (For example, a normally quiet person might become loud and talkative, or a normally mild-mannered person might become quick to anger.)

____ 19. Does the person avoid social functions where alcohol will not be served or where drugs will not be available or permitted?

____ 20. Does the person insist on going only to restaurants that serve alcohol?

____ 21. To your knowledge, has the person ever driven a car while intoxicated or under the influence of drugs?

____ 22. Has the person ever received a summons for driving while intoxicated (DWI) or driving under the influence (DUI)?

____ 23. Are you afraid to ride with the person after he or she has been drinking or using?

____ 24. Has anyone else talked to you about the person's drinking or using behavior?

____ 25. Has the person ever expressed remorse for his or her behavior during a drinking or using episode?

____ 26. If you are married to the person and have children, are the children afraid of the person while he or she is drinking or using?

____ 27. Does the person seem to have a poor self-image?

____ 28. Have you ever found alcohol or drugs that the person has hidden?

____ 29. Is the person having financial difficulties that seem to be related to his or her drinking or drug use?

____ 30. Does the person look forward to times when he or she can drink or use the drugs?

Scoring: If you answered yes to any three of these questions, then there is a good chance that the person you care about has a drinking or drug problem. If you answered yes to any five, then the chance is even greater. And if you answered yes to seven or more, the likelihood is great that the person has a problem with chemical dependency.

Survival Rules of the Pharmaceutical Age

Name: _____ Date: _____

Purpose: Our culture has been described as drug-dependent. We are constantly urged, from screen and print, to depend on medication to cure headaches, upset stomachs, coughs, colds, and sleep problems. Can you survive this pharmaceutical dilemma? Find out below.

Directions: Look in your medicine cabinet or wherever you store and keep medications. Pull out some of the drugs, prescription and nonprescription, and answer the following questions about each.

1. Do you know why the drug was prescribed (if a prescription drug)?	YES	NO
2. Do you know what the side effects are?	YES	NO'
3. Is it an old medicine that you saved for self-treatment at a later time?	YES	NO
4. Have you ever forgotten to take it?	YES	NO
5. Have you ever forgotten to take it and doubled the dosage the next time?	YES	NO
6. Have you ever taken a larger dose than is prescribed, thinking that if one dose is helpful, two would be even better?	YES	NO
7. Have you taken doses at the wrong time?	YES	NO
8. Have you ever discontinued it without notifying your physician (if a prescription drug)?	YES	NO
9. Have you stretched it out to make it last longer than the period for which it was intended?	YES	NO
10. Have you sought a refill long after the rational need for it has disappeared?	YES	NO
11. Have you borrowed this medicine?	YES	NO
12. Have you ever lent this medicine to someone else?	YES	NO
13. Is this particular medicine (if prescription) not prescribed for you by a physician?	YES	NO
14. Have you taken duplicate medicines prescribed by two different physicians?	YES	NO
15. Have you mixed this drug with alcohol?	YES	NO

Scoring: Check your answers to see if you may be misusing the medications by considering the notes below.

Notes to the Preceding Questions
1. If you do not know why it was prescribed, throw it out.
2. Some side effects can be uncomfortable or hazardous enough to warrant discontinuing the drug.

3. Just as food does not last forever, neither do drugs. Medications should be replaced when they expire, or at least every 3 years.
4. Drugs do not work unless you take them.
5-9. Drugs depend on a regular, steady course of administration. They do not work otherwise.
10. Watch it--this may be sign of addiction.
11-12. This is serious business. You have no idea of that person's medical history or the possible side effects, if it is a prescription drug.
13-14. Caution: It may be hazardous to your health.
15. If it is a tranquilizer, barbiturate, or antihistamine, you are on a collision course with fate. Many persons have combined alcohol with these drugs and never awakened.

Source: Sandra Kammerman, et al. Wellness RSVP. Menlo Park, CA: Benjamin Cummings, 1983, 161-62.

What are the Signs of Alcoholism?

Name: _____   Date: _____

Directions: Respond to the following questions by answering "yes" or "no."

YES   NO   1. Do you occasionally drink heavily after a disappointment, a quarrel, or when the boss gives you a hard time?

YES   NO   2. When you have trouble or feel under pressure, do you drink more heavily than usual?

YES   NO   3. Have you noticed that you are able to handle more liquor than you did when you were first drinking?

YES   NO   4. Did you ever wake up on the "morning after" and discover that you could not remember part of the evening before, even though your friends tell you that you did not pass out?

YES   NO   5. When drinking with other people, do you try to have a few extra drinks when others will not know it?

YES   NO   6. Are there certain occasions when you feel uncomfortable if alcohol is not available?

YES   NO   7. Have you recently noticed that when you begin drinking you are in more of a hurry to get the first drink than you used to be?

YES   NO   8. Do you sometimes feel a little guilty about your drinking?

YES   NO   9. Are you secretly irritated when your family or friends discuss your drinking?

YES   NO   10. Have you recently noticed an increase in the frequency of your memory blackouts?

YES   NO   11. Do you often find that you wish to continue drinking after your friends say that they have had enough?

YES   NO   12. Do you have a reason for the occasions when you drink heavily?

YES   NO   13. When you are sober, do you often regret things you did or said while drinking?

YES   NO   14. Have you tried switching brands or following different plans for controlling your drinking?

YES   NO   15. Have you often failed to keep the promises you have made to yourself about controlling or cutting down your drinking?

YES   NO   16. Have you ever tried to control your drinking by making a change in jobs, or moving to a new location?

YES   NO   17. Do you try to avoid family or close friends while you are drinking?

YES   NO   18. Are you having an increasing number of financial and work problems?

YES   NO   19. Do more people seem to be treating you unfairly without good reason?

YES   NO   20. Do you eat very little or irregularly when you are drinking?

YES   NO   21. Do you sometimes have "the shakes" in the morning and find that it helps to have a little drink?

YES   NO   22. Have you recently noticed that you cannot drink as much as you once did?

YES   NO   23. Do you sometimes stay drunk for several days at a time?

YES   NO   24. Do you sometimes feel very depressed and wonder whether life is worth living?

YES   NO   25. Sometimes after periods of drinking, do you see or hear things that aren't there?

YES   NO   26. Do you get terribly frightened after you have been drinking heavily?

Interpretation: If you answered "yes" to two or more of these questions you may wish to evaluate your drinking behavior in terms of consistency and frequency. Use the following guide to score yourself on questions related to the various stages of alcoholism.

* Questions 1 through 8 represent the early stage of alcoholism. If you checked one or more of these, it would be wise to watch your drinking behaviors carefully. Although many people stay at this stage throughout their lives, many others miss the chance to control their drinking before it progresses.

* Questions 9 through 21 represent the middle stage of alcoholism. If you checked one or more of these, your dependence on alcohol is probably well established. Outside counseling might be helpful at this stage.

* Questions 22 through 26 represent the final stage of alcoholism. If your answers indicate that you are in this stage, you should seek medical help.

Source: Adapted from the brochure, <u>What are the Signs of Alcoholism?</u> National Council of Alcoholism.

Tracing Alcohol

Name: _____   Date: _____

Weight: _____

Directions: Imagine you are attending a party. During a 1-hour period (7-8 P.M.) you consume eight drinks. One drink is a 12-ounce can of bear, or a 4-ounce glass of table wine, or a 1-ounce glass of 100-proof distilled liquor. Each contains 1/2 ounce of "pure" alcohol.

Chart your blood alcohol level (BAL), psychological changes, and physiological reactions. After doing this for all eight drinks, complete the questions at the end of this paper.

Drink Number   BAL   Behavioral Effects

    1.
_____

    2.
_____

    3.
_____

    4.
_____

    5.
_____

    6.
_____

    7.
_____

    8.
_____

1. How much of the alcohol you are drinking is metabolized by the liver? Where does the rest go?

2. How much alcohol is *metabolized* per hour?

120

3. At what time would a person have all traces of alcohol removed?

4. Does this exercise seem realistic? Why or why not? Please be specific. If you have never consumed alcohol, please indicate.

5. Amount of alcohol is only one factor regarding intoxication. What other factors play a role in intoxication?

Source: Girdano, et al. Drug Education: Content and Methods, 3rd ed. Reading MA: Addison-Wesley, 1980.

Drunk Driving

Name: _____ Date: _____

Directions: Write a sentence or two on your reaction to the consequences for drunk driving in other countries. Write the law as you would prefer it to be in the United States.

Australia: The names of the drivers are sent to the local newspaper and are printed under the following heading: "He's drunk and in jail."

_____

_____

_____

_____

Malaysia: The driver is jailed, and if he's married, his wife is jailed too. _____

_____

_____

_____

_____

El Salvador: Your first offense may be your last. Execution by a firing squad is said to have been ordered. _____

_____

_____

_____

_____

Turkey: Drunk drivers are taken 20 miles from town by the police and forced to walk back under escort. _____

_____

_____

_____

_____

Norway: Three weeks in jail at hard labor, one year loss of license. Second offense within 5 years, license is revoked for life. _____

_____

_____

_____

_____

United States: _____

_____

_____

_____

_____

Source: Yoder, Barbara. The Recovery Resource Book. New York: Simon & Schuster, Inc. 1990

Why Do You Smoke?

Name: _____ Date: _____

Directions: Here are some statements made by people to describe what they get out of smoking cigarettes. How often do you feel this way when smoking? Circle one number for each statement. ANSWER EVERY QUESTION.

Response Scale:	5 Always	4 Frequently	3 Occasionally	2 Seldom	1 Never

A. I smoke cigarettes in order to keep myself from slowing down.
Always   5   4   3   2   1   Never

B. Handling a cigarette is part of the enjoyment of smoking it.
Always   5   4   3   2   1   Never

C. Smoking cigarettes is pleasant and relaxing.
Always   5   4   3   2   1   Never

D. I light up a cigarette when I feel angry about something.
Always   5   4   3   2   1   Never

E. When I have run out of cigarettes I find it almost unbearable until I can get them.
Always   5   4   3   2   1   Never

F. I smoke cigarettes automatically without even being aware of it.
Always   5   4   3   2   1   Never

G. I smoke cigarettes to stimulate me, to perk myself up.
Always   5   4   3   2   1   Never

H. Part of the enjoyment of smoking a cigarette comes from the steps I take to light up.
Always   5   4   3   2   1   Never

I. I find cigarettes pleasurable.
Always   5   4   3   2   1   Never

J. When I feel uncomfortable or upset about something I light up a cigarette.
Always   5   4   3   2   1   Never

K. I am very much aware of the fact when I am not smoking a cigarette.
Always   5   4   3   2   1   Never

L. I light up a cigarette without realizing I still have one burning in the ashtray.
Always   5   4   3   2   1   Never

M. I smoke cigarettes to give me a "lift."
Always   5   4   3   2   1   Never

N. When I smoke a cigarette, part of the enjoyment is watching the smoke as I exhale it.
Always   5   4   3   2   1   Never

O. I want a cigarette most when I am comfortable and relaxed.
Always   5   4   3   2   1   Never

P. When I feel "blue" or want to take my mind off cares and worries, I
   smoke cigarettes.
Always   5   4   3   2   1   Never

Q. I get a real gnawing hunger for a cigarette when I haven't smoked for a
   while.
Always   5   4   3   2   1   Never

R. I've found a cigarette in my mouth and didn't remember putting it there.
Always   5   4   3   2   1   Never

Scoring:
1. Enter the number you have circled for each question in the spaces below,
putting the number you have circled to Question A over line A, to Question
B over line B, etc.

2. Add the 3 scores on each line to get your totals. For example, the sum
of your scores over lines A, G, and M give you your score on Stimulation;
lines B, H, and N give the score on Handling, etc. Scores can vary from 3
to 15. Any score 11 and above is high; any score 7 and below is low.

                                                    Totals

____ + ____ + ____ = _____
 A   G   M   Stimulation

____ + ____ + ____ = _____
 B   H   N   Handling

____ + ____ + ____ = _____
 C   I   O   Pleasurable Relaxation

____ + ____ + ____ = _____
 D   J   P   Crutch: Tension Reduction

____ + ____ + ____ = _____
 E   K   Q   Craving: Psychological Addiction

____ + ____ + ____ = _____
 F   L   R   Habit

Interpretation: In this test examining reasons why you smoke, a score of 11
or above on any factor indicates that it is an important source of
satisfaction for you. The higher you score (15 is the highest), the more
important a particular factor is in your smoking and the more useful an
examination of that factor can be in your attempt to quit.

   If you do not score high on any of the six factors, chances are that you
do not smoke very much or have not been smoking for very many years. If so,
giving up--and staying off--smoking should be easy.

1. *Stimulation*
If you score high or fairly high on this factor, it means that you are one
of those smokers who is stimulated by the cigarette-you feel that it helps
wake you up, organize your energies, and keep you going. If you try to give
up smoking, you may want a safe substitute--a brisk walk or moderate
exercise, for example--for whenever you feel the urge to smoke.

2. *Handling*
Handling things can be satisfying, but there are many ways to keep your
hands busy without lighting up or playing with a cigarette. Why not toy
with a pen or pencil? Or try doodling. Or play with a coin, a piece of
jewelry, or some other harmless object.

3. *Accentuation of Pleasure--Pleasurable Relaxation*
It is not always easy to find out whether you use the cigarette to feel
good--that is, get real, honest pleasure out of smoking (Factor 3)--or to
keep from feeling so bad (Factor 4). About two-thirds of smokers score high
or fairly high on *accentuation of pleasure*, and about half of those also
score as high or higher on *reduction of negative feelings*.

If you get real pleasure out of smoking, you may find that an honest
consideration of the harmful effects of your habit is enough to help you
quit. You may substitute social and physical activities and not seriously
miss your cigarettes.

4. *Reduction of Negative Feelings, or "Crutch"*
Many smokers use the cigarette as a kind of crutch in moments of stress or
discomfort. But the heavy smoker, the person who tries to handle severe
personal problems by smoking many times a day, is apt to discover that
cigarettes do not help in dealing with problems effectively.

When it comes to quitting, this kind of smoker may find it easy to stop
when everything is going well, but may be tempted to start again in a time
of crisis. If you are such a smoker, physical exertion or social activity
may serve as a useful substitute for cigarettes, even in times of tension.

5. *"Craving" or Dependence*
Quitting smoking is difficult for the person who scores high on this
factor. For the addicted smoker, the craving for a cigarette begins to
build up the moment the cigarette is put out, so tapering off is not likely
to work. This smoker must go "cold turkey."

If you are dependent on cigarettes, it may be helpful for you to smoke
more than usual for a day or two, so that you spoil your taste for
cigarettes, and then isolate yourself completely from cigarettes until the
craving is gone.

6. *Habit*
If you are smoking out of habit, you no longer get much satisfaction from
your cigarettes. You just light them frequently without even realizing you
are doing so. You may find it easy to quit and stay off if you can break
the habit patterns you have built up. Cutting down gradually may be quite
effective if you change the way you smoke cigarettes and the conditions
under which you smoke them. The key to success is to become aware of each
cigarette you smoke. This can be done by asking yourself, "Do I really want
this cigarette?" You may be surprised at how many you do not want.

You must make two important decisions: (1) whether to try to do without the satisfactions you get from smoking or find an appropriate, less hazardous substitute activity; and (2) whether to try to cut out cigarettes all at once or to taper off. Your scores on this test should guide you in making these decisions.

Additional Resources:
- American Cancer Society*
  777 Third Avenue
  New York, NY 10017

- American Lung Association*
  1740 Broadway
  New York, NY 10019

- Office on Smoking and Health
  5600 Fishers Lane
  Room 1-10
  Park Building
  Rockville, MD 20857

American Heart Association*
7320 Greenville Avenue
Dallas, TX 75231

Office of Cancer Communications
National Cancer Institute
National Institutes of Health
Bethesda, MD 20205

* Consult your local telephone directory for listings of local chapters.

Source: U.S. Department of Health, Education and Welfare, Public Health Service, National Institute of Health, Publication No. (NIH) 79-182. This is Test III of the Smoker's Self-Testing Kit developed by Daniel H. Horn, Ph.D. and originally printed by the National Clearinghouse for Smoking and Health, DHEW.

What Do You Think the Effects of Smoking Are?

Name: _____ Date: _____

Directions: For each statement, circle the number that shows how you feel about it. Do you strongly agree, mildly agree, mildly disagree, or strongly disagree? *Important: Answer every question.*

Response Scale:	1 Strongly Agree	2 Mildly Agree	3 Mildly Disagree	4 Strongly Disagree

A. Cigarette smoking is not as dangerous as many other health hazards.
Strongly Agree   1   2   3   4   Strongly Disagree

B. I don't smoke enough to get any of the diseases that cigarette smoking is supposed to cause.
Strongly Agree   1   2   3   4   Strongly Disagree

C. If a person has already smoked for many years, it probably won't do him or her much good to stop.
Strongly Agree   1   2   3   4   Strongly Disagree

D. It would be hard for me to give up smoking cigarettes.
Strongly Agree   1   2   3   4   Strongly Disagree

E. Cigarette smoking is enough of a health hazard for something to be done about it.
Strongly Agree   1   2   3   4   Strongly Disagree

F. The kind of cigarette I smoke is much less likely than other kinds to give me any of the diseases that smoking is supposed to cause.
Strongly Agree   1   2   3   4   Strongly Disagree

G. As soon as a person quits smoking cigarettes, he begins to recover from much of the damage that smoking has caused.
Strongly Agree   1   2   3   4   Strongly Disagree

H. It would be hard for me to cut down to half the number of cigarettes I now smoke.
Strongly Agree   1   2   3   4   Strongly Disagree

I. The whole problem of cigarette smoking and health is a minor one.
Strongly Agree   1   2   3   4   Strongly Disagree

J. I haven't smoked long enough to worry about the diseases that cigarette smoking is supposed to cause.
Strongly Agree   1   2   3   4   Strongly Disagree

K. Quitting smoking helps a person to live longer.
Strongly Agree   1   2   3   4   Strongly Disagree

L. It would be difficult for me to make any substantial change in my smoking habits.
Strongly Agree   1   2   3   4   Strongly Disagree

Scoring:

1. Enter the numbers you have circled in the test questions in the spaces below, putting the number you have circled for question A over line A, for question B over line B, and so on.
2. Add the three scores across on each line to get your totals. For example, the sum of your scores over A, E, and I give you your score on *Importance*; lines B, F, and J give the score on *Personal relevance*; and so on.

Totals

___	+	___	+	___	=
A		E		I	

_____ Importance — 6 or below indicates that you may shrug off evidence available.

___	+	___	+	___	=
B		F		J	

_____ Personal relevance — 6 or below may indicate the "it-can't-happen-to-me" attitude.

___	+	___	+	___	=
C		G		K	

_____ Value of stopping — 6 or below suggests an ignorance of health benefits occurring when you quit.

___	+	___	+	___	=
D		H		L	

_____ Capability for stopping — 6 or below suggests that you feel stopping would be difficult.

Scores can vary from 3 to 12. Any score of 9 or above is *high*; any score 6 or below is *low*.

Source: National Clearinghouse for Smoking and Health (USPHS).

Passive Smoking

Name: _____ Date: _____

Directions: Answer the following questions to assess your attitudes toward and exposure to passive smoke. Describe your thoughts, feelings, or behavior in response to each question.

1. How many people in your home, apartment, or dorm room smoke?

   _____

   _____

2. Does your employer provide separate work/break areas for smokers and nonsmokers?

   _____

   _____

3. Are smokers in your home or work environment considerate of nonsmokers (If you smoke, are you considerate of nonsmokers)?

   _____

   _____

4. When I go to a restaurant with smokers, (or with nonsmokers and you are a smoker), I:

   _____

   _____

5. When I travel in a car with smokers (or with nonsmokers and you are a smoker), I:

   _____

   _____

6. The things that bother me most about being around smokers are:

   _____

   _____

Interpretation: Perhaps use these questions to initiate discussion with family, friends, employers, or co-workers about the effects of passive smoking and the rights of non-smokers.

Marijuana Attitudes

Name: _____   Date: _____

Directions: What do you think? How strongly do you feel about the following items? Place each letter in a numbered box to rank order the lettered items according to your depth of feeling about each statement.

A. The smoking of pot in public places.
B. People getting long prison sentences for possession of marijuana.
C. Organizations that advocate legalization of marijuana.
D. Merchants and magazines that specialize in "head" products.
E. Younger people you know and care about using marijuana.
F. Friends who make a habit of turning on their nondrug-using friends.

Strongest feeling   Weakest feeling

1	2	3	4	5	6

What values are reflected by your feelings? Do you need to examine some issues further in order to render values to choices regarding marijuana? What ones?

Source: Corry, et al., <u>Drugs: Facts, Alternatives and Decisions</u>. New York: Wadsworth, 1985.

Why People Use Drugs

Name: _____ Date: _____

Directions: What Are Your Psychoactive Drug Use Motives? Rank order the
following questions according to the ones most appropriate for you (if you
have never used any psychoactive drugs, try to imagine what your answers
might be).

I use drugs because

____ 1. Drugs allow me to escape from an annoying world.

____ 2. Drugs help me to achieve an altered state of consciousness.

____ 3. Drugs allow me to hang around some interesting people.

____ 4. I'm not afraid of life when I'm using drugs.

____ 5. Drugs are a part of my culture; they're just natural to use.

____ 6. Drug use allows me to feel good about myself.

____ 7. Drugs help me to be a more spiritual person.

____ 8. Drugs are my way of protesting the ugliness of the world.

____ 9. My drug use is a social protest against the system.

____ 10. Drugs are the only thing of interest about me or my life.

____ 11. Drugs are a source of enjoyment; they're just playthings.

____ 12. My drugs are really food (e.g., beer, wine, tea or coffee).

____ 13. My friends would think less of me if I didn't use drugs.

____ 14. I need drugs to get me through a day.

____ 15. Drugs help me to experience the world in a very special way, and I
can't duplicate this without drugs.

____ 16. Drugs are a source of relief from tension.

____ 17. Drugs allow me to be more social.

____ 18.*_____

____ 19.*_____

____ 20.*_____

* (Add your own)

Source: Corry et al., <u>Drugs: Facts, Alternatives and Decision</u>. New York: Wadsworth, 1985.

Do You Have A Drug Problem?

Name: _____ Date: _____

Directions: Answer the following questions by placing a check next to the appropriate boxes.

1. Which of the following have you tried more than once outside the direct care of a physician? (Score 2 points for each box checked)
   [ ] caffeine
   [ ] cannabis (hashish, marijuana)
   [ ] cocaine powder
   [ ] crack
   [ ] PCP (angel dust)
   [ ] heroin, methadone, morphine
   [ ] LSD
   [ ] amphetamines
   [ ] barbiturates
   [ ] benzodiazapines (Valium and Librium)

2. How often do you use some form of psychoactive drug?
   [ ] daily or almost daily (16 points)
   [ ] more often than once a week but less than daily (8 points)
   [ ] about once a week (4 points)
   [ ] about once a month (2 points)
   [ ] rarely if ever (1 point)

3. How would you feel if you did not use any psychoactive drug for more than three days?
   [ ] I would be very nervous and upset and have an uncontrollable urge to find a drug to use. (16 points)
   [ ] I would want to use a drug very much but could definitely control myself. (8 points)
   [ ] I would think quite a bit about using a drug. (4 points)
   [ ] I would think a little about using a drug. (2 points)
   [ ] I wouldn't notice that I hadn't used it. (1 point)

4. Which of the following have you recently experienced that accompanied your use of drugs? (Score 3 points for each box checked)
   [ ] missing work or school
   [ ] fighting with family or friends
   [ ] becoming belligerent, insulting, or fighting
   [ ] chest pains
   [ ] difficulty breathing
   [ ] feelings of dizziness, nausea, or vertigo

5. Which of the following have you experienced recently? (Score 2 points for each box checked.)
   [ ] withdrawal symptoms when drug use has been delayed
   [ ] an ability to take increased doses of a drug
   [ ] a need to take an increased dose of a drug to get a desired effect
   [ ] no effect from a drug that used to get you high

[ ] the use of a drug at the same time every day
[ ] losing track of how many times you have used a drug or how much you have taken
[ ] using more than one drug during the same time period.

Scoring: Total the points as indicated with each question.

Interpretation:

Score	Label	Danger Rating
2-5	Nonuser	x
6-19	Experimenter	xx
20-35	Moderate user	xxxxx
36-50	Heavy user	xxxxxxxxx
51-90	Problem user	xxxxxxxxxxx-see a counselor *now*

Source: Joan Luckman, Your Health! Englewood Cliffs, NJ: Prentice Hall, 1990.

Evaluating Drug Use Presentation in Movies

Name: _____ Date: _____

Directions: For the film being observed, respond to the following statements by circling one of the following choices located under each statement.

SA = Strongly Agree
 A = Agree
 U = Undecided
 D = Disagree
SD = Strongly disagree
NA = Not Applicable (drug-related scenes not in film)

Title of Film _____

Number of drug use scenes in the film ____

Generally the scene in the film or movie:

1. Encourages or condones the use of mood modifying substances.
   SA   A   U   D   SD   NA

2. Does not show the negative effects of using mood modifying substances.
   SA   A   U   D   SD   NA

3. Promotes use of mood modifying substances as a solution to boredom.
   SA   A   U   D   SD   NA

4. Associates the use of mood modifying substances with fun or pleasure.
   SA   A   U   D   SD   NA

5. Encourages the use of mood modifying substances as a problem-solving behavior.
   SA   A   U   D   SD   NA

6. Suggests that use of mood modifying substances is a "norm" (in other words, "everyone is doing it!").
   SA   A   U   D   SD   NA

7. Portrays people who abstain from using mood modifying substances as immature, not adult, or "nerds."
   SA   A   U   D   SD   NA

8. Shows an easy solution to the results of misuse or abuse of mood modifying substances.
   SA   A   U   D   SD   NA

9. Portrays the hero or heroine as one who uses mood modifying substances.
   SA   A   U   D   SD   NA

10. Portrays the use of mood modifying substances as a means of enhancing performance (intellectual, physical, spiritual, etc.).
    SA   A   U   D   SD   NA

Scoring and Interpretation:

Step   I: Scoring: Use the following method of scoring your responses:
            [SA] Strongly Agree   = 5 points
            [A] Agree   = 4 points
            [U] Undecided   = 3 points
            [D] Disagree   = 2 points
            [SD] Strongly Disagree   = 1 point
            [NA] Not Applicable   = 0 points

Step II: Add your points as follows:

Statement 1:   _____ Points   Statement 6:   _____ Points
   +   +
Statement 2:   _____ Points   Statement 7:   _____ Points
   +   +
Statement 3:   _____ Points   Statement 8:   _____ Points
   +   +
Statement 4:   _____ Points   Statement 9:   _____ Points
   +   +
Statement 5:   _____ Points   Statement 10:   _____ Points
   +   =
                                             Total Points   _____

Step III: After you have added up the total points, place an "X" on the
            appropriate point on the following line that best represents your
            total points. Once you've placed the "X" that represents the
            total points, you can easily see the film's position regarding
            drug use.

"Anti" Drug Use   "Pro" Drug Use
Position   Position

          < ---------- | ---------- | ---------- | ---------->
            10   20   30   40   50

Step IV: Comments regarding analysis of movie (e.g., what kind of closure
            was reached?).

136

Heart-Rate Recovery Test

Name: _____   Date: _____

Purpose: A useful procedure for assessing your cardiorespiratory fitness is the *step test*, a heart-rate recovery measure. Stepping on and off a bench for a 3-to-5 minute time period at a selected cadence (24 or 30 steps a minute) has long been used for rating the physical capacity for hard work and evaluating the effects of training. Although not recognized as the best predictor of cardiorespiratory fitness, the heart-rate reaction during recovery from a standardized step test is a simple way to evaluate the heart's response to exercise. The test is easy to administer to individuals or to a large group. It takes little time, does not require special skills to perform, and, more important, requires a minimum of equipment (locker room bench or bleachers, watch, and a card for recording pulse counts). The testing can easily be done with the methods and procedures described here.

Step-Test Procedure

1. A locker room bench (generally 18 inches high) is recommended for both men and women. A roll-out bleacher seat (usually 16 inches high) can be used. If neither is available, a sturdy chair (17 inches high) can be used. (Step-test norms presented in the T-Score charts are based on stepping up on an 18-inch bench.)

2. Work with a partner.

3. As soon as the signal is given to "begin," the watch is started and start stepping on to the bench--first the left foot up, then the right foot up; then the left foot down, then the right foot down.
   This represents four counts. Step in cadence at the following pace:

Men: 120 counts/minute or 30-step executions/minute (4-step count every 2 seconds--up, up, down, down).

Women: 96 counts/minute or 24-step executions/minute (4-step count every 2.5 seconds--up, up, down, down).

4. Continue the exercise for 3 minutes. Keep the tempo and be sure to straighten the knees as you step on the bench. (In a group situation, the instructor will keep the cadence.)

5. Measurements
   a. After stepping for 3 minutes, sit on the bench or chair.
   b. One minute after the exercise period stops, the tester counts the pulse for 30 seconds. (In a group situation, the instructors calls out BEGIN and STOP for each 30-second period.)
   c. Record the pulse for the following periods.
      1-1 1/2 minutes of recovery
      2-2 1/2 minutes of recovery
      3-3 1/2 minutes of recovery

6. Measuring the pulse: The tester presses lightly with the index and middle fingers in the regions just below the jawbone, and just behind the Adam's apple. For added accuracy the performer can check his or her pulse also at the radial artery site, located on the inside of the wrists, thumbside. This measurement provides a double check for accuracy, and the rate should not differ more than two beats from the tester's count during a 30-second period. A stethoscope, if available, proves the best means for accuracy.

7. Improper procedures:
   a. Not keeping the cadence of 30 or 24 step executions per minute.
   b. Failure to straighten the knees to full extension on the steps ups.

8. Scoring: The sum of the three 30-second pulses is your *recovery index*. On a 3x5 inch card make a testing card, as shown, for recording each recovery pulse. Be sure to mark the time of day and the date. Refer to this when you repeat the step test at a later date.

Name _____   Age _____

Date _____ Time _____   Bench Ht ____

STEP TEST (_____ min.)

Stepping Rate _____

RECOVERIES (beats) 1-1 1/2 min. _____   2-2 1/2 min. ___   3-3 1/2 min. ___

3-Minute Step Test - Cardiorespiratory

	Women	Men
	95	97
Super	107	107
	118	117
	126	122
Excellent	130	127
	135	132
	141	137
Good	147	142
	153	147
	158	152
Average	164	157
	170	162
	176	167
Fair	181	172
	187	177
	193	182
Poor	199	187
	204	192
	210	197
Very Poor	222	207
	233	217

Source: Adapted from B. Hafen, A. Thygerson, and R. Rhodes, Health Perspectives Provo, UT: Brigham Young University Press, 1979, 207-208.

	You	Other	Other
Bone			
Are you experiencing ...			
1. Pain in the bone or joint	____	____	____
2. Swelling in the bone or joint	____	____	____
3. Unusual warmth in the bone or joint	____	____	____
4. Protruding veins along the bone or joint	____	____	____
Breast			
Are you experiencing ...			
1. Thickening or lump in the breast	____	____	____
2. Lump under the arm	____	____	____
3. Thickening or reddening of skin of the breast	____	____	____
4. Puckering or dimpling of skin of the breast	____	____	____
5. Nipple discharge	____	____	____
6. Inverted nipple, if nipple was previously erect	____	____	____
7. Persistent pain and tenderness of the breast	____	____	____
8. Unusual changes in the nipple and areolae	____	____	____
9. Benign breast lumps	____	____	____
Colon/Rectum			
Are you experiencing ...			
1. Continuous constipation or diarrhea	____	____	____
2. Rectal bleeding	____	____	____
3. Change in bowel habit	____	____	____
4. An increase in intestinal gas	____	____	____
5. Abdominal discomfort	____	____	____
Larynx			
Are you experiencing ...			
1. Persistent and progressive hoarseness	____	____	____
2. Change in voice pitch	____	____	____
3. Difficulty in breathing or swallowing	____	____	____
4. Continuous coughing	____	____	____
5. Nagging earache	____	____	____
Lung			
Are you experiencing ...			
1. An unusual cough	____	____	____
2. Shortness of breath	____	____	____
3. Sputum streaked with blood	____	____	____
4. Chest pain	____	____	____
5. Recurring attacks of pneumonia or bronchitis	____	____	____

	You	Other	Other

Lymphomas
Are you experiencing ...

1. Painless enlargement of a lymph node or cluster of lymph nodes

2. Profuse sweating and fever

3. Weight loss

4. Unexplained weakness

5. Unusual itching

Oral
Are you experiencing ...

1. A sore in the mouth that does not heal

2. Lump or thickening that bleeds easily

3. Difficulty in chewing or swallowing food

4. The sensation of something in the throat

5. Restricted movement of the tongue or jaw

6. Poor oral hygiene

Prostate (for men only)
Are you experiencing ...

1. Weak or interrupted flow of urine

2. Inability to urinate or difficulty in starting urination

3. A need to urinate frequently, especially at night

4. Blood in urine

5. Urine flow that is not easily stopped

6. Painful or burning urination

7. Continuing pain in lower back, pelvis, or upper thighs

Skin
Are you experiencing ...

1. Obvious change in wart or mole

2. Unusual skin condition

3. Chronic swelling, redness, or warmth of the skin

4. Unexplained itching

5. Overexposure to the ultraviolet rays of the sun

	You	Other	Other
Stomach			
Are you experiencing ...			
1. Indigestion	___	___	___
2. Vague discomfort or mild pain	___	___	___
3. Blood in the stool	___	___	___
4. Uncontrollable belching or regurgitation of food	___	___	___
5. Rapid weight loss	___	___	___
Testicular (for men only)			
Are you experiencing ...			
1. An enlargement and change in the consistency of the testes	___	___	___
2. A dull ache in the lower abdomen and groin	___	___	___
3. Sensation of dragging and heaviness	___	___	___
4. Difficulty with ejaculation	___	___	___
Thyroid			
Are you experiencing ...			
1. A lump or mass in the neck	___	___	___
2. Persistent hoarseness	___	___	___
3. Difficulty in swallowing	___	___	___
4. Overexposure to head and neck X-ray treatments	___	___	___
Uterine/Cervical (for women only)			
Are you experiencing ...			
1. Irregular bleeding	___	___	___
2. Unusual vaginal discharge	___	___	___
3. Positive Pap smear, Class 2-5, some signs of abnormality	___	___	___
4. Recurring herpes simplex virus	___	___	___
5. Fibroid tumors of the uterus	___	___	___

Interpretation: If you answered YES to any of the statements you should carefully examine each symptom, then seek professional help when you are dissatisfied with the symptom's progress. This could be from the day of discovery up to 14 days, depending on the seriousness of the symptom (that is, from the nagging cough to blood in the stool). If the symptom persists beyond 14 days, see your physician as soon as possible for medical diagnosis. For example, if you checked YES to a multiple of mild symptoms, you should not wait or postpone visiting your physician or health clinic. When dealing with cancer, patients who treat themselves are foolish. Remember, when in doubt have a physical check you out.

Source: Kammerman and Doyle, Wellness RSVP. Menlo Park, CA: Benjamin Cummings, 1983. 179-82.

Positive Attitude to Preventing Heart Disease

Name: _____   Date: _____

I. Place a check mark in front of each behavior that you now practice:

___ 1. I know my normal blood pressure reading. **(blood pressure)**

___ 2. I maintain a low level of saturated fat in my diet. **(saturated fat)**

___ 3. I encourage my family members and friends to have their blood pressures checked regularly and to maintain healthy diets. **(encourage)**

___ 4. I avoid being overweight or obese. **(overweight)**

___ 5. I participate in a regular program of aerobic exercise. **(aerobic exercise)**

___ 6. I control the amount of salt in my diet. **(salt)**

___ 7. I do not smoke cigarettes. **(cigarettes)**

___ 8. If I am being treated by my physician with drugs for hypertension. I follow his or her instructions and take my medication regularly. **(medication)**

II. For each behavior that you DO NOT ENGAGE IN write, in the appropriate space below, the KEY WORD(S) located in the parentheses at the end of the above statements. Then indicate whether you intend to keep or change that behavior.

Behaviors I Don't Engage in: KEEP/CHANGE

_____   _____/_____

_____   _____/_____

_____   _____/_____

_____   _____/_____

_____   _____/_____

_____   _____/_____

_____   _____/_____

_____   _____/_____

III. For each of the preceding behaviors that you choose to KEEP, write a statement indicating why you are choosing to keep that behavior.

I choose to keep behavior _____ because:

For each of the preceding behaviors that you choose to CHANGE, write a statement indicating how you plan to implement that change.

I will change behavior _____ by:

Source: Boskin, Warren, Graf, Gerald, Kreisworth, Virginia. Health Dynamics Attitudes and Behaviors. New York: West Publishing Company, 1990.

AIDS Questionnaire

Name: _____   Date: _____

Directions: This survey was developed to assess your knowledge level of AIDS. Please answer the following questions to the best of your ability.

____ 1. Male = A   Female = B

____ 2. Freshman = A Sophomore = B
       Junior = C   Senior = D

Which of the following has been shown to spread the disease of AIDS? Mark A if it has been shown to spread the disease; mark B if has not been shown.

____ 3. Hugging an infected AIDS victim.

____ 4. Having an infected AIDS victim bite and break the skin.

____ 5. Sharing of cigarettes, cigars, or pipes with an infected person.

____ 6. Donating blood.

____ 7. Receiving blood from an infected person.

____ 8. Infected mother to fetus.

____ 9. Infected father to fetus.

____ 10. Mosquitos to person.

____ 11. Lip kissing with an AIDS victim.

____ 12. Tongue kissing with an AIDS victim.

____ 13. Sharing of eating utensils with an AIDS victim.

____ 14. Sharing of toilet facilities with an AIDS victim.

____ 15. Sharing of razors with an AIDS victim.

____ 16. Sharing of toothbrushes with an AIDS victim.

____ 17. Sharing of beds, linens, pillows with an AIDS victim.

____ 18. Infected mother's breast milk to infant.

____ 19. Having tears of a person with AIDS touch you.

____ 20. Being sneezed upon by an AIDS victim.

____ 21. Being coughed upon by an AIDS victim.

____ 22. Being breathed upon by an AIDS victim.

____ 23. Mouth to penis contact with an infected person.

____ 24. Mouth to vulva/vagina contact with an infected person.

____ 25. Mouth to anus contact with an infected person.

____ 26. Monogamous sexual relationships.

____ 27. Multiple sexual partners.

___ 28. Vaginal intercourse with an infected person.

___ 29. Anal intercourse with an infected person.

___ 30. Infected male to male intercourse.

___ 31. Infected male to female intercourse.

___ 32. Infected female to male intercourse.

___ 33. Infected female to female sexual intimacies.

___ 34. Male to animal intercourse.

___ 35. Animal to male intercourse.

___ 36. Female to animal intercourse.

___ 37. Animal to female intercourse.

___ 38. CPR instruction on manikin.

___ 39. CPR on actual human infected with AIDS.

___ 40. AIDS infected medical worker to patient.

___ 41. AIDS patient to medical worker.

___ 42. Receiving injections from medical workers.

___ 43. Swimming in a pool with a person who has AIDS.

___ 44. A positive AIDS antibody test means that you have the disease.

___ 45. A positive AIDS antibody test means you have been exposed to the virus.

___ 46. AIDS can be transmitted even if the person has no symptoms.

___ 47. Most babies born with AIDS develop natural immunities; thus, can live a normal life.

___ 48. Less than 1% of pregnant women with AIDS transmit the disease to the fetus.

___ 49. A significant number of AIDS cases have been transmitted in school settings from student to student.

___ 50. A majority of AIDS victims are gay or bisexual.

___ 51. A majority of AIDS victims are I.V. drug users/abuser.

___ 52. A majority of AIDS victims are heterosexuals.

___ 53. The contraction of AIDS can be prevented or reduced significantly by the use of a condom.

___ 54. The contraction of AIDS can be prevented or reduced significantly by the use of the Public Health's Approved Vaccine.

___ 55. The contraction of AIDS can be prevented or reduced significantly if a person abstains from sexual intercourse.

___ 56. The contraction of AIDS can be prevented or reduced significantly by having the male withdraw his penis just prior to ejaculation (coming).

___ 57. AIDS can be cured by large doses of antibiotics.

___ 58. If one does not belong to one of the dominant risk groups, there is no chance of getting AIDS.

___ 59. The AIDS virus can remain active for several hours outside the body.

___ 60. Nobody under 18 years of age has died (yet) from AIDS.

___ 61. My chances of catching AIDS are
A. Almost impossible   B. Improbable   C. Quite Possible

SOURCE: This survey was developed by Dr. Mark J. Kittleson, Youngstown State University, and Francine E. Glista, Tod Children's Hospital, Youngstown, Ohio. Permission granted for classroom use only.

Your Risks of STDs

Name: _____ Date: _____

Directions: For each category below, circle the *one* answer that best describes you, your attitudes, and/or your behavior.

AGE

Age	Points if Male	Points if Female
0-10	1	1
11-14	2	3
15-19	4	6
20-30	5	4
31-35	3	3
36+	2	2

SEXUAL PREFERENCE

Preference	Points
Celibate	0
Heterosexual	3
Bisexual	6
Gay male, multiple partners	8
Gay female	1
Gay male, monogamous	5

NUMBER OF PARTNERS

Number	Points
Never engage in sex	0
One sex partner only	1
More than one sex partner, but never more than one relationship at a time	2
2-5 sex partners	4
5-10 sex partners	6
10+ sex partners	8

SEXUAL ATTITUDES

Attitude	Points
Will not engage in non-marital sex	0
Monogamous relationship only	1
Sex OK if relationship is long-term	1
An occasional fling OK	4
Sex OK with multiple or casual partners	8
Believe in *complete* sexual freedom	8

ATTITUDES TOWARD CONTRACEPTION

Attitude	Points
Not now sexually active	0
Would use condom to prevent pregnancy	1
Would use condom with all but steady partner	2
Would not use condom ever	6
Self or partner would use the pill	5
Would use other contraceptive measures	4
Sexually active and use nothing, but don't worry about STDs or pregnancy	8

ATTITUDES TOWARD STDs

Attitude	Points
Not now sexually active, so no need to worry	1
Would definitely tell my partner(s) if I had an STD	2
Would see a doctor at first sign of symptoms	2
Would wait to see if symptoms go away	6
Am sexually active, but low risk because all partners are clean	6
STDs no sweat because I know I'll never have it.	5

Scoring: Total the points circled.

Interpretation:

5-10	Well below average
11-15	Below average
16-20	Average
21-24	Moderate risk
25+	High risk

Do You Have Allergies?

Directions: For each of the following questions, circle either "Yes" or "No."

1. Do you *ever* have any of the following symptoms?
   (a) wheezing   Yes No
   (b) shortness of breath   Yes No
   (c) hives   Yes No
   (d) eczema (red, itchy, scaly, rash)   Yes No
   (e) nasal congestion (except during cold and flu)   Yes No

2. Does exposure to any of the following make your symptoms worse?
   (a) cold weather   Yes No
   (b) house dust   Yes No
   (c) grass, weeds, or flowering trees   Yes No
   (d) dogs, cats, or other animals   Yes No
   (e) feather pillows or comforters   Yes No
   (f) damp, musty basements or barns   Yes No
   (g) cooking odors   Yes No
   (h) perfumes   Yes No
   (i) cigarette smoke   Yes No
   (j) exhaust fumes   Yes No
   (k) periods of emotional strain   Yes No

3. Does eating or drinking any specific substance make your
   symptoms worse?   Yes No

4. Do any medications make your symptoms worse?   Yes No

5. Do you wheeze when exercising?   Yes No

6. Do soaps, detergents, wool, plant, chemicals, cosmetics,
   or other agents produce a skin rash?   Yes No

7. Do any of your blood relatives have allergies?   Yes No

8. Did you have a milk or other food allergy as a child?   Yes No

9. Do colds usually settle in your chest?   Yes No

10. Has your chest x-ray ever been abnormal?   Yes No

11. Do you have a chronic cough?   Yes No

12. Do you smoke cigarettes?   Yes No

13. Is your sense of taste or smell impaired?   Yes No

14. Do you use nose sprays?   Yes No

15. Have you ever had any of the following?
    (a) pneumonia   Yes No
    (b) severe flu in the chest   Yes No
    (c) tuberculosis   Yes No
    (d) any other serious lung ailment   Yes No
    (e) sinusitis   Yes No
    (f) nasal polyps   Yes No

16. Do you consider yourself a nervous person?   Yes No

17. Do you have any of the following in your current residence?
    (a) an air-circulating ducted heating system   Yes No
    (b) a mattress of the usual type   Yes No
    (c) a mattress without a dust-proof cover   Yes No
    (d) feather pillows   Yes No
    (e) pets   Yes No
    (f) hair or fiber pads beneath your carpet   Yes No
    (g) upholstered furniture   Yes No
    (h) bookcases   Yes No
    (i) stuffed toys   Yes No

18. Are you exposed to irritating dusts or vapors in your
    work?   Yes No

19. Do you have any hobbies that involve dusts or odors? Yes No

Scoring: Count up the number of times you circled "Yes" above.

Interpretation: The higher your "Yes" score, the greater the chances that you have an allergy and/or are at risk for allergic reactions.

Name: _____   Date: _____

Directions: Answer the following fifteen questions either True or False.
The answers will be provided after you have completed the quiz.

____ 1. Epileptics suffer from either grand mal, petit mal, or psychomotor
         seizures.

____ 2. A grand mal seizure may be a life-threatening experience.

____ 3. Epilepsy, if untreated, will lead to insanity.

____ 4. The onset of an acute infectious disease in an infant may be
         accompanied by convulsions.

____ 5. Convulsions can be caused by a head injury.

____ 6. In most instances, epileptic seizures cannot be controlled or
         prevented.

____ 7. A bystander should place an object between the teeth of a victim of
         convulsions in order to prevent the tongue from being swallowed.

____ 8. It is important that the jerking and rigidity of muscle groups that
         occur during some seizures be prevented and restrained.

____ 9. The best thing for a bystander to do for a person suffering a
         seizure is nothing.

____ 10. Bystanders should attempt to make a person "walk it off" after
         suffering a grand mal seizure.

____ 11. A grand mal attack can last between 5 and 10 minutes.

____ 12. Bystanders watching a grand mal seizure often think the victim is
         in great pain.

____ 13. All seizures are indicative of epilepsy.

____ 14. Epilepsy cannot occur in people over age 18.

____ 15. Epilepsy is contagious.

Answers to Self-Test on Epilepsy

1. True. The grand mal seizure is the characteristic epileptic seizure. The victim often has tightening of the jaw, arms, and other body parts. Spasms may occur in these limbs, and often the eyes are turned back into the head. The victim will lose control of his or her bowels and bladder. The person may also turn slightly blue. Petit mal, the most common type of epilepsy in children, is often outgrown by the time a child reaches mid-aloescence. Petit mal seizures consist of brief (seconds) loss of consciousness, but once a seizure is over, the person continues as if the seizure never occurred. Psychomotor seizures act upon the mental processes as well as the muscles. These seizures are often ignored by the epileptic and others.

2. False. Although bystanders often feel that the individual is in great danger there is no serious danger unless the victim has fallen and his or her head.

3. False. Epilepsy is a symptom of a physical disorder in the brain. This is not indicative of the person's intelligence. The myth that epilepsy leads to insanity goes back many years, before modern medicine determined what epilepsy is. It in no way leads a person to insanity.

4. True. Convulsive seizures do not occur only with grand mal epilepsy. Many young children experience seizures without having epilepsy. The seizure may indicate an unsuspected illness or poisoning. In the case of children under the age of 10, high fevers often trigger seizures.

5. True. One of the main causes of epilepsy and/or convulsions is head injuries. The large number of automobile accidents has dramatically increased the number of epileptics in this country (estimated at around 3 million). Children, as well as adults, are prime candidates when they are not restrained by seat belts. There is no good reason why you should not wear seat belts. Preventing epilepsy is just one of these many good reasons why you should.

6. False. Once a person has been diagnosed as having epilepsy, he or she can easily be treated by medication. As long as this person takes the medication, there is very little chance of having a seizure. Almost all states now allow epileptics to drive if under the proper medication.

7. False. There are three reasons why this statement is false. First, it is virtually impossible to open the jaws of a person having a grand mal seizure. The muscles holding the jaw are often in such a spasmatic state they they clinch the jaw very tight. Second, the damage to the interior of the mouth could be extensive if an object is placed in the mouth. Could you imagine the damage to the teeth, tongue, and cheeks if a spoon were placed in the mouth? As ridiculous as this sounds, this very same belief was common not too many years ago. The third reason why this statement is false is that it is impossible to swallow your tongue.

   Often an epileptic will experience an "aura." This aura is a signal to the person that he or she will be having a seizure within a few minutes. Many times a person who is experiencing an aura will place a handkerchief between the teeth and lie down. However, this is the only time a person should have something placed between the teeth.

8. False. The epileptic should not be restrained in any way. It has been shown that the more a person is restrained, the greater the chance that a repeat seizure of greater magnitude will occur.

9. True. As strange as it sounds, this is really the best thing to do. Leave the victim alone and protect him or her from injuring him or herself on objects in the room (e.g., tables, chairs). Also protect the person from other well-meaning but wrong bystanders.

10. False. After a grand mal seizure a person is often extremely tired, confused, and sleepy. It is best to let this person sleep as long as he or she desires. It is also recommended that you do not discuss the seizure with the individual unless he or she initiates the discussion.

11. True. During a grand mal seizure the person is actually unconscious. When a person becomes unconscious, the tongue often falls to the back of the throat (mistakenly referred to as swallowing the tongue). There is no memory of the seizure because the person was unconscious. If a seizure lasts longer than 10 minutes, it is recommended that a physician be contacted.

12. True. As referred to in question 11, the victim is unconscious and does not feel any pain. However, it is quite common for bystanders to want to aid the victim, whom they feel is suffering tremendous pain. The person suffering the most is often the bystander.

13. False. Epilepsy is characterized by seizures, but seizures are not necessarily signs of epilepsy. Illness and poison are important causes of seizures as well.

14. False. There are more than 3 million epileptics in the United States. Only strokes are more common. Epilepsy can occur at any age; however, in many instances, adult onset has been triggered by head injury.

15. False. Epilepsy is no more contagious than a stroke. In fact, it is not considered hereditary. The likelihood that an epileptic will have a child who will become an epileptic is very slim indeed.

Source: Adapted from a quiz constructed by Dr. Mark J. Kittleson, Assistant Professor, Health Education, Department of Health and Physical Education, Youngstown State University, Youngstown, Ohio 44555

Are Your Bones at Risk?

Name: _____ Date: _____

Directions: For each of the following questions, circle the response that best describes you and your lifestyle.

1. Do you smoke cigarettes?
   a. No (0 points)   b. Yes (4 points)

2. Do you drink alcoholic beverages daily?
   a. No (0 points)
   b. 1-2 oz. of hard liquor or 2 glasses of wine or beer per day (2 points)
   c. 3 or more oz. of hard liquor or 2 or more glasses of wine or beer per day (4 points)

3. Do you generally avoid milk, cheese, and other dairy products in your diet?
   a. No (0 points)   b. Yes (3 points)

4. Do you get regular exercise?
   a. No (3 points)   b. Yes (0 points)

5. Are you a female who exercises a great deal with irregular or no menstruation?
   a. No (0 points)   b. Yes (4 points)

6. Do you have an eating disorder or consume only small amounts of nutritious food?

7. Do you eat a diet high in animal protein such as red meats?
   a. No (0 points)   b. Yes (4 points)

8. Do you add salt to your food at the table?
   a. No (0 points)   b. Yes (3 points)

9. Are you a vegetarian or do you eat a diet heavily weighted toward vegetables?
   a. No (0 points)   b. Yes (2 points)

10. Do you include high amounts of fiber in your diet?
    a. No (0 points)   b. Yes (2 points)

11. Do you drink three or more cups of coffee each day or consume an equivalent amount of caffeine from other sources, such as cola-type beverages?
    a. No (0 points)   b. Yes (2 points)

12. Do you have a family history of osteoporosis or other bone disease?
    a. No (0 points)   b. Yes (4 points)

13. Are you of white, northern European, or Asian background?
    a. No (0 points)   b. Yes (3 points)

14. Do you have a fair complexion?
    a. No (0 points)   b. Yes (2 points)

15. Do you have a small-boned frame?
    a. No (0 points)   b. Yes (4 points)

16. Do you have a low percentage of body fat (less than 15 percent of total body weight-see Chapter 6) or a lean build?
    a. No (0 points)   b. Yes (4 points)

17. Are you over 40 years of age?
    a. No (0 points)   b. Yes (2 points)

18. Are you over 70 years of age?
    a. No (0 points)   b. Yes (4 points)

19. Have you had your ovaries removed?
    a. No (0 points)   b. Yes (4 points)

20. Have you breast-fed just one child?
    a. No (0 points)   b. Yes (1 point)

21. Are you allergic to milk or other dairy products?
    a. No (0 points)   b. Yes (3 points)

22. Are you a woman who has never borne children?
    a. No (0 points)   b. Yes (2 points)

23. Did you experience early menopause?
    a. No (0 points)   b. Yes (3 points)

24. Do you use or have you used steroid drugs?
    a. No (0 points)   b. Yes (4 points)

25. Do you have an overactive thyroid gland?
    a. No (0 points)   b. Yes (4 points)

26. Do you suffer from excessive secretion of the parathyroid glands?
    a. No (0 points)   b. Yes (3 points)

27. Do you have biliary cirrhosis or an inflammatory disease of the bile system connecting the liver and the intestines?
    a. No (0 points)   b. Yes (3 points)

28. Do you have chronic kidney disease?
    a. No (0 points)   b. Yes (3 points)

29. Do you use anticonvulsants or medications designed to prevent convulsions or fits?
    a. No (0 points)   b. Yes (2 points)

30. Do you have a history of stomach or small-bowel disease?
    a. No (0 points)   b. Yes (4 points)

Scoring: Add up the total number of points associated with your responses.

Interpretation:
 0-18:   Low risk
 9-16:   Moderate risk
17-24:   High risk
25+:   Very high risk

Source: Kenneth H. Cooper, Preventing Osteoporosis. New York: Bantam Books, 1989.

Personal Immunization Record

Name: _____ Date: _____

Directions: This is an exercise to check your active immunization history. From your best recollection, record the following information. Perhaps consult with your parents or physicians who may have records of your immunizations and childhood diseases. Keep it for your records.

Immunization	Date	Booster?
Smallpox		
Rubella		
Mumps		
Measles		
Polio		
Tetanus		
Pertussis		
Diphtheria		

Childhood Disease Or Immunization	Date	Booster?
Influenza		
TB		
Typhoid		
Cholera		
Hepatitis		
Strep		
Chickenpox		

Interpretation: You may also want to check any instances of passive acquired immunity.

How Accurate Are Your Perceptions of Aging?

Name: _____ Date: _____

Directions: Indicate whether each of the following questions is true or false about the aged (defined as those over 65).

____ 1. The majority of the aged are senile.

____ 2. The majority of the aged only seldom become irritated or angry.

____ 3. Most of the aged have no interest in, or capacity for, sexual relations.

____ 4. Lung capacity tends to decline in old age.

____ 5. Most of the aged feel miserable all the time.

____ 6. Physical strength tends to decline in old age.

____ 7. Most of the aged live in extended care institutions (nursing homes, mental hospitals, etc.).

____ 8. Aged drivers have fewer accidents per person than drivers under age 65.

____ 9. Most older workers cannot work as effectively as younger workers.

____ 10. The vast majority of the aged are healthy enough to carry out their normal activities.

____ 11. Most of the aged are set in their ways and cannot change.

____ 12. Old people usually take longer to learn something new.

____ 13. It is almost impossible for the aged to learn new things.

____ 14. The reaction of most older people tends to be slower than the reaction of most younger people.

____ 15. In general, most of the aged are pretty much alike.

____ 16. The majority of the aged are seldom bored.

____ 17. The majority of the aged are socially isolated and lonely.

____ 18. Older workers have fewer accidents than younger workers.

____ 19. The health and socioeconomic status of older people (compared to younger people) in the year 2000 will probably be about the same as that of today's older people.

____ 20. Most medical practitioners tend to give low priority to the aged.

____ 21. The majority of the aged have incomes below the poverty level (as defined by the federal government).

____ 22. The majority of the aged are working or would like to have some kind of work to do (including housework and volunteer work).

____ 23. Older people tend to become more religious as they age.

Scoring: Compare your responses with the following answer key and add up the number of wrong answers you scored.

Answer key: All odd-numbered statements are false; all even-numbered statements are true.

Interpretation: The more wrong answers you got, the more likely it is that you have a negative view of aging and the aged. Unless you plan to die young, reconsider aging in terms of what senior citizens *can* do.

Source: Dr. Erdman Paimore, Duke University Center for the Study of Aging and Human Development, Durham, NC. Initially published in <u>The Gerontologist</u>, Vol. 20, No. 6, 1980.

I'd Pick More Daisies

Name: _____ Date: _____

If I had my life to live over,
I'd try to make more mistakes next time.
I would relax. I would limber up.
I would be sillier than I have been on this trip.
I would be crazier, I would be less hygienic.
I know of very few things I would take seriously.
I would take more chances. I would take more trips.
I would climb more mountains, swim more rivers, and watch more sunsets.
I would burn more gasoline.
I would eat more ice cream, less beans.
I would have more actual troubles and fewer imaginary ones.
You see, I am one of those sensible people who lives sensibly and sanely,
  hour after hour, day after day.
Oh, I've had my moments.
And, if I had it to do over again, I'd have more of them.
In fact, I'd try to have nothing else.
Just moments, one after another,
Instead of living so many years ahead each day.
I have been one of those people who never go anywhere without a
  thermometer, a hot water bottle, a gargle, a raincoat, a parachute.
If I had it to do over again I would go places and do things, and travel
  lighter than I have.
If I had my life to live over, I would start barefooted earlier in the
  spring, and stay that way later in the fall,
I would play hooky more.
I wouldn't make such good grades except by accident.
I would ride more merry-go-rounds.
I'd pick more daisies.

Anonymous

React to this poem: _____

_____

_____

_____

_____

_____

_____

_____

_____

_____

Death Attitude Scale

Name: _____ Date: _____

Purpose: The following items are not intended to test your knowledge. There are no right or wrong answers.

Directions: Reach each item carefully. Place a check mark next to each item with which you *agree*. Make *no marks* next to items with which you disagree.

249 ___ The thought of death is a glorious thought.

247 ___ When I think of death I am most satisfied.

245 ___ Thoughts of death are wonderful thoughts.

243 ___ The thought of death is very pleasant.

241 ___ The thought of death is comforting.

239 ___ I find it fairly easy to think of death.

237 ___ The thought of death isn't so bad.

235 ___ I do not mind thinking of death.

233 ___ I can accept the thought of death.

231 ___ To think of death is common.

229 ___ I don't fear thoughts of death, but I don't like them either.

227 ___ Thinking about death is over-valued by many.

225 ___ Thinking of death is not fundamental to me.

223 ___ I find it difficult to think of death.

221 ___ I regret the thought of death.

219 ___ The thought of death is an awful thought.

217 ___ The thought of death is dreadful.

215 ___ The thought of death is traumatic.

213 ___ I hate the sound of the word death.

211 ___ The thought of death is outrageous.

Scoring: The death attitude scale you have just taken in a pre-post fashion is a reliable and valid attitude scale. (For a detailed explanation of the validity and reliability of the scale, see Dale V. Hardt, "Development of an Investigating Instrument to Measure Attitudes toward Death," *Journal of School Health,* 45, no. 2 (February, 1975), 96-99.)

To score, simply disregard the first number (2), place a decimal point between the two remaining numbers, and average the responses. The average will fall either on an attitude statement or between two attitude statements. Example: An individual checks items 237 (3.7), 235 (3.5), and 227 (2.7). By adding these together and dividing by the total number of items checked, an average of 3.3 is found. Hence, we can say that this person's attitude toward death, at the time he or she took the test, is best described by statement 233-that is, "I can accept the thought of death."

Source: Dale Hardt, <u>Death, The Final Frontier</u>. Englewood Cliffs, NJ: Prentice Hall, 1979. 185-86.

Death and Life's Human Relationships

Name: _____   Date: _____

Purpose: To make better use of human relationships by considering them finite.

Directions:
1. List fifteen people with whom you like to spend time.
2. Place an O next to anyone older than 50.
3. Place a Y next to anyone younger than 10.
4. Place a D next to the five people most likely to die first.
5. Place a T next to the five people you would most trust in a life-and-death situation.
6. Think of your three most valuable possessions. Place a G next to the three people to whom you would give one of these possessions if you were to die today.
7. If you were told you were dying and could only say goodbye to five of the people on your list, who would they be? Place an M next to these people.

Name

1. _____   ___ ___ ___ ___ ___ ___
2. _____   ___ ___ ___ ___ ___ ___
3. _____   ___ ___ ___ ___ ___ ___
4. _____   ___ ___ ___ ___ ___ ___
5. _____   ___ ___ ___ ___ ___ ___
6. _____   ___ ___ ___ ___ ___ ___
7. _____   ___ ___ ___ ___ ___ ___
8. _____   ___ ___ ___ ___ ___ ___
9. _____   ___ ___ ___ ___ ___ ___
10. _____   ___ ___ ___ ___ ___ ___
11. _____   ___ ___ ___ ___ ___ ___
12. _____   ___ ___ ___ ___ ___ ___
13. _____   ___ ___ ___ ___ ___ ___
14. _____   ___ ___ ___ ___ ___ ___
15. _____   ___ ___ ___ ___ ___ ___

Results: Silently contemplate your responses to each of these questions:

1. Can you think of other people you would like to add to your list? Who are they? Why did you not include them originally?
2. Do you enjoy spending time with younger people, people your own age, or older people? Why?

3. Relative to the five people you identified as most likely to die first:
   a) Are they the oldest on your list?
   b) Do you now want to spend more time with them?
   c) What do you want to do with them before they die?
   d) Do you think they would guess that you would include them on such a list? Should you tell them you did?
4. If you were dying in a hospital, would you want any of the five people you designated as the ones you most trust to decide when to "pull the plug"? Or is there someone else to whom you would rather assign that responsibility?
5. How would you feel giving one of your most valued possessions to the people you designated with a G *now* rather than when you are dying? Would the meaning behind the gift be more valuable to you than the possession itself?

The class should then discuss what they have learned from this activity and how their behavior will be changed (if at all).

Source: Adapted from Jerrold S. Greenberg, <u>Student-Centered Health Instruction: A Humanistic Approach.</u> Reading, MA: Addison-Wesley, 1978. 246-47.

Death Concern Scale

Name: _____ Date: _____

Directions: Assign a number reflecting your attitudes regarding each of the statements below as follows:

For questions 1-11: Never = 1; Rarely = 2; Sometimes = 3; Often = 4

For questions 12-30: Strongly agree = 1; Somewhat agree = 2; Somewhat disagree = 3; Strongly disagree = 4

___ 1. I think about my own death.

___ 2. I think about the death of loved ones.

___ 3. I think about dying young.

___ 4. I think about the possibility of my being killed on a city street.

___ 5. I have fantasies of my own death.

___ 6. I think about death just before I go to sleep.

___ 7. I think of how I would act if I knew I were to die within a given period of time.

___ 8. I think of how my relatives would act and feel upon my death.

___ 9. When I am sick I think about death.

___ 10. When I am outside during a lightning storm I think about the possibility of being struck by lightning.

___ 11. When I am in an automobile I think about the high incidence of traffic fatalities.

___ 12. I think people should first become concerned about death when they are old.

___ 13. I am much more concerned about death than those around me.

___ 14. Death hardly concerns me.

___ 15. My general outlook just doesn't allow for morbid thoughts.

___ 16. The prospect of my own death arouses anxiety in me.

___ 17. The prospect of my own death depresses me.

___ 18. The prospect of the death of my loved ones arouses anxiety in me.

___ 19. The knowledge that I will surely die does not in any way affect the conduct of my life.

___ 20. I envision my own death as a painful nightmarish experience.

___ 21. I am afraid of dying.

___ 22. I am afraid of being dead.

___ 23. Many people become disturbed at the sight of a new grave but it does not bother me.

___ 24. I am disturbed when I think about the shortness of life.

___ 25. Thinking about death is a waste of time.

___ 26. Death should not be regarded as a tragedy if it occurs after a productive life.

___ 27. The inevitable death of man poses a serious challenge to the meaningfulness of human existence.

___ 28. The death of the individual is ultimately beneficial because it facilitates change in society.

___ 29. I have a desire to live on after death.

___ 30. The question of whether or not there is a future life worries me considerably.

Scoring: Using the key below, convert the numbers of your answers into points and add these points together to reach a total score.

Key:
- Score the same number of points as your answer for questions 1-12,14, 15,19,23,25,26, and 28.
- Score the inverse (see below) of your answer for questions 13,16,17,18, 20,21,22,24,27,29, and 30.
- To invert, if you answered "1," score 4 points
  - "2," score 3 points
  - "3," score 2 points
  - "4," score 1 point

Interpretation:
30-67   Low anxiety about death
68-80   Average anxiety about death
81-120 High anxiety about death

Source: L.S. Dickstein, <u>Death Concern: Measurement and Correlates</u>. Psychological Reports, 1972, 30, Table 1, 565.

Planning: Dying and Death

Name: _____   Date: _____

Purpose: It is important to acknowledge the inevitability of death and to entertain the thought that if something were to happen to you and you were unable to discuss your ideas regarding your own care, you have taken the time to have your views known. This exercise provides you with the opportunity to assess your current actions regarding the planning for the possibility of your own death.

Directions: In the space provided, check off the appropriate answer. If you intend to complete the task within the next month, you may check off the "will do."

	Yes	No	Will do (1 month)
1. I have a Last Will and Testament.	___	___	___
2. I have completed a uniform donor card.	___	___	___
3. I carry a Uniform Donor Card in my wallet.	___	___	___
4. I have a Living Will.	___	___	___
5. I have a power of attorney for health care.	___	___	___
6. I have talked with someone about what I would like to happen to my body when I die.	___	___	___
7. I have talked with someone about what type of ceremony I would like when I die.	___	___	___
8. I have talked with someone about who I would like to have present at the ceremony.	___	___	___
9. I have talked with someone about what I would like to have happen with my body or ashes.	___	___	___

Behaviors Affecting the Environment

Name: _____ Date: _____

Directions: For each of the following statements, identify how you feel about the behavior:

  1 = Very Strongly   2 = Strongly   3 = Mildly   4 = No opinion

___ 1. Zimi Corporation is secretly dumping huge amounts of chemicals and solid wastes into a nearby stream.

___ 2. A local elected official knows that Zimi Corporation is dumping wastes bu says nothing because the company supports him for office.

___ 3. While you are out boating, the people in the boat ahead of you dump their leftover food and trash into the lake.

___ 4. A small, quiet mountain lake is opened to motorboats.

___ 5. The government is allowing homes to be built along the coast as long as they cost at least $300,000.

___ 6. A large dog defecates on your front lawn.

___ 7. Dogs are allowed to run free in public parks.

___ 8. The person ahead of you throws a cigarette butt out the care window.

___ 9. Someone emptied an ash tray in the supermarket parking lot.

___ 10. The Cuyahoga River catches on fire-again.

___ 11. Local zoning is permitting cabins and houses to be built around a beautiful mountain reservoir.

___ 12. Your next-door neighbor buys a huge gas-hog car.

___ 13. Your mother uses an electric can opener to open a can of soup.

___ 14. Your roommate writes on one side of the paper.

___ 15. The people across the street have their lawn sprinklers on in the same spot for three hours.

___ 16. Your brother uses the toilet as a wastebasket, flushing it each time.

___ 17. The city buses leave behind a horrible odor.

___ 18. Your friends honk their horns each time they drive by your apartment or house.

___ 19. The local housing contractor burns all his leftover lumber cuttings in the field next door.

___ 20. You see in your office "What's News" that George and Irene Jacoby announce the birth of their eighth child.

___ 21. The city of Deerfield, 50 miles away, files an application to build nuclear power plant.

170

_____ 22. You read in the newspaper that the local power company is proposing to build a hydroelectric plant at Feather River Falls, second in height in California to Yosemite Falls.

_____ 23. As you drive down the Sacramento and San Joaquin valleys in California, you observe many crop dusting planes operating over the fields.

Observations and Reactions

1. Do you see any patterns in your responses? If so, what?

2. Are there some behaviors that you feel strongly about? Which ones? Why?

3. Are there some behaviors that you do not feel as strongly about? Which ones? Why?

4. Would you rate yourself as very concerned, mildly concerned, or unconcerned about the environment?

5. Are your behaviors consistent with your personal concerns about the environment? Why? Why not?

6. What situations might you add to this list?

Source: Reprinted by permission from Health Behaviors, 2nd ed. By Reed and Lang, Copyright 1987 by West Publishing Company. All rights reserved. pp 518-519.

Annual Exposure to Radiation

Name: _____ Date: _____

Directions: For each of the following categories, place the score of the answer that best reflects your life in the blank to the right.

Where You Live

1. To find the cosmic radiation, determine the approximate elevation of your town/city above sea level.
   (a) sea level, score 26 points   _____
   (b) 1000 feet, score 28 points   _____
   (c) 2000 feet, score 31 points   _____
   (d) 3000 feet, score 35 points   _____
   (e) 4000 feet, score 41 points   _____
   (f) 5000 feet, score 47 points   _____
   (g) 6000 feet, score 55 points   _____
   (h) 7000 feet, score 66 points   _____
   (i) 8000 feet, score 79 points   _____
   (j) 9000 feet, score 96 points   _____

2. For ground radiation in the United States, score 26 points   __26__

3. What is your home constructed of?
   (a) stone, concrete and/or masonry, score 7 points   _____
   (b) Other, score 0 points   _____

4. On an average day, how many hours do you spend close to a nuclear plant?
   (a) For each hour at the site boundary, score 0.2 points   _____
   (b) For each hour one mile away, score 0.02 points   _____
   (c) for each hour five miles away, score 0.002   _____

What You Eat, Drink and Breathe

1. For average food, water, and air radiation in the United States, score 24 points   __24__

2. For average weapons-test fallout in the United States, score 4 points   __4__

How You Live

1. For each chest x-ray you have in a year, score 10 points   _____

172

2. For each lower gastrointestinal tract x-ray you have in a
   year, score 500 points   _____

3. For each radiopharmaceutical examination you have in a year,
   score 300 points   _____

4. For each 2,500 miles you travel by jet plane, add 1 point   _____

5. For each hour per day you view television, add 0.15 points   _____

Scoring: Add up all the points in the right-hand column for an estimate of
the number of milliards of radiation you are receiving annually.

Interpretation: Compare your score to the United States annual average dose
of 180 milliards; if it is substantially higher, your health could be in
danger.

Are You Doing Enough to Prevent Accidents?

Name: _____ Date: _____

Directions: For each of the following questions, answer "Yes" or "No."

Group 1: Safety at Home

		Yes	No
1.	Do you make it a point never to smoke in bed?	___	___
2.	If you have fireplaces, do you keep screens around them?	___	___
3.	When cooking, do you guard against accidental tipping by positioning pan handles so that they do not extend outwards?	___	___
4.	Do you keep electric cords out of the reach of children and avoid overloading the outlets?	___	___
5.	Are you careful never to leave small children unsupervised in the kitchen or bathroom?	___	___
6.	Are children's nightclothes and soft toys labeled to show they are made of nonflammable materials?	___	___
7.	Are medicines in your house kept in a secure place out of children's reach and away from beds?	___	___
8.	Are you careful never to store drugs or dangerous chemicals (bleach, paint-stripper, etc.) within children's reach or in incorrectly labeled containers?	___	___
9.	If you own a gun, do you keep it unloaded, separate from the ammunition, and locked away?	___	___
10.	Do you make it a point to prevent children from playing with objects small enough to be swallowed or inhaled?	___	___
11.	Do you keep plastic bags away from children?	___	___
12.	When working around the house, do you wear safety glasses, ear plugs, and protective clothing such as sturdy shoes?	___	___
13.	Are your carpets firmly fixed, with no ragged spots or edges, and are loose rugs placed to minimize the risk of sliding or tripping?	___	___
14.	Are your stairs, halls, and other passages well lit (brightly enough to read a newspaper)?	___	___
15.	Is it a rule in your house that nothing is left on the stairs?	___	___
16.	If you spill or drop something that might be slippery on the floor, do you always clean it up right away?	___	___
17.	Do you keep non-slip mats both in and alongside the bath or shower?	___	___
18.	Do you have a written and updated escape plan in event of a fire?	___	___

	Yes	No

19. Are there fire extinguishers in your residence that are adequately charged and everyone knows how to operate? ___ ___

20. Do you check the smoke detectors every few months to make sure they work? ___ ___

21. Do you know where the shut-off valves or switches for water, electricity, and gas are in your residence and how to turn them off? ___ ___

22. Do you know the phone number for emergency medical aid in your community and is this phone number listed on all phones in your residence? ___ ___

23. Do you have the phone number for the Poison Control Center listed on your phone? ___ ___

Group 2: Safety on the Road

24. Have you taught your children exactly how, when, and where to cross streets safely? ___ ___

25. Have your children been taught the basic rules of the road to use when bicycling? ___ ___

26. When walking in streets or on open roads at twilight or in the dark, do all members of your family wear a markedly visible outer garment such as white or luminous jacket? ___ ___

27. Do you always drive within the speed limit and drive defensively? ___ ___

28. Are you always careful to drink very little alcohol or none at all if you are going to drive a car soon afterwards? ___ ___

29. Do you avoid driving when you feel unusually tired or ill, or if you are taking drugs such as antihistamines that are known to impair alertness? ___ ___

30. Do you have your car carefully serviced, including lights, tires, windshield washer and wipers, brakes, and steering, either every 6,000 miles or at least every 6 months? ___ ___

31. Do you check at least once a week to make sure that your car windows, lights, mirrors, and reflectors are clean? ___ ___

32. When driving, do you always try to keep a gap of at least a yard for each mile-per-hour of speed between your car and the one in front? ___ ___

33. Do you always make sure than you and all passengers in your car use available seatbelts? ___ ___

34. Are any infants or toddlers riding in your car securely strapped into infant car seats? ___ ___

Group 3: Safety on Vacations

35. Are all members of your family able to swim or in the process of learning to swim?   ___ ___

36. Do you test the depth of the water and go in feet first? ___ ___

37. In a boat, does everyone always wear a life jacket?   ___ ___

38. If you do any skiing, hiking, or climbing, do you always go prepared with the right clothing and equipment?   ___ ___

39. When going on an excursion for a day or longer, do you tell someone what your route is and when you expect to be back?   ___ ___

40. Do you and your family take full safety precautions and have the proper equipment when you engage in contact sports and other possibly dangerous sports?   ___ ___

41. Before taking up a new and potentially dangerous activity such as hang gliding, do you make sure you get proper instruction?   ___ ___

42. During a vacation, do you make sure you get adequate rest and relaxation?

Scoring: Add up the number of times you checked "No." Add up the number of times you checked "Yes."

Interpretation: Although there are no hard and fast rules, in general, the more "No's" you had the more likely it is that you have *not* accident-proofed your environment adequately and run the risk of injury. The more "Yes's" you had, the more likely it is that you *have* accident-proofed your environment adequately and run only a small risk of injury.

Source: Adapted from J.Kunz and A. Finkel, The American Medical Association Family Medical Guide, revised and updated New York; Random House, 1987.

Free Health Care in Your Community

Name: _____ Date: _____

Purpose: To identify the free healthcare services available in your community.

Size of Group: Five to seven students per group.

Directions:
1. Each group chooses one of the following:
   Health Maintenance Organizations
   Mental health clinics,
   Medical clinics (including abortion, treatment of STDs),
   Other free clinics.
2. Each group prepares a list of all the free clinics within the area chosen and assigns one or two clinics to each group member.
3. Students visit the clinics and health maintenance organizations and complete the information on the chart that follows.

Results:
1. Each group prepares copies of its findings (chart) for distribution to the entire class.
2. One student from each group is selected to summarize findings to the class.

County and City Health Clinics/Agencies Providing Free Services

Name of Clinic	Location	Telephone	Primary Services Rendered	Cost	Who is Eligible

Source: George B. Dintiman and Jerrold S. Greenberg, Health through Discovery, 2nd ed. Reading, MA; Addison-Wesley, 1983, p. 498.

Is an HMO Right For You?

Name: _____ Date: _____

Directions: Select a local HMO and visit the facilities to get answers to the following questions:

Questions About the HMO

1. Technical Quality of Care
[ ] What kinds of training have the doctors had?
[ ] What proportion of doctors is board certified or board eligible?
[ ] What percentage of your care will be handled by doctors, and what percentage by nurses or other non-physician personnel?
[ ] What is the reputation of the plan in terms of quality of care, based on the information you can get from current and/or former members?
[ ] Is there any medical condition that the plan will not cover?

2. Are of Care
[ ] How effectively do the doctors in the HMO deal with patients as people?
[ ] Are there members of the staff who speak other languages or who are willing to help senior citizens or other special-needs groups when necessary?
[ ] How does the HMO keep in touch with the needs of patients, and how comfortable would you feel making a complaint if it were necessary?
[ ] What proportion of HMO members has dropped out voluntarily because of dissatisfaction in the last year? (The HMO should keep a record of this and will make it available to you if you ask.)

3. Accessibility of Care
[ ] How convenient is the location for you?
[ ] Is it easy to get there?
[ ] Are the hours convenient?
[ ] Do you have to wait long when you go in for visits?
[ ] Where are the hospitals that are part of the plan?
[ ] What do you do in an emergency, either in town or out? Whom do you call, and in what instances do you need permission before you can get covered care?

4. Finance
[ ] How much does than plan cost?
[ ] What's covered for that price, and what isn't?
[ ] What portion of that will your employer pay, and will there be any payroll deduction?
[ ] What are the copayments, the deductibles (if any), and other out-of-pocket costs?
[ ] Is there a high- or low-option plan to choose from?
[ ] What do you pay for emergency services, and how do you handle the paperwork?
[ ] How fiscally sound is the plan itself?

5. Physical Environment
[ ] What do the waiting rooms and examining rooms look like?
[ ] Are they clean and comfortable?
[ ] How crowded are they?

6. Availability of Care
[ ] How quickly can you be seen by a doctor or nurse?
[ ] What are your doctor's phone-in times, and are they convenient?
[ ] How hard is it to get an appointment to see a specialist?
[ ] Is there a wide variety of specialist services available?
[ ] What are they?
[ ] What is the plan's second-opinion policy?
[ ] When and how can you see someone outside the plan?
[ ] What are the procedures for emergency care?
[ ] What are the procedures for out-of-town care?

7. Continuity of Care
[ ] How long do doctors stay with the plan on the average?
[ ] How many doctors are there to chose from?
[ ] How do you go about changing doctors if you want to?
[ ] Can you count on your doctor to see you through a major illness, or to help you cope with a new infant's changing needs? Again, to determine this you may have to rely on the experiences of other HMO members.

8. Outcomes of Care
[ ] How successful is the care according to the HMO's morbidity and mortality rates? These statistics should be available to the public.
[ ] What are the grievance procedures if you are not satisfied?
[ ] What have the major complaints been in the past year? Most HMOs have open records on the outcomes of grievance procedures and complaints.
[ ] What are the procedures if you wish to cancel your membership?

Questions About Doctors Assigned as Primary Caregivers
[ ] What is the doctor's professional background? Schools? Training? Area of concentration?
[ ] What is the doctor's general philosophy and health care? Does he or she smoke? Exercise regularly? Believe in alternative health care, nutrition, stress control? To what extent does he or she agree with the plan's general philosophy if there is one?
[ ] What does the doctor see as his or her responsibilities to you? As your responsibilities as a patient?
[ ] Is the doctor financially at risk for your care? What happens if you need extensive care?
[ ] What is the doctor's referral network? What would happen if you requested a referral other than that recommended by your doctor?
[ ] What is the doctor's availability for call-ins or visits?
[ ] What is the doctor's commitment to the HMO? How long does he or she plan to be around?
[ ] Whom would the doctor recommend you see if he or she were not available? Why?
[ ] What is the doctor's general attitude about life?

179

Questions for You
[ ] Is the center convenient to work as well as home?
[ ] How many children do you have? Do they already have pediatric care? How willing are you--or they--to give it up?
[ ] Does everyone in your family live at home? If not, can the members who don't live at home get care easily?
[ ] Do some members of your family travel a lot? What kind of coverage will they need?
[ ] Does someone in your family need long-term care? What kind of coverage is available?
[ ] Do you feel comfortable with the preventive-care aspects of your HMO? With the attitudes of its doctors? With the limitations on access to care, if any?
[ ] Are there financial burdens under the terms of the plan that you might not be able to handle? What if you leave your job and are no longer covered? Can you continue on an individual basis? Can you leave the plan and then rejoin if necessary?

Scoring: There are no right or wrong answers to this questionnaire. Put a plus sign before those answers that you feel would fit your needs and a minus sign before those that you feel would *not* fit your needs. Then add up the number of plus and minus responses in each category.

Interpretation: If you have a great many more positive (plus) than negative (minus) answers, then HMOs in general--and this one in particular--may be a good option for you. But if your negative answers greatly outnumber your positive ones, you will need to decide whether to examine other managed care facilities or to remain with a more traditional private doctor and indemnity plan.

Source: J. Bloom. HMOs: What They Are, How They Work, and Which One is Best for You. Tuscon, AZ: The Body Press, 1987, pp.146-154.

Seeking and Evaluating a Physician

Name: _____ Date: _____

Directions: Use the checklist below to evaluate your current physician or to choose a new one.

Yes No

___ ___ 1. The office appears to be run efficiently.

___ ___ 2. The office atmosphere is friendly and reassuring.

___ ___ 3. The receptionist is helpful when I call to make an appointment for a visit.

___ ___ 4. Phone messages are passed on and phone calls returned in a timely manner.

___ ___ 5. I am informed ahead of time if there will be any delays.

___ ___ 6. The waiting area is rarely crowded.

___ ___ 7. Privacy is provided when I am asked personal questions.

___ ___ 8. The office accepts insurance, and requirements for payment are clearly explained.

___ ___ 9. The physician seems thorough when taking my medical history.

___ ___ 10. The physician gives me sufficient time and encouragement to completely describe my problem.

___ ___ 11. The physician is receptive to my questions and concerns.

___ ___ 12. The physician answers all my questions.

___ ___ 13. The physician explains things clearly; he or she does not use so much medical jargon that I have difficulty understanding.

___ ___ 14. The physician explains the purpose and procedure for all medical tests.

___ ___ 15. The physician clearly explains the diagnosis.

___ ___ 16. The physician explains the reasons a particular drug is prescribed. He or she provides complete instructions for using the drug safely and efficiently.

___ ___ 17. Follow-up instructions are clearly given. I understand what my next steps should be.

___ ___ 18. The physician supports my decision to seek a second opinion when I feel it's necessary.

___ ___ 19. The physician refers me to a specialist when indicated.

___ ___ 20. The physician is willing to consult with me on the telephone when needed.

___ ___ 21. Overall, the physician makes me feel comfortable with and confident of the services he or she is providing.

Interpretation: "No" answers indicate areas where your relationship with your physician or the running of the office may be less than ideal. Discuss any areas of concern with your physician. If things do not improve, consider changing physicians. Remember, your physician works for you.

Rating Your Health Insurance

Name: _____   Date: _____

Directions: Before selecting a health insurance plan you should consider several very important factors. Completing the following checklist and making notes about any special features or exclusions in a policy will help you select the plan with the most benefits for the money.

Questions   **Comments/Notes**

Types of Services Covered

1. How many days of hospitalization are covered?

2. How much is the maximum per-day payment?

3. Are surgical procedures paid in full? What percentage must I pay? (co-insurance)

4. Are physicians' visit covered?

5. What about radiation therapy? Physical therapy? Are transfusions covered?

6. Are emergency-room services covered?

7. Are outpatient provisions and ambulance services provided?

8. Are prescription medications and hospital medications covered?

9. Does the policy have provisions for pregnancy coverage?

10. Does the policy contain restrictions for communicable diseases such as AIDS?

11. Are routine examinations such as Pap tests covered?

12. Which treatments, if any, require preauthorization?

Questions	Comments/Notes

Waiting periods/Cancellations

13. Is the policy effective immediately?
    How long before coverage is in effect?

14. What constitutes a preexisting condition?
    How long must I be free of symptoms before
    a condition is covered?

15. Under what circumstances, if any, could
    the policy be canceled?

16. If I quit or lose my job, can I keep the
    insurance by paying my own premiums? How
    long can I continue doing this?

17. If I am no longer employed by a firm and
    I cannot continue in the group plan, can
    I convert to an individual policy?

18. How long is the grace period for nonpayment
    of my premium?

Co-Insurance and Out-Of-Pocket Expenses

19. What is the yearly deductible per family
    or per individual?

20. What is the co-insurance ratio for most
    procedures?

21. What is the maximum major medical payment?

Aggressiveness Questionnaire

Name: _____ Date: _____

Directions: Circle the number of each statement that describes aggression.

1. A spider eats a fly.
2. Two wolves fight for the leadership of the pack.
3. A soldier shoots an enemy at the front line.
4. The warden of a prison executes a convicted criminal.
5. A juvenile gang attacks members of another gang.
6. Two men fight for a piece of bread.
7. A man viciously kicks a cat.
8. A man, while cleaning a window, knocks over a flowerpot, which, in falling, injures a pedestrian.
9. A girl kicks a wastebasket.
10. Mr. X, a notorious gossip, speaks disparagingly of many people in his acquaintance.
11. A man mentally rehearses a murder he is about to commit.
12. An angry son purposely fails to write to his mother, who is expecting a letter and will be hurt if none arrives.
13. An enraged boy tries with all his might to inflict injury on his antagonist, a bigger boy, but is not successful.
14. A man daydreams of harming his antagonist, but has no hope of doing so.
15. A senator does not protest the escalation of bombing to which he is morally opposed.
16. A farmer beheads a chicken and prepares it for supper.
17. A hunter kills an animal and mounts it as a trophy.
18. A dog snarls at a mail carrier, but does not bite.
19. A physician gives a flu shot to a screaming child.
20. A boxer gives his opponent a bloody nose.
21. A girl scout tries to assist an elderly woman, but trips her by accident.
22. A bank robber is shot in the back while trying to escape.
23. A tennis player smashes his racket after missing a volley.
24. A person commits suicide.
25. A cat kills a mouse, parades around with it, and then discards it.

Source: L.T. Benjamin, Jr. Defining aggression: an exercise for classroom discussion."Teaching of Psychology," 1985: 12, 41.

Rating the Evening News

I - Aggressive Acts

Name: _____ Date: _____

1. Which network news program did you watch? (circle one)
   ABC   CBS   NBC   Other _____

2. What time was the broadcast? From _____ until _____

3. Who was the anchor reading the news? _____

4. How many separate stories or news items were presented during the broadcast? _____

5. How many separate stories focused on some kind of aggressive act or aggressive behavior? _____

6. Briefly describe each of the news stories that focused on aggression. In which position did each story appear during the newscast (i.e., was it the first story? the fifth story? the last story?)

             Description   Position

   _____   _____

   _____   _____

   _____   _____

   _____   _____

   _____   _____

   _____   _____

   _____   _____

   _____   _____

   _____   _____

   _____   _____

7. Divide the number of stories that focused on aggression by the total number of stories presented during the broadcast.

Number of stories on aggression _____ divided by

Total number of stories _____ = _____

II - Prosocial Acts

1. Which network news program did you watch? (circle one)
   ABC   CBS   NBC   Other _____

2. What time was the broadcast? From _____ until _____

3. Who was the anchor reading the news? _____

4. How many separate stories or news items were presented during the broadcast? _____

5. How many separate stories focused on some kind of prosocial act or prosocial behavior (i.e., someone who gave help or someone who acted unselfishly)? _____

6. Briefly describe each of the news stories that focused on prosocial behavior. In which position did each story appear during the newscast (i.e., was it the first story? the fifth story? the last story?)

Description	Position
_____	_____
_____	_____
_____	_____
_____	_____
_____	_____
_____	_____
_____	_____
_____	_____
_____	_____
_____	_____
_____	_____

7. Divide the number of stories that focused on aggression by the total number of stories presented ruing the broadcast.

Number of stories on aggression _____ divided by

Total number of stories _____ = _____

Coercive Sex Questionnaire

Name: _____ Date: _____

Sexual coercion places both men and women in "victim" roles, although women are victimized more often.

The development of effective strategies to deal with the problem of coercive sex requires changing the traditional gender role socialization that makes females vulnerable to sexual abuse and pushes males into the "victimizer" role. Decisions to make such changes are usually based upon our values and attitudes toward the use of power and influence.

Purpose: The exercise that follows is designed to assist you in clarifying your choices about ways to deal the problem of coercive sex.

Directions: Write in the feelings and behaviors you would most likely experience or engage in for each of the first eight questions. In question 9, check the appropriate box to identify your choice.

1. If you were witnessing a rape of a stranger in a public place (e.g., bus depot)...

   a) How would you feel?

   b) What would you do?

2. If your spouse were the victim of a forcible rape...

   a) How would you feel?

   b) What would you do?

3. If you learned that a child in your neighborhood was being subjected to an incestuous relationship with his or her parent...

a) How would you feel?

b) What would you do?

4. If you learned that two of your children (e.g., son and daughter) were involved in brother-sister incest...

a) How would you feel?

b) What would you do?

5. If you learned that your spouse was asked to participate in sexual activity with his or her boss in order to keep a job or get a promotion...

a) How would you feel?

b) What would you do?

6. If you were applying for a position of employment that you wanted very badly and the prospective employer made it clear that hiring depended on your sexual "availability" and requested a "sample" as a sign of "good faith"...

   a) How would you feel?

   b) What would you do?

7. If you were constantly stared at, touched, and visually and verbally "raped" and generally taken advantage of at work...

   a) How would you feel?

   b) What would you do?

8. If you were invited to a private showing of sexually explicit movies at a neighbor's home and realized that the films you were viewing were of young children engaged in sexual activity...

   a) How would you feel?

   b) What would you do?

9. If a referendum appeared on the ballot in your state to require mandatory sentence for coercive sexual behavior, how would you vote on the following? Place a check mark in the appropriate space.

	Sentence		
	Long Term	Short Term	None
Coercive Sex	_____	_____	_____
Forcible rape	_____	_____	_____
Statutory rape	_____	_____	_____
Parent-child incest	_____	_____	_____
Sibling incest	_____	_____	_____
Sexual harassment at work	_____	_____	_____

Scoring: Responses to this inventory would be very specific to each individual. Taking a closer look at these issues and discussing them with significant others may help you clarify your feelings in regard to coercive sex.

Source: Robert F. Valois and Sandra Kammerman. Your Sexuality: A Self-Assessment, 2nd Ed. New York, McGraw-Hill, 1992. 113-116

Review
and
Practice Tests

1 Promoting Healthy Behavior Change

General Review Questions

1. What are the major dimensions of health?
2. Define prevention and list the three forms of prevention.
3. What are the major factors that influence behavior and behavior-change decisions?
4. According to the Health Belief Model, what factors must support a belief in order for a change to be likely to occur?
5. What are the components for analyzing a behavior you want to change?

Practice Test #1

1. Prior to the 1800s, poor health was often associated with:
   a. The lack of penicillin
   b. The lack of medical care
   c. Poor hygiene and unsanitary conditions
   d. Diseases of heart and circulatory system

2. Statistics that are used to measure death rates are called:
   a. Morbidity
   b. Mortality
   c. Wellness
   d. Health evaluation

3. The leading cause of death for all 15 to 24-year-olds in the United States is:
   a. Cancer
   b. Accidents and adverse effects
   c. Stroke
   d. Heart disease

4. The performance of tasks of everyday living such as bathing or walking up the stairs are called:
   a. Improved quality of life
   b. Physical health
   c. Health promotion behaviors
   d. Activities of Daily Living

5. An appraisal of the relationship between some objcct, action, or idea and some attribute of that object, action or idea, is called:
   a. An attitude
   b. A cue to action
   c. A predisposing factor
   d. A belief

6. Life experiences, knowledge, cultural and ethnic inheritance, and cultural beliefs and values are called:
   a. Predisposing factors
   b. Enabling factors
   c. Readiness factors
   d. Reinforcing factors

7. Attending a health education seminar to stop cigarette intake is an example of:
   a. Primary prevention
   b. Health promotion
   c. Secondary prevention
   d. Tertiary prevention

8. The number of existing cases of a disease or disability is called
   a. Prevalence
   b. Incidence
   c. Health status
   d. Cumulative percentage

9. Reinforcers that include such things as loving looks, affectionate hugs, and praise are called:
   a. Consumable reinforcers
   b. Activity reinforcers
   c. Manipulative reinforcers
   d. Social reinforcers

10. The type of disease prevention that involves treatment and/or rehabilitation after the person is already sick and is typically offered by medical specialists is referred to as:
    a. Primary prevention
    b. Secondary prevention
    c. Tertiary prevention
    d. Disease prevention

11. Taking prevention steps that stop a health problem before it starts is called:
    a. Primary prevention
    b. Secondary prevention
    c. Wellness
    d. Health promotion

12. The state of being that precedes a behavioral change is called:
    a. Cue to action
    b. Readiness
    c. Values
    d. Locus of control

13. Using positive self-affirmations to promote positive self-esteem and behaviors is a form of:
    a. Thought stopping
    b. Cues to action
    c. Modeling
    d. Self-talk

14. The setting events for a behavior that cue or stimulate a person to act in certain ways are called:
    a. Antecedents
    b. Frequency of events
    c. Consequences
    d. Cues to action

15. Programs that combine educational, organizational, procedural, environmental and financial supports to help individuals and groups change negative health behaviors and promote positive change are called:
    a. Health promotion programs
    b. Wellness programs
    c. Prevention programs
    d. Prevalence

Practice Test #2

1. According the Health Belief Model, the process in which a person takes into consideration the severity of potential medical and social consequences if a health problem were to develop or is left untreated is called:
    a. Perceived seriousness of the health problem
    b. Perceived susceptibility of the health problem
    c. Cue to action
    d. Sociopsychological variables

2. The key behaviors that will help people live longer include:
    a. Maintaining healthy eating habits
    b. Sleeping a minimum of seven hours
    c. Weight management
    d. All of the above

3. Our ability to think clearly, reason objectively, and use one's "brain power" effectively to meet life's challenges is defined as:
    a. Social health
    b. Intellectual health
    c. Emotional health
    d. Spiritual health

4. The number of new cases of a disease or disability is called:
    a. Prevalence
    b. Incidence
    c. Health status
    d. Cumulative percentage

5. An academically trained health educator who has passed a national competency examination for prevention/intervention programming is a:
    a. Primary prevention specialist
    b. Health promotion specialist
    c. Certified health education specialist
    d. Certified prevention specialist

6. The dimension of health that refers to the ability to have satisfying interpersonal relationships is called:
    a. Spiritual health
    b. Emotional health
    c. Social health
    d. Mental health

7. Which of the following is(are) reason(s) for the exclusion of women from clinical trials?
    a. Their childbearing potential
    b. Variations caused by women's menstrual cycles
    c. Women's physiology
    d. All of the above

8. The theory that proposes that our behaviors result from our intentions to perform actions is called:
    a. Social Learning Theory
    b. Modeling
    c. Cues to Action
    d. Theory of Reasoned Action

9. Which of the following is *not* a factor that influences behavior and behavior-change decisions?
   a. Circumstantial factors
   b. Enabling factors
   c. Reinforcing factors
   d. Predisposing factors

10. Spiritual health includes all of the following *except*:
    a. The belief in a supreme being
    b. A specified way of living as prescribed by a particular religion
    c. To experience love, joy, pain, sorrow, peace, contentment
    d. To have satisfying interpersonal relationships

11. Learning behaviors through careful observation of other people is called:
    a. Thought stopping
    b. Modeling
    c. Reinforcing factors
    d. Cues to action

12. You want to bicycle for exercise but do not have access to a bicycle. This is an example of:
    a. Predisposing factors
    b. Enabling factors
    c. Reinforcing factors
    d. Cues to action

13. A relatively stable set of beliefs, feelings, and behavioral tendencies in relation to something or someone is called:
    a. Belief
    b. Value
    c. Social environment
    d. Attitude

14. Delicious edibles such as candy, cookies, or gourmet meals are examples of:
    a. Consumable reinforcers
    b. Activity reinforcers
    c. Extrinsic rewards
    d. Manipulative reinforcers

15. A form of cognitive therapy that is based on the premise that there is a close connection between what people say to themselves and how they feel is:
    a. Theory of Reasoned Action
    b. Thought blocking
    c. Locus of Control
    d. Rational-Emotive Therapy

2 Psychosocial Health

General Review Questions

1. What are the basic elements shared by psychologically healthy people?
2. Describe the characteristics of a dysfunctional family
3. What internal factors shape psychological well-being?
4. List the risk factors for suicide
5. What are ways to develop and maintain self-esteem?

Practice Test #1

1. The "feeling" part of psychosocial health that includes your emotional reactions to life is called:
   a. Emotional health
   b. Social health
   c. Spiritual health
   d. Self-esteem

2. A mentally healthy student who receives a D on an exam may be very disappointed by their grade and will:
   a. Reassess his or her course options and withdraw from the course
   b. Try to assess the reasons why s/he did poorly
   c. Make an appointment with the teacher to re-evaluate the test results
   d. Become cynical about passing the class and stop trying to get an A

3. Belief in some unifying force that gives a sense of purpose or meaning to life is called:
   a. Mental health
   b. Psychological health
   c. Spiritual health
   d. Egocentric health

4. Strong social bonds function to:
   a. Provide intimacy
   b. Provide opportunities for giving or receiving nurturance
   c. Provide reassurance of one's worth
   d. All of the above

5. A complex interaction of one's mental, emotional, social, and spiritual health is known as:
   a. Wellness
   b. Psychosocial health
   c. Health promotion
   d. Psychosocial prevention

6. A psychologically unhealthy person is characterized by all of the following *except*:
   a. Laughs, usually at others
   b. High energy, resilient, and enjoys challenges
   c. Has little fun, no time for him- or herself
   d. Has serious bouts of depression

7. A negative evaluation of an entire group of people that is typically based on unfavorable ideas about the group is called:
   a. Personal control
   b. Prejudice
   c. Phobia
   d. Learned helplessness

8. Our family, the greater environment, and social supports/social bonds are examples of:
   a. Internal factors
   b. External factors
   c. Intrinsic factors
   d. Self-efficacy

9. Marty flunked a math class two times and does not believe that he is good at math. He has resolved himself to not being able to graduate because he will never pass a required math class. This is known as:
   a. Learned helplessness
   b. External locus of control
   c. Seasonal affective disorder
   d. Post-traumatic shock syndrome

10. Anxiety disorders are characterized by:
    a. Fatigue
    b. Back pain
    c. Fear of losing control
    d. All of the above

11. To overcome the effects of insomnia, a person can use which of the following methods?
   a. Don't drink alcohol or smoke before bedtime
   b. Read, listen to music, watch TV, or take a warm bath
   c. Avoid reproaching yourself
   d. All of the above

12. Anxiety disorders that result from experiencing such traumatic events as rape, assault, war, or airplane crashes is called:
   a. Phobias
   b. Depression
   c. Panic attacks
   d. Posttraumatic Stress Disorder

13. After a shooting that left two students dead, the students at a local high school may experience:
   a. Posttraumatic stress disorder
   b. Depression
   c. Manic-depressive mood disorder
   d. Panic attack

14. A person with a Ph.D. degree and training in psychology, is called:
   a. A psychiatrist
   b. A psychologist
   c. A social worker
   d. A psychoanalyst

15. People suffering from schizophrenia may:
   a. Be unfailingly pleasant
   b. Be confused by multiple stimuli and respond inappropriately
   c. Have a clear sense of self
   d. Suffer from carbohydrate cravings

Practice Test #2

1. Susie is worried about the clothes she wears and says that she needs to buy a car that projects her as successful. What stage of Jung's View of Personal Growth and Spiritual Development is she experiencing?
   a. The dawn of life
   b. The morning of life
   c. The noon of life
   d. The evening of life

2. Sam is fatigued and is sleeping too much. He has no interest in hanging out with his friends or family. In addition, he no longer cares to snowboard or participate in other hobbies. Sam may be experiencing:
   a. Anxiety
   b. A phobia
   c. Depression
   d. Posttraumatic Stress Disorder

3. Disorders such as compulsions, phobias, and obsessive thinking are most responsive to:
   a. Behavioral and drug therapy
   b. Cognitive therapy
   c. Family therapy
   d. Psychodynamic therapy

4. Continual failure that causes people to give up and fail to take any action to help themselves is called:
   a. Learned helplessness
   b. Protective factors
   c. Learned failure
   d. Learned survival

5. The cause(s) of obsessive-compulsive disorders are:
   a. Low self-esteem
   b. Fear of losing control
   c. Alteration in a person's senses
   d. Difficult to isolate

6. One's sense of self-respect or self-confidence refers to:
   a. Self-esteem
   b. Social support
   c. Ego
   d. Developmental capabilities

7. All of the following are warnings of suicide *except*:
   a. A preoccupation with themes of death
   b. Increased interest in classes or work
   c. Failure to recover from a personal loss or crisis
   d. Giving away prized possessions

8. Depression that has a biochemical origin is known as:
   a. Manic-depressive mood disorder
   b. Exogenous depression
   c. Androgynous depression
   d. Endogenous depression

9. Which of the following is *not* true about phobias?
   a. They tend to be more prevalent in men than in women
   b. They are deep and persistent fears of specific objects, activities, or situations
   c. Simple phobias may be treated successfully with behavioral therapy
   d. Social phobias may require more extensive therapy

10. A psychological disorder among women that is characterized by depression, irritability, and other symptoms of increased stress is called:
    a. Depression
    b. Phobia
    c. Premenstrual syndrome depression
    d. Panic attack

11. A medical doctor who specializes in treating emotional disorders is:
    a. An Oncologist
    b. A Psychoanalyst
    c. A Psychologist
    d. A Psychiatrist

12. Therapy that aims to help a patient look at life rationally and to correct habitually pessimistic thought patterns is called:
    a. Family therapy
    b. Psychodynamic therapy
    c. Cognitive therapy
    d. Behavioral therapy

13. Suicide is more likely to occur:
    a. among college students
    b. among high school dropouts
    c. among high school students
    d. among middle age males

14. Panic attacks are caused by:
    a. Previously experienced trauma
    b. No obvious link to environmental stimuli
    c. Learned responses to environmental stimuli
    d. Both b and c

15. The type of phobia that occurs spontaneously and has no obvious link to environmental stimuli is called:
    a. Triskaidekaphobia
    b. Simple phobia
    c. Claustrophobia
    d. Agoraphobia

3 Managing Stress

General Review Questions

1. List the phases of Selye's General Adaptation Syndrome.
2. What are the sources of both eustress and distress?
3. What are the characteristics of the Type A personality?
4. Describe the characteristics of psychological hardiness.
5. Describe stress inoculation.

Practice Test #1

1. The sudden burst of energy and strength that is believed to be one of our most basic, innate survival instincts is called:
   a. Eustress
   b. Adjustment
   c. Strain
   d. The fight-or-flight response

2. Stress that presents positive opportunities for personal growth are called:
   a. Homeostasis
   b. Strain
   c. Eustress
   d. Distress

3. The branch of the Autonomic Nervous System that is responsible for energizing the body for either fight or flight and triggering many other stress responses is:
   a. The central nervous system
   b. The parasympathetic nervous system
   c. The sympathetic nervous system
   d. The endocrine system

4. The hormone secreted by the adrenal glands that is responsible for stimulating the body is:
   a. Epinephrine
   b. Adrenocorticotropic Hormones (ACTH)
   c. Adrenaline
   d. Both a and c

5. The key region of the brain responsible for controlling the sympathetic nervous system and directing the stress response is:
   a. The pituitary gland
   b. The hypothalamus
   c. The adrenal glands
   d. The adrenal cortex

6. The phase of the General Adaptation Syndrome in which the physical and psychological energy used to fight the stressors have been depleted is called:
   a. Alarm phase
   b. Resistance phase
   c. Endurance phase
   d. Exhaustion phase

7. Conflict occurs when:
   a. We are forced to face two incompatible demands, opportunities, needs, or goals
   b. We are forced to speed up, intensify or shift the direction of our performance
   c. We must make adjustments to change
   d. None of the above

8. The wear and tear that our bodies and minds sustain during the process of adjusting to or resisting a stressor is called:
   a. Strain
   b. Eustress
   c. Stress
   d. Resistance

9. Overload occurs when we suffer from:
   a. Excessive time pressure
   b. Excessive responsibility
   c. Lack of support
   d. All of the above

10. Type C personalities:
    a. Thrive in stress-filled environments
    b. Succeed more often than Type A
    c. Have better health while displaying negative Type A patterns
    d. All of the above

11. During the Alarm phase of the General Adaptation Syndrome:
    a. The stressor disturbs homeostasis
    b. The body reacts to the stressor and adjusts to allow the system to return to homeostasis
    c. The body's adaptation energy stores release cells for energy and renew the energy reserves
    d. The energy stores are depleted and the organism dies

12. Mood-elevating, pain-killing chemicals that have a morphinelike action on the body and are produced by exercise are called:
    a. Endorphins
    b. Adrenaline
    c. Cortisol
    d. Norepinephrine

13. Symptoms of stress overload among college students include(s) all of the following, *except*:
    a. Prone to accidents
    b. Lethargy caused by lack of sleep or excessive frustration
    c. Increased ability to keep up with classes or concentrate on and finish tasks
    d. Frequent mood changes or overreaction to minor problems

14. The ability of the immune system to respond to assaults is called:
    a. Psychoneuroimmunology
    b. Adaptation
    c. Resistance
    d. Immunocompetence

15. According to Eliot, to reduce stress you should:
    a. Don't sweat the small stuff
    b. Remember that it's all small stuff
    c. Stress is only temporary
    d. Both a and b

Practice Test #2

1. The adaptive response to stress occurs when:
    a. The body attempts to return to homeostasis
    b. The stressor is no longer present
    c. There is a sense of relief that survival has been achieved
    d. Resistance to the stress has adjusted to a positive result

2. Events that can result in debilitative stress or strain are known as:
    a. Strain
    b. Stress
    c. Distress
    d. Adjustment

3. A balanced physical state in which all of the body's systems function smoothly results in:
    a. Homeostasis
    b. Distress
    c. Eustress
    d. General Adaptation Syndrome

4. The pituitary hormone that signals the adrenal glands to release cortisol is:
    a. Epinephrine
    b. Adrenocorticotropic hormone
    c. Endorphin
    d. Adrenaline

5. Feeling forced to speed up, intensify, or shift the direction of your behavior to meet a higher standard of performance, can result in:
    a. Hassles
    b. Pressure
    c. Change
    d. Conflict

6. A state of physical and mental exhaustion caused by excessive stress is called:
    a. Conflict
    b. Overload
    c. Hassles
    d. Burnout

7. There is evidence that suggests a strong relationship between excessive exposure to stress and:
    a. Depression
    b. Drug abuse
    c. Self-esteem
    d. All of the above

8. Rachel has just begun college and is having a hard time adjusting to her new demands. What types of chronic stressors can she expect as she continues in college?
    a. Lack of privacy
    b. Time management
    c. Loneliness
    d. All of the above

9. Overcrowding, discrimination, unemployment, inflation, and poverty are examples of:
   a. Burnout
   b. Conflict
   c. Psychosocial stress
   d. Background distressors

10. The part of the autonomic nervous system that functions to slow all the systems stimulated by the stress response is called the:
   a. Parasympathetic nervous system
   b. Sympathetic nervous system
   c. Central nervous system
   d. Cerebral cortex

11. Preliminary research data on stress levels and immune functioning supports that during periods of prolonged stress, elevated adrenal hormones:
   a. Destroy or reduce the ability of natural killer-T cells to aid the immune response
   b. Improve the ability of natural killer-T cells to aid the immune response
   c. Have no known affect on natural killer-T cells
       to aid the immune response
   d. None of the above

12. Deep adaptive energy stores:
   a. Seem to be influenced primarily by heredity
   b. Release glycogen for energy in response to stressors
   c. Store nutrients for the body's immune response
   d. Are the resources that individuals possess to maintain the balance between their body and minds

13. A conscious attempt to simplify life in an effort to reduce the stresses and strains of modern living is called:
   a. Adaptation
   b. Conflict resolution
   c. Burnout reduction
   d. Downshifting

14. A stress management technique that involves self-monitoring by machine our physical responses to stress is:
   a. Meditation
   b. Biofeedback
   c. Hypnosis
   d. Deep-muscle relaxation

15. Losing your keys or having the grocery bag rip on the way to the door are examples of:
   a. Pressure
   b. Incongruent goals and behaviors
   c. Hassles
   d. Conflict

4 Intentional and Unintentional Injuries

General Review Questions

1. List the phases of the " cycle of violence."
2. Describe the factors that increase the likelihood of violent acts.
3. What are the most important assumptions in our society that prevent the realization of the true nature of sexual assault.
4. What causes young people to join gangs?
5. What preventive actions can be taken to ensure that sexual harassment will not be repeated?

Practice Test #1

1. A set of behaviors that produces injuries, regardless of whether they are intentional or unintentional is called:
   a. Aggression
   b. Accidents
   c. Abuse
   d. Violence

2. Which of the following is vulnerable to violence?
   a. Children
   b. Black males
   c. The elderly
   d. All of the above

3. The best way(s) to prevent a person from joining a gang is to:
   a. Keep that person connected to positive influences and programs
   b. Involve families, social service organizations, and law enforcement, school, and city officials
   c. Provide for programs staff who are well-trained, empathic, competent in dealing with emotionally charged issues, and understanding of the underlying factors that make youths chose the gang way of life
   d. All of the above

4. The threat of abuse and violence, including slapping, shoving, or breaking bones by someone in the home environment, is called:
   a. Rape
   b. Sexual assault
   c. Domestic assault
   d. Domestic violence

5. The single greatest cause of injury to women is:
   a. Auto accidents
   b. Rape
   c. Domestic violence
   d. Muggings

6. Child abusers tend to:
   a. Have been abused as a child
   b. Have feelings of isolation
   c. Have a tendency to abuse alcohol and/or drugs
   d. All of the above

7. The most frequent sexual abusers of children is(are):
   a. Parents
   b. Parents companions
   c. Spouses of the child's parent
   d. All of the above

8. All of the following statements about the impact of child abuse in later life are true, *except*:
   a. Ninety-nine percent of the inmates in the maximum security prison at San Quentin were either abused or raised in abusive households.
   b. Three hundred thousand children between the ages of 8 and 15 are living on the nation's streets and would rather prostitute themselves than return to abusive households.
   c. Most people who are abused as children do not end up as convicts or prostitutes.
   d. Male deviance or mental illness accounts for most incidents of sexual abuse among children.

9. Child abuse refers to the systematic harm of a child by a caregiver, generally a parent. This includes:
   a. Sexual harm
   b. Psychological harm
   c. Physical harm
   d. All of the above

10. Acquaintance or date rape is most common among:
    a. Minority high school females
    b. College women
    c. Mothers with small children
    d. Women in professional jobs

11. Rape by one person known to the victim and that does not involve a physical beating or use of a weapon is called:
    a. Simple assault
    b. Sexual assault
    c. Simple rape
    d. Aggravated rape

12. Much of the violence on college campuses is fueled by:
    a. Alcohol abuse
    b. Excessively high academic standards
    c. Personal problems
    d. Both a and c

13. Self-defense against rape should include:
    a. Learning self-defense techniques
    b. Taking reasonable precautions
    c. Developing the self-confidence and judgment to determine appropriate responses to different situations
    d. All of the above

14. Any act in which one person is sexually intimate with another without the other's consent is called:
    a. Sexual assault
    b. Sexual abuse
    c. Rape
    d. Sexual harassment

15. Injuries that occur without anyone planning or intending that harm occur are called:
    a. Assaults
    b. Intentional injuries
    c. Unintentional injuries
    d. Circumstantial injuries

Practice Test #2

1. Anger that is goal-directed, hostile self-assertion, and/or self-destructive in character is called:
    a. Violence
    b. Primary aggression
    c. Suicide
    d. Violence

2. For the average American, the lifetime probability of being murdered is:
    a. 1 in 450
    b. 1 in 153
    c. 1 in 28
    d. 1 in 3

3. Hate crimes tend to be characteristically:
    a. Excessively brutal
    b. Perpetrated at random on total strangers
    c. Perpetrated by multiple offenders
    d. All of the above

4. An abused wife will remain in an abusive relationship because:
    a. She is financially dependent on her partner
    b. She loves her partner and fears what will happen to him if she leaves
    c. Her cultural or religious beliefs prohibit her from leaving
    d. All of the above

5. Risk factors for gang membership include all of the following *except*:
    a. High self-esteem
    b. History of family violence
    c. Living in gang-controlled neighborhoods
    d. Academic problems

6. Susan was brutally murdered. The person most likely to have caused her death is:
    a. A stranger she met at the grocery store
    b. Her husband
    c. A man who was an ex-partner
    d. Most likely b or c

7. To reduce the risk of personal assaults while on the street, a person should:
    a. Walk with others
    b. At night, avoid dark parking lots, wooded areas, and any place that offers an assailant good cover
    c. Carry change to make a phone call
    d. All of the above

8. Injuries within the home typically occur in the form of:
    a. Falls
    b. Burns
    c. Intrusions by others
    d. All of the above

9. Which of the following is among the most dangerous occupations?
   a. Commercial fishing
   b. Bus drivers
   c. Postal workers
   d. School teachers

10. Based on research findings, men are more likely to commit sexual assaults:
    a. When attending large social gatherings
    b. During their senior year of high school or freshman year of college
    c. When they did not know the victim
    d. When their dates were dressed in a provocative manner

11. Why do people tend to be abusive in relationships?
    a. Alcohol abuse
    b. Marital dissatisfaction
    c. Dysfunctional communication patterns
    d. There is no single explanation

12. Rape that involves multiple attackers, strangers, weapons, or a physical beating is called:
    a. Sexual assault
    b. Simple rape
    c. Aggravated rape
    d. Simple assault

13. Which of the following is a common ploy by rapists to initiate their attacks?
    a. Requests for help
    b. Guilt
    c. Purposeful accident
    d. All of the above

14. Date rape is:
    a. A miscommunication between two individuals
    b. An act of violence
    c. A misperception on the part of males
    d. An inconsistent message that women give to men

15. Violence that is directed randomly at persons affiliated with a particular group is called:
    a. Physical abuse
    b. Psychological violence
    c. Social abuse
    d. Ethnoviolence

5 Communicating Effectively

General Review Questions

1. What are the major steps in the communication process?
2. List the barriers to communication.
3. What barriers interfere with good communication between patients and medical practitioners?
4. What are the barriers to effective listening?
5. How can listening skills be improved?

Practice Test #1

1. Communication in our daily interactions is important because:
   a. It improves our self-esteem
   b. It reduces our level of stress
   c. It helps us learn about health
   d. All of the above

2. A pessimistic explanatory style is important to our health because:
   a. It improves our self-esteem
   b. It allows us to communicate effectively by making our needs known
   c. It explains negative life events and predicts poor health
   d. It provides opportunities to share our feelings

3. Raul is an international student who has come to the United States from Columbia. He is having difficulty communicating with his new peers. This may be the result of:
   a. He does not share the same experiences as his new peers
   b. He may not understand the "jargon" of his new peers
   c. His eye contact is too direct
   d. Both a and b

4. Aggressive persons tend to employ all of the following communication characteristics, *except*:
   a. Acceptance of others
   b. Verbally abusive
   c. Blaming others when they don't get their own way
   d. Typically loud and confrontational

5. In order for communication to be successful:
   a. Both parties must understand the information communicated
   b. Both parties must understand the meaning of the information communicated
   c. Both parties must increase their understanding of each other's repertoire of actions and behavior
   d. Both a and b

6. The percentage of campus rapes that take place under the influence of alcohol is:
   a. 15%
   b. 34%
   c. 56%
   d. 90%

7. People who lack communication skills:
   a. Do not take care of themselves
   b. May blame themselves rather than seek medical attention for curable problems
   c. Often suffer from self-esteem problems
   d. All of the above

8. People who use direct, honest communication that maintains and defends their rights in a positive manner are called:
   a. Nonassertive communicators
   b. Aggressive communicators
   c. Assertive communicators
   d. Nonaggressive communicators

9. Women are more likely than males to:
   a. Give advice when trouble arises
   b. Remain silent when trouble arises
   c. Share a similar problem when trouble arises
   d. Tell a joke when trouble arises

10. According to your textbook, students listen with a ____ level of listening effectiveness.
    a. 98%
    b. 75%
    c. 50%
    d. 25%

11. The process of censoring comments that would be intentionally hurtful or irrelevant to the conversation is called:
    a. Documenting
    b. "I" messages
    c. Validating
    d. Editing

12. The statement "I don't agree with you but I can see how you might view things that way" is an example of:
    a. Editing
    b. Validating
    c. Documenting
    d. Paraphrasing

13. The process of revealing one's inner thoughts, feelings, and beliefs to another person is called:
    a. Self-disclosure
    b. Paraphrasing
    c. "I" messages
    d. Assertiveness

14. Sara is very angry with her boyfriend. She tells him, "When you don't call me when you can't keep our date, I feel angry because I have planned on being with you when I could have done something else." Sara is using:
    a. Documenting
    b. "I" messages
    c. Validating
    d. Editing

15. When angered, men tend to:
    a. Interpret the cause as something or someone in their environment
    b. Turn their anger outward in an aggressive manner
    c. Suppress the direct expression of their anger
    d. Both a and b

Practice Test #2

1. Self-disclosure may be difficult because of:
    a. Fear of rejection
    b. Fear that confidential chats will be violated
    c. Fear of alienation
    d. All of the above

2. According to the text, a person may overcome his or her fears of self-disclosure by:
    a. Getting to know him- or herself
    b. Becoming more accepting of him- or herself
    c. Choosing a safe context for self-disclosure
    d. All of the above

3. Stress is reduced by:
    a. An ability to get along better with family, friends, and co-workers
    b. Expressing our needs better and in order to get what you want
    c. Becoming a more effective listener and giving others what they want
    d. All of the above

4. David is loud and confrontational when he talks to others. When things do not go his way, he becomes verbally abusive and hostile. David would be considered a(n):
    a. Nonassertive communicator
    b. Nonverbal communicator
    c. Aggressive communicator
    d. Assertive communicator

5. The goal of good communication is:
    a. To have everyone agree with you
    b. To express one's religious, cultural, and political beliefs
    c. To have others understand you
    d. Both a and b

6. An open climate for communication is more likely to occur when:
    a. Descriptive statements are used to reveal feelings without labeling them as good, bad, right, or wrong
    b. Giving qualifying statements that allows others a chance to state their opinion
    c. Showing respect for other's opinions
    d. All of the above

7. All unwritten and unspoken messages, both intentional and unintentional, are called:
    a. Assertive communication
    b. Nonverbal communication
    c. Incongruent communication
    d. Congruent communication

8. Body movements, hand gestures, and eye contact are important to communication because:
   a. These nonverbal cues influence the way we interpret messages
   b. These nonverbal cues are important in determining the sexual orientation of the speaker
   c. These nonverbal cues must be considered within the context of a person's cultural background to be properly understood
   d. All of the above

9. Conflicts revolve around:
   a. Content
   b. Relationship
   c. Aggression
   d. Both a and b

10. The communication of a clear and honest message is:
   a. Conflict resolution
   b. Assertive communication
   c. Leveling
   d. Genderlect

11. A concerted effort by all parties to resolve points of contention in a constructive manner is called:
   a. Conflict resolution
   b. Editing
   c. Leveling
   d. Self-disclosure

12. The "dialect," or individual speech pattern and conversational style, of each gender, refers to:
   a. Leveling
   b. Genderlect
   c. Editing
   d. Documenting

13. According to Tannen, communication between men and women can be improved through:
   a. Learning to interpret others messages while explaining your own unique way of communicating
   b. Avoid talking to one's partner about issues that may elicit negative reactions
   c. Expecting persons of the opposite sex to change their style of communication
   d. All of the above

14. Giving specific examples of issues being discussed is called:
   a. Editing
   b. Validating
   c. Documenting
   d. Leveling

15. Emotional states that arise when the behaviors of one person interfere with the behaviors of another are called:
   a. Documents
   b. Conflicts
   c. Nonassertiveness
   d. Aggressiveness

6 Healthy Relationships

General Review Questions

1. What psychological needs do intimate relationships fulfill?
2. Describe the characteristics of intimate sexual relationships.
3. List the characteristics of a dysfunctional family.
4. What are the causes of jealousy?
5. Discuss the reasons for divorce.

Practice Test #1

1. Intimate relationships are characterized by all of the following, *except*:
   a. Behavioral interdependence
   b. Need fulfillment
   c. Financial commitment
   d. Emotional attachment

2. The type of intimacy that involves the sharing of feelings is known as:
   a. Creative intimacy
   b. Commitment intimacy
   c. Intellectual intimacy
   d. Emotional intimacy

3. According to McAdams, most people are fortunate to develop _____ lasting friendships in a lifetime.
   a. one or two
   b. two or four
   c. four or five
   d. five or seven

4. The type of family that includes unrelated people living together for ideological, economic, or other reasons, is called a:
   a. Communal family
   b. Polygamous family
   c. Extended family
   d. Family of origin

5. Friendships are characterized by all of the following *except*:
   a. Prearranged roles
   b. Respect
   c. Confiding
   d. Acceptance

6. According to the "Triangular Theory of Love," which of the following is *not* a key ingredient of love?
   a. Intimacy
   b. Infatuation
   c. Passion
   d. Decision/Commitment

7. Regardless of the form or structure of families, the one unique characteristic that is common is:
   a. Shared finances
   b. Shared cultural practices
   c. Societally approved structure
   d. The special caring, regard, and bonding that a group of people having shared interests has for each other

8. The percentage of all Americans who marry at least once is:
   a. 35%
   b. 50%
   c. 75%
   d. 90%

9. If selecting the "right" partner is only half of the battle for success in a committed relationship, what other variables are needed?
   a. Communication
   b. Respect for one another
   c. A genuine fondness for one another
   d. All of the above

10. The only available relationship option for lesbian and gay couples is:
    a. Open-relationship marriage
    b. Cohabitation
    c. Common-law marriage
    d. Polygamy

11. Divorce rates are highest among people:
    a. Below 30 years of age
    b. 30-40 years of age
    c. 40-50 years of age
    d. 65 years or older

12. Fundamentally, trust includes:
    a. Predictability
    b. Dependability
    c. Faith
    d. All of the above

13. The chances for balanced intimacy are greater for people who:
    a. Are raised in an environment where close relationships are valued
    b. Have positive role models or friends
    c. Have close family bonds
    d. All of the above

14. To maintain a good relationship, self-nurturance involves:
    a. Being responsible for one's own decisions and actions
    b. Maintaining a balance of sleeping, eating, exercising, working, relaxing, and socializing
    c. Learning from one's bad choices
    d. All of the above

15. Breakdowns in relationships usually begin with:
    a. Unresolved conflicts over money
    b. Changes in communication
    c. Sexual difficulties
    d. Spending time apart

Practice Test #2

1. The mutual impact that people have on each other as their lives and daily activities become intertwined is called:
    a. Need fulfillment
    b. Social integration
    c. Assistance
    d. Behavioral interdependence

2. Close relationships with another person in which you offer and are offered validation, understanding, and a sense of being valued intellectually, emotionally, and physically are called:
    a. Friendship
    b. Intimate relationships
    c. Need fulfillment
    d. Nurturing relationships

3. The skills needed for developing friendships include all of the following, *except*:
    a. Self-disclosure
    b. Negotiation
    c. Compromise
    d. Intimidation

4. According to Fisher, attraction and falling in love follow a predictable pattern based on:
    a. Imprinting
    b. Attraction
    c. Attachment
    d. All of the above

5. In comparison to friendship, love relationships are characterized by all of the following, *except*:
    a. Fascination
    b. Sexual desire
    c. Mutual assistance
    d. Giving the utmost

6. Which of the following best describes the differences between men and women in selecting partners?
    a. Men are more likely than women to select their partners on the basis of youth and physical attractiveness.
    b. Women are more likely to select partners who are opposite of themselves in attitudes and values.
    c. Women are more likely than men to select their partners on the basis of youth and physical attractiveness.
    d. Men are more likely than women to place greater emphasis on financial prospects.

7. Adult children of alcoholics:
    a. Are no different from others in their ability to develop and maintain intimate relationships
    b. Have difficulty trusting others
    c. Have few or no problems communicating with their partners
    d. Have the skills necessary to develop a healthy relationship

8. Which of the following factors are important when choosing a partner?
   a. Proximity
   b. Similarities
   c. Reciprocity
   d. All of the above

9. Of those people who divorce, nearly _____ percent will remarry.
   a. 30
   b. 55
   c. 67
   d. 80

10. Although physical attractiveness is an important criterion for women in mate selection, they place a greater emphasis on partners who:
    a. Are at least five years younger
    b. Have good financial prospects
    c. Maintain strong family ties, especially with their mothers
    d. Possess athletic prowess

11. The practice of having monogamous sexual relationships with one partner before moving on to another is called:
    a. Serial monogamy
    b. Cohabitation
    c. An open relationship
    d. Common-law marriage

12. Developing individual potential through a balanced and realistic appreciation of self-worth and ability is known as:
    a. Accountability
    b. Self-nurturance
    c. Trust
    d. Mutuality

13. A type of couples therapy that teaches crucial psychological skills that give people knowledge so they can help themselves is called:
    a. Marital therapy
    b. Psychoeducation
    c. Relationship enhancement
    d. Marriage survival

14. The median age for first marriages is:
    a. 23.3 years for males; 21.6 years for females
    b. 26.3 years for males; 24.0 years for females
    c. 26.1 years for males; 23.9 years for females
    d. 27.9 years for males; 25.5 years for females

15. By the year 2000, it s estimated that over ___ percent of all people will never marry.
    a. 3
    b. 10
    c. 13
    d. 17

7 Sexuality

General Review Questions

1. What are the secondary sex characteristics for males and females?
2. List the phases of the human sexual response.
3. Define and give examples of erogenous zones.
4. What are "normal" sexual behaviors?
5. Explain the effects of alcohol on sexual performance.

Practice Test #1

1. Sexual identity is defined by a person's:
   a. Biological sex
   b. Gender identity
   c. Gender roles
   d. All of the above

2. Which of the following statements is true about androgyny?
   a. Androgyny is a combination of traditional masculine and feminine traits in a single person
   b. Androgyny is the personal sense or awareness of being either masculine or feminine
   c. Androgyny is the process by which a society transmits behavioral expectations to its individual members
   d. Androgyny is the generalized way in which males and females express themselves the characteristics of each process

3. All of the following are part of the vulva, *except*:
   a. Labia minora
   b. Glans clitoris
   c. Vagina
   d. Mons veneris

4. The ovaries:
   a. Contain tiny hairlike fibers called fimbriae
   b. Are the reservoir for immature eggs
   c. Are a hollow, muscular tube capable of expanding to accommodate the passage of an infant during birth
   d. Are the most common sites of fertilization

5. Ovulation usually occurs on the:
   a. Seventh day of the proliferatory phase
   b. Fourteenth day of the proliferatory phase
   c. Twenty-first day of the proliferatory phase
   d. Twenty-eighth day of the proliferatory phase

6. Menopause is the result of:
   a. An increase in the production of testosterone
   b. The presence of human chorionic gonadotropin
   c. A sudden and permanent release of epinephrine
   d. A decrease in estrogen levels

7. Testes are responsible for the manufacture of:
   a. Progestin
   b. Follicle stimulating hormone
   c. Testosterone
   d. Androgens

8. The structure where immature sperm ripen and reach full maturity is the:
   a. Testosterone
   b. Cowper's gland
   c. Vasa deferentia
   d. Epididymis

9. The organ that deposits sperm in the vagina is called:
   a. The testes
   b. The prostate gland
   c. The penis
   d. The ejaculatory organ

10. People who are emotionally and sexually attracted to members of both sexes are:
    a. Heterosexual
    b. Homosexual
    c. Bisexual
    d. Homogeneous

11. During the human sexual response, vasocongestion occurs in the _____ phase.
    a. Excitement/arousal
    b. Plateau
    c. Orgasm
    d. Resolution

12. The avoidance or abstention from sexual activities with others is called:
    a. Celibacy
    b. Homosexuality
    c. Limerence
    d. Autoerotic behaviors

13. A condition in which a person experiences sexual arousal by looking at or touching inanimate objects, such as underclothing or shoes, is called:
    a. Transvestitism
    b. Fetishism
    c. Voyeurism
    d. Sadomasochism

14. The most frequent problem that causes people to seek out a sex therapist is:
    a. Erectile dysfunction
    b. Inhibited sexual desire
    c. Premature ejaculation
    d. Dyspareunia

15. Ejaculation that occurs prior to or almost immediately following penile penetration of the vagina is called:
    a. Impotence
    b. Premature ejaculation
    c. Retarded ejaculation
    d. Erectile dysfunction

Practice Test #2

1. The differential development of male and female gonads occurs at about:
    a. The 8th week of fetal life
    b. The 20th week of fetal life
    c. The last trimester of fetal life
    d. The 2nd week after birth

2. A personal sense or awareness of being masculine or feminine is called:
    a. Androgyny
    b. Gender identity
    c. Gender roles
    d. Gender role stereotypes

3. The hollow, muscular tube through which menstrual flow leaves the female's body is:
    a. Fallopian tubes
    b. Vagina
    c. Uterus
    d. Cervix

4. The lower end of the uterus that opens into the vagina is called:
    a. The vagina
    b. The hymen
    c. The fallopian tubes
    d. The cervix

5. The hormone that signals the ovaries to begin producing estrogen is:
    a. Gonadotropin-releasing hormone
    b. Follicle-stimulating hormone
    c. Luteinizing hormone
    d. Human Chorionic Gonadotropin

6. The internal male genitals include all of the following *except*:
    a. Testes
    b. Scrotum
    c. Vasa deferentia
    d. Prostate

7. Homophobia is:
    a. The irrational hatred or fear of homosexuality in
       others
    b. The fear of homosexual feelings within
       one's self
    c. Self-loathing because of one's homosexuality
    d. All of the above

8. The oral stimulation of a male's genitals is called:
    a. Cunnilingus
    b. Fellatio
    c. Coitus
    d. Autoerotic behaviors

9. The exposure of one's genitals to strangers in public places is called:
    a. Pedophilia
    b. Exhibitionism
    c. Voyeurism
    d. Transsexualism

10. Difficulty in achieving or maintaining a penile erection sufficient for intercourse is called:
    a. Erectile dysfunction
    b. Premature ejaculation
    c. Inhibited sexual desire
    d. Performance anxiety

11. Sexual activities in which gratification is received by inflicting pain are called:
   a. Transvestitism
   b. Fetishism
   c. Pedophilia
   d. Sadomasochism

12. Which of the following theories best explains the origin of sexual orientation?
   a. Prenatal hormone levels and structural differences in the brain determine sexual orientation
   b. Environmental factors such as being sexually abused during childhood cause an individual to become homosexual
   c. Social and psychological factors such as an overbearing mother and passive father cause an individual to become homosexual
   d. The cause or causes of sexual orientation are complex and is best understood using a multi-factorial model which incorporates biological, socioenvironmental, and psychological factors

13. Which of the following is(are) a common form of nonverbal sexual communication?
   a. Kissing
   b. Touching
   c. Sexual fantasies
   d. Both a and b

14. The most widely practiced form of sexual expression for most couples is:
   a. Cunnilingus
   b. Anal intercourse
   c. Vaginal intercourse
   d. Fellatio

15. The most common side effect(s) reported for Viagra is(are):
   a. Stomach ache
   b. Urinary tract infection
   c. Diarrhea
   d. All of the above

8 Birth Control, Pregnancy, and Childbirth

General Review Questions

1. What conditions are necessary for conception?
2. Discuss the major purposes of prenatal care.
3. What are the signs of pregnancy?
4. How does the Norplant implant prevent pregnancy?
5. What are the risks associated with abortion?

Practice Test #1

1. Birth control pills, condoms, and abstinence are examples of:
   a. Permanent methods of contraception
   b. Reversible methods of contraception
   c. Temporary methods of contraception
   d. Transitional methods of contraception

2. Which of the following is(are) an early warning sign(s) for possible complications associated with oral contraceptive use?
   a. Abdominal pain
   b. Eye problems
   c. Headache
   d. All of the above

3. Women who smoke more than 10 to 15 cigarettes a day during pregnancy have higher rates of:
   a. Miscarriages
   b. Stillbirth
   c. Premature births
   d. All of the above

4. Modern pregnancy tests are designed to detect the presence of:
   a. HCG
   b. LH
   c. FSH
   d. RU-486

5. Toxic chemicals, pesticides, X-rays and other hazardous compounds that cause birth defects are referred to as:
   a. Carcinogens
   b. Teratogens
   c. Mutants
   d. Environmental assaults

6. Detection of major health defects in a fetus as early as the fourteenth to eighteenth weeks of pregnancy can be determined by what procedure?
   a. Ultrasound
   b. Fetoscopy
   c. Amniocentesis
   d. Sonography

7. During the second stage of labor:
   a. The amniotic sac breaks
   b. The baby shifts into a head down position
   c. The junction of the pubic bones loosens to permit expansion of the pelvic girth
   d. The uterus works to push the baby through the birth canal

8. The most popular birth alternative in the United States is:
   a. Leboyer method
   b. Harris method
   c. Lamaze method
   d. Eclectic method

9. Postpartum depression is characterized by:
   a. Energy depletion
   b. Anxiety
   c. Mood swings
   d. All of the above

10. During the third stage of labor:
    a. Contractions become more rhythmic and painful
    b. The amniotic sac breaks
    c. The baby shifts into a head-down position
    d. The placenta or afterbirth is expelled from the womb

11. Which of the following contraceptive method has the greatest failure rate?
    a. Chance
    b. Condoms
    c. Withdrawal
    d. Foams, suppositories, jellies, and creams

12. A soft, shallow cup made of thin latex rubber that is designed to cover the cervix and block access to the uterus is called:
    a. A condom
    b. A diaphragm
    c. An IUD
    d. A spermicidal sponge

13. The type of contraceptive that consists of six silicon capsules that are surgically inserted under the skin of a woman's upper arm is called:
    a. Depo-Provera
    b. Norplant
    c. Progesterone inserts
    d. Intradermal devices

14. The leading cause of infertility in women in the United States is:
    a. Pelvic inflammatory disease
    b. Endometriosis
    c. Low sperm count
    d. Psychological stress

15. The fertilization of an egg in a test tube followed by transfer to a nutrient medium and subsequent transfer to the mother's body is called:
    a. Alternative insemination
    b. In vitro fertilization
    c. Gamete intrafallopian transfer
    d. Nonsurgical embryo transfer

Practice Test #2

1. A collection of symptoms, including mental retardation, slowed nerve reflexes and small head size, that can appear in infants of women who drink too much alcohol during pregnancy is called:
    a. Teratogenic poisoning
    b. Fetal Alcohol Syndrome
    c. Down's syndrome
    d. Tay-Sachs disease

2. The most common birth defect found in babies born to older mothers is:
    a. Hemophilia
    b. Anencephaly
    c. Down's syndrome
    d. Sickle cell anemia

3. Pregnancy usually lasts:
    a. 23 weeks
    b. 32 weeks
    c. 40 weeks
    d. 53 weeks

4. The surgical procedure in which the female's fallopian tubes are closed or cut and cauterized to prevent access by sperm to released eggs is called:
    a. Tubal ligation
    b. Vasectomy
    c. Hysterectomy
    d. Abortion

5. Medical care that is received prior to becoming pregnant and helps a woman assess her potential maternal health is called:
    a. Precoital care
    b. Preconception care
    c. Prenatal care
    d. Genetic counseling

6. The estimated expense of raising a child from birth to 21 years of age, not including the cost of a college education, is:
    a. $75,000
    b. $150,000
    c. $200,000
    d. Over $250,000

7. Sudden Infant Death Syndrome is believed to occur when:
    a. A baby is exposed to high levels of folic acid
    b. A mother has undergone an extremely difficult delivery
    c. A mother experiences a traumatic shock during the prenatal development of the fetus
    d. An infant is under the age of one and suddenly dies for no apparent reason

8. An ectopic pregnancy occurs when:
    a. The fertilized egg implants outside the uterus
    b. There is a chromosomal birth defect present
    c. The mother is Rh positive and the fetus is Rh negative
    d. The fetus is not viable

9. While fetuses that are born during the seventh month may live, in order to survive:
   a. The fetus needs the layer of fat it acquires during the eighth month
   b. The fetus needs time for its organs to develop to their full potential
   c. The baby will usually require intensive medical care
   d. All of the above

10. Most oral contraceptives work through:
    a. The use of synthetic follicle-stimulating hormones
    b. The combined effects of synthetic estrogen and progesterone
    c. The combined effects of synthetic testosterone and follicle-stimulating hormones
    d. The use of estrogen-only hormones

11. Depo-Provera:
    a. Must be taken orally every 24 hours
    b. Consists of six silicone capsules that contain progesterone
    c. Is a long-acting synthetic progesterone that is injected intramuscularly every three months
    d. Must be inserted in the vagina at least 15 minutes prior to intercourse and left in place at least six hours afterwards

12. A released ovum can survive for up to ___ hour(s) after ovulation, while sperm can live for as long as ___ day(s) in the vagina.
    a. 24 hours; 1 day
    b. 30 hours; 2 days
    c. 43 hours; 3 days
    d. 48 hours; 5 days

13. A chemical substance that kills sperm is known as:
    a. Spermatogenesis
    b. Sperm barrier
    c. Spermicide
    d. All of the above

14. Sterilization of the male that consists of cutting and tying both vas deferens is called a:
    a. Vasectomy
    b. Tubal ligation
    c. Circumcision
    d. None of the above

15. Low sperm count in males can result from:
    a. The mumps virus
    b. Excessively tight underwear or outerwear
    c. Varicose veins
    d. All of the above

9 Addictions and Addictive Behaviors

General Review Questions

1. What are the criteria for diagnosis of an addiction?
2. What are the signs of addiction?
3. Describe the phases of addiction.
4. IIow can college students avoid problems with credit card use?
5. What are the components of effective treatment programs?

Practice Test #1

1. Habits differ from addictions in that:
   a. Habits can be broken without too much discomfort
   b. The repetition of the behavior occurs by compulsion and considerable comfort is experienced if the behavior is not performed
   c. They result in such negative consequences as physical damage, financial problems, and/or family dissolution
   d. They are self-destructive

2. Michael is in a fraternity and drinks heavily at social events or other functions. He does not believe that his drinking pattern is a problem. He is experiencing:
   a. A habit
   b. An obsession
   c. A compulsion
   d. Denial

3. Psychic withdrawal symptoms for addictive behaviors include all of the following, *except*:
   a. Anxiety
   b. Exuberance
   c. Frustration
   d. Preoccupation or craving for another exposure to the behavior

4. Biochemical messengers that exert influence at specific receptor site(s) on the nerve cells are called:
   a. Neurons
   b. Hormones
   c. Neurotransmitters
   d. Euphoric cells

5. The phenomenon in which progressively larger doses of a drug are needed to produce the desired effects is called:
   a. Tolerance
   b. Withdrawal
   c. Dependency
   d. Addiction

6. Common addictions that are mood-altering are called:
   a. Process addictions
   b. Obsessions
   c. Compulsion addictions
   d. Interdependence

7. Which of the following characterizes work addictions?
   a. Work addictions are found in all age and racial groups
   b. Male work addicts outnumber their female counterparts
   c. Work addictions develop in people who are in their 40s and 50s
   d. All of the above

8. All of the following are characteristics of money addictions, *except*:
   a. Money addictions are more common among men than women
   b. Women tend to be compulsive gamblers
   c. Money addictions are common among all socioeconomic groups
   d. One or both parents of the addict were typically absent or emotionally unavailable and often had addictions of their own

9. The major life event that is the most common trigger for excessive drinking among the elderly is:
   a. A second marriage
   b. Divorce
   c. Retirement
   d. Death of a spouse

10. The hallmark of addiction is:
    a. Codependence
    b. Anxiety
    c. Denial
    d. Withdrawal

11. The model of addiction that proposes that people learn behaviors by watching parents, caregivers, and significant others is known as:
   a. Societal Influences Model
   b. Stimulus-Response Model
   c. Social Learning Theory
   d. Behavioral Intent Model

12. The relationship pattern in which a person is thought to be "addicted to the addict" is known as:
   a. Enabling
   b. Codependent
   c. Post-traumatic stress
   d. Control-Controller relationship

13. The early abstinence period during which an addict adjust physically and cognitively to being free from the influences of the addiction refers to:
   a. Denial
   b. Abstinence
   c. Detoxification
   d. Interdependence

14. Issues that lead to spending as a way of coping with daily stressors include all of the following, *except*:
   a. Anxiety
   b. Self-doubt
   c. Contentment
   d. Anger

15. An isolated occurrence of or full return to addictive behaviors is called:
   a. Response mechanism
   b. Relapse
   c. Withdrawal
   d. Recovery

Practice Test #2

1. A series of temporary physical and psychological symptoms that occur when the addict stops the addictive behavior is known as:
   a. Physiological dependence
   b. Withdrawal
   c. Tolerance
   d. Addiction

2. The inability to reliably predict whether any isolated involvement with the addictive object or behavior will be healthy or damaging is called:
   a. Compulsion
   b. Loss of control
   c. Denial
   d. Tolerance

3. To be addictive, a behavior must:
   a. Have the potential to produce a positive mood change
   b. Produce a positively reinforcing response
   c. Result in a physiological dependency
   d. Be reinforced by a set of events that support the addiction

4. The most common stimulus for alcoholism for women is:
   a. Death of a spouse
   b. Birth of a child
   c. Divorce
   d. The loss of a child

5. The severest side effect of withdrawal is:
   a. Depression
   b. Delirium tremens
   c. Irritability
   d. Convulsions

6. The theory that proposes that addiction is caused by a variety of factors operating together is known as the:
   a. Sociocultural Influences Theory
   b. Social Learning Theory
   c. Life Events Model
   d. Biopsychosocial Model

7. Which of the following factors contributes to the development of addiction?
   a. Biological factors
   b. Psychological factors
   c. Environmental factors
   d. All of the above

8. The only addiction that wins the admiration of others is:
   a. Money addiction
   b. Exercise addiction
   c. Work addiction
   d. Eating addiction

9. Which of the following life events may trigger addictive behaviors?
   a. Marriage
   b. Change in work status
   c. Death of a loved one
   d. All of the above

10. People who knowingly or unknowingly protect addicts from the natural consequences of their behavior are called:
    a. Codependents
    b. Enablers
    c. Coaddicts
    d. Rescuers

11. Sexual addicts may participate in:
    a. Prostitution
    b. Voyeurism
    c. Cross-dressing
    d. All of the above

12. Codependents have difficulty:
    a. Experiencing appropriate levels of self-esteem
    b. Setting healthy boundaries
    c. Taking care of their own adult needs and desires
    d. All of the above

13. A planned process of confrontation by significant others including spouse, parents, children, boss, and friends is called:
    a. An intervention
    b. Denial
    c. The treatment process
    d. Enabling

14. People who work out compulsively to try to meet needs of nurturance, intimacy, self-esteem, and self-competency have a(n):
    a. Money addiction
    b. Work addiction
    c. Exercise addiction
    d. Shopping addiction

15. A person may be a compulsive shopper if:
    a. They feel a rush of euphoria mixed with feelings of anxiety
    b. Many of their purchases are seldom or never worn or used
    c. They lie to family or friends about what they buy and how much they spend
    d. All of the above

10 Pharmaceutical Drugs

General Review Questions

1. What is the current theory of how drugs work?
2. What environmental factors influence the main effects and side effects of psychoactive drugs?
3. Define *prostaglandin inhibitors* and give examples of these analgesics.
4. Describe rebound effects and list the severe withdrawal symptoms of stimulants?
5. What general precautions should OTC users consider?

Practice Test #1

1. Painkillers that are manufactured in the body are called:
   a. Neurotransmitters
   b. Endorphins
   c. Psychoactive drugs
   d. Illegal drugs

2. Substances that can be obtained only with a written prescription from a physician are called:
   a. Prescription drugs
   b. Recreational drugs
   c. Herbal drugs
   d. Over-the-counter drugs

3. The most frequently used route of administration of drugs is:
   a. Inhalation
   b. Oral ingestion
   c. Intravenous injection
   d. Subcutaneous injection

4. Applying a small adhesive patch to introduce a prescription medication into the body through the skin is called:
   a. Inhalation
   b. Inunction
   c. Subcutaneous injection
   d. Oral administration

5. A severe allergic reaction that may result in respiratory failure and cardiac arrest is called:
   a. Anaphylactic shock
   b. Cardiopulmonary arrest
   c. Pulmonary hypersensitivity
   d. Aneurysm shock

6. A synergistic interaction is most likely to occur when:
   a. Central nervous system depressants are combined
   b. Central nervous system stimulants are combined
   c. Hallucinogenic drugs are combined
   d. None of the above

7. When drugs combine in the body to produce extremely uncomfortable reactions, the reaction is called:
   a. Intolerance
   b. Potentiation
   c. Antagonism
   d. Interaction

8. Drugs used to fight bacterial infection are called:
   a. Analgesics
   b. Sympathomimetics
   c. Antibiotics
   d. Antagonizers

9. The most common form(s) of NSAID (nonsteroidal anti-inflammatory drug) types is (are):
   a. Naproxen sodium
   b. Acetaminophen
   c. Ibuprofen
   d. Both a and c

10. The most frequently prescribed antidepressant is:
    a. Morphine
    b. Librium
    c. Prozac
    d. Anaprox

11. Drugs that are marketed by their chemical names rather than a brand name are called:
    a. Generic drugs
    b. OTC drugs
    c. Recreational drugs
    d. Commercial drugs
12. Aspirin is used to:
    a. Bring down a fever
    b. Reduce inflammation and swelling due to arthritis
    c. Reduce the chances of repeat heart attacks
    d. All of the above

13. Drugs that are generally recognized as effective when used properly are called:
    a. GRAE list drugs
    b. GRAS list drugs
    c. FDA policy drugs
    d. Over-the-counter drugs

14. The active ingredient in OTC stimulants is:
    a. Amphetamines
    b. Caffeine
    c. Phenylpropanolamine
    d. Pyrilamine maleate

15. Drugs advertised as "appetite suppressants" contain:
    a. Amphetamines
    b. Caffeine
    c. Phenylpropanolamine
    d. Pyrilamine maleate

Practice Test #2

1. Drugs work by:
   a. Interfering with the body's processes
   b. Short circuiting the body and redirecting the chemicals that are produced abnormally
   c. Resembling physically the chemicals produced naturally within the body
   d. Reducing the amount of chemicals that are produced at abnormally high rates

2. Alcohol, tobacco, caffeine, tea, and chocolate products are categorized as:
   a. Over-the-counter drugs
   b. Recreational drugs
   c. Herbal preparations
   d. Illicit drugs

3. Antibiotics and vaccinations are normally administered by:
   a. Intramuscular injection
   b. Inhalation
   c. Intravenous injection
   d. Suppositories

4. Administration of a drug through the nostrils is called:
   a. Oral ingestion
   b. Intravenous injection
   c. Inhalation
   d. Inunction

5. Taking a drug for a longer time or more often than is intended is an example of:
   a. Drug abuse
   b. Drug misuse
   c. Synergistic drug use
   d. Illicit drug use

6. Rebecca takes a number of medications for various medical conditions, including prinivil (an anti-hypertensive), insulin (a diabetic medication), and claridin (an antihistamine). This is an example of:
   a. Synergism
   b. Illegal drug use
   c. Polydrug use
   d. Antagonism

7. When a person develops a physiological tolerance to one drug and shows a similar tolerance to selected other drugs as a result, it is known as:
   a. Synergism
   b. Antagonism
   c. Cross-tolerance
   d. Ploydrug use

8. The less-powerful tranquilizers used in the treatment of psychiatric illnesses are called:
   a. Analgesics
   b. Antidepressants
   c. Minor tranquilizers
   d. Major tranquilizers

9. The type of interaction in which the effects of one drug are eliminated or reduced by the presence of another drug at the receptor site is called:
   a. Antagonism
   b. Cross-tolerance
   c. Intolerance
   d. Inhibition

10. Which of the following medicines can keep birth control pills from working and result in an accidental pregnancy?
    a. Penicillin
    b. Tuberculosis medicines
    c. Anxiety medicines
    d. All of the above

11. Drugs that are used to relieve pain are classified as:
    a. Analgesics
    b. Antibiotics
    c. Depressants
    d. Psychoactives

12. Amphetamines:
    a. Cause elevated blood pressure
    b. Suppress appetite
    c. Adversely affect respiration
    d. All of the above

13. To reduce the incidence of problems from OTC drug use, it is important to:
    a. Always know what you are taking by identifying the active ingredient(s) in the product
    b. Read the warnings and cautions
    c. Don't use anything for more than one or two weeks
    d. All of the above

14. It is spring and Roy is experiencing allergy symptoms, including a runny nose, sinus congestion, and tearing. When he goes to the store to buy an over-the-counter preparation, Roy would most likely buy a(n):
    a. Decongestant
    b. Expectorant
    c. Antihistamine
    d. Antitussive

15. Herbal products are unique because:
    a. Their active ingredients have little or no federal regulation
    b. Their ingredients are natural and harmless
    c. They are safe due to thousands of years of use without any complications
    d. They can be purchased without a prescription

11 Drinking Responsibly

General Review Questions

1. What are the factors that influence how quickly alcohol is absorbed by the body?
2. How does alcohol affect the immune system?
3. What are the unique problems of adult children of alcoholics?
4. What are the annual costs of alcohol abuse to society?
5. When does an alcoholic seek help?

Practice Test #1

1. Approximately ___ percent of students consume alcoholic beverages.
   a. 20
   b. 45
   c. 65
   d. 85

2. Lindsay has joined a sorority, and when she goes to a social with a fraternity she usually has five or six drinks in a row. This type of high risk drinking is called:
   a. Alcohol overconsumption
   b. Binge drinking
   c. Drinking overabuse
   d. Alcoholic addiction

3. The alcohol content in beer is usually:
   a. 2-6 percent
   b. 6-10 percent
   c. 12-15 percent
   d. 15-19 percent

4. Doug likes to have a drink to help him feel slightly relaxed. The blood alcohol concentration level that produces this effect is:
   a. .02
   b. .05
   c. .08
   d. .10

5. How many calories are contained in alcohol?
   a. 4
   b. 7
   c. 9
   d. 13

6. At a party, Roger has been "shooting" tequila in large amounts over a short time. He has become unconscious and cannot be aroused. In addition, his breathing is irregular and his skin is bluish. Unless he gets immediate help, he can die from:
   a. Alcohol abuse
   b. Pancreatitis
   c. Alcohol poisoning
   d. Delirium tremors

7. Liver deterioration caused by fibrous scar tissue is called:
   a. Cardiomyopathy
   b. Antithrombotic disease
   c. Liver hepatitis
   d. Liver fibrosis

8. When a mother consumes alcohol during pregnancy, which of the following disorders can result?
   a. Sudden infant death syndrome
   b. Pancreatitis
   c. Fetal alcohol syndrome
   d. Osteoporosis

9. Drinkers who had at least one parent of either sex who was a problem drinker and who grew up in an environment that encouraged heavy drinking are classified as:
   a. Binge drinkers
   b. Type 1 alcoholics
   c. Type 2 alcoholics
   d. Type 3 alcoholics

10. Women who have the highest risk for alcohol-related problems are:
    a. Those who are unmarried but living with a partner
    b. Those who are in their 20s or early 30s
    c. Those who have a husband or partner who drinks heavily
    d. All of the above

11. The primary action of ethanol within the central nervous system is:
   a. To reduce the frequency of nerve transmissions and impulses at the synaptic junctions
   b. To increase the frequency of nerve transmissions and impulses at the synaptic junctions
   c. To reduce the frequency of nerve transmissions and increase the impulses at the synaptic junctions
   d. To increase the frequency of nerve transmissions and decrease the impulses at the synaptic junctions

12. The most common preventable cause of mental impairments in the Western world is:
   a. Down's syndrome
   b. Cerebral palsy
   c. Fetal alcohol syndrome
   d. Tay-Sachs disease

13. Ed is an alcoholic who grew up in a family with an alcoholic father. Alcohol was an accepted practice by his parents and grandparents. In fact, his father took him out drinking to celebrate his 21st birthday. Ed is a:
   a. Type I alcoholic
   b. Type II alcoholic
   c. Type III alcoholic
   d. Type II reactive alcoholic

14. Over ____ percent of all child abuse cases are the result of alcohol-related problems.
   a. 25
   b. 50
   c. 75
   d. 100

15. The process by which addicts end their dependence on a drug and which is commonly carried out in a medical facility is called:
   a. Recovery
   b. Intervention
   c. Detoxification
   d. Aversion therapy

Practice Test #2

1. The process whereby yeast organisms break down plant sugars to yield ethanol is called:
   a. Fermentation
   b. Distillation
   c. Mashation
   d. Alcoholization

2. Most distilled alcoholic beverages are:
   a. 40% or higher alcohol
   b. 12% to 15% alcohol
   c. 8% to 10% alcohol
   d. 2% to 6% alcohol

3. Blood alcohol concentration (BAC) is:
   a. The concentration of plant sugars in the blood stream
   b. The percentage of alcohol in a beverage
   c. The level of alcohol content in the blood before becoming drunk
   d. The ratio of alcohol to the total blood volume

4. The majority of alcohol is absorbed into the blood stream in the:
   a. Mouth
   b. Stomach
   c. Small intestine
   d. Large intestine

5. A cardiovascular condition that results from drinking alcohol is:
   a. Cirrhosis
   b. High blood pressure
   c. Myocardial infarction
   d. Alcoholic hepatitis

6. Among women, drinking alcohol has been linked with:
   a. Vaginal cancer
   b. Ovarian cancer
   c. Uterine cancer
   d. Breast cancer

7. Fetal alcohol syndrome can cause:
   a. Mental retardation
   b. Small head
   c. Abnormalities of the face, limbs, heart, and brain
   d. All of the above

8. Approximately ___ percent of all traffic fatalities are alcohol related.
   a. 25
   b. 37
   c. 41
   d. 53

9. Margie is a junior at a prestigious university. She does not work so that she can have time for studying since her major is extremely demanding. She lives with her boyfriend, with whom she has a couple of beers on the weekend. Margie usually drinks more when they go to the local college bar, however. Why is Margie at risk for alcoholism?
   a. Because young women who attend college drink more frequently than those who do not attend college
   b. Because young women who drink and are un-employed are at increased risk for alcoholism
   c. Because young women drink and live with a partner but not are not married are at increased for alcoholism
   d. All of the above

10. Only 14 percent of women who need treatment for alcoholism get it. What is the reason(s) that more women do not get treatment?
    a. The loss of potential income prohibits some women from getting treatment
    b. The lack of child care prohibits some women from getting treatment
    c. The fear that treatment is not confidential prohibits some women from getting treatment
    d. All of the above

11. Research indicates that less than ___ percent of recovering alcoholics are able to resume drinking on a limited basis.
    a. 1
    b. 9
    c. 12
    d. 21

12. If whisky is 80 proof, what is the percentage of alcohol in the drink?
    a. 20%
    b. 40%s
    c. 60%
    d. 80%

13. A driver's BAC depends on:
    a. His or her weight and body fat
    b. The water content in his or her body tissue
    c. The volume of the alcohol
    d. All of the above

14. People who drink moderately experience which of the following effects:
    a. Shrinkage in brain size
    b. Shrinkage in brain weight
    c. A loss in some degree of intellectual ability
    d. All of the above

15. A syndrome describing children with a history of prenatal alcohol exposure but without all of the physical or behavioral symptoms of FAS is:
    a. Alcoholic Behavioral Syndrome
    b. Fetal Alcoholic Hepatitis
    c. Fetal Alcohol Effects
    d. Fetal Alcoholic Abuse

12 Tobacco and Caffeine

General Review Questions

1. List the dangerous chemicals in tobacco smoke.
2. What are the physical effects of nicotine?
3. Describe the warning signs of oral cancer.
4. Describe the most common therapy techniques for quitting smoking.
5. What health problems are associated with long-term caffeine use?

Practice Test #1

1. The single most preventable cause of death in the United States is:
   a. Alcohol use
   b. Illegal drug use
   c. Tobacco use
   d. Prescription drug abuse

2. The most common form of tobacco use is:
   a. Chewing tobacco
   b. Snuff
   c. Smoking
   d. Clove cigarettes

3. The type of tobacco that comes in the form of loose leaf, plug, or twist is:
   a. Snuff
   b. Chewing tobacco
   c. Cigarettes
   d. Cigars

4. While smoking her first cigarette, Nancy begins to get dizzy, lightheaded, nauseated, and clammy skin. Most likely Nancy is experiencing:
   a. Nicotine poisoning
   b. Nicotine withdrawal
   c. Nicotine intolerance
   d. Nicotine overdose

5. Nicotine acts as a(n) _____ on the central nervous system.
   a. Stimulant
   b. Analgesic
   c. Depressant
   d. Hallucinogenic

6. Smokers have a ___ percent higher death rate from heart disease than do nonsmokers.
   a. 25
   b. 36
   c. 47
   d. 70

7. A chronic disease in which the alveoli are destroyed, making breathing difficult is:
   a. Chronic Obstructive Lung Disorder
   b. Stroke
   c. Emphysema
   d. Sudden Infant Death Syndrome

8. The cigarette, pipe, or cigar smoke breathed by nonsmokers is called:
   a. Secondhand smoke
   b. Sidestream smoke
   c. Nicotine poisoning
   d. Both a and b

9. Which of the following is *not* a symptom of nicotine withdrawal?
   a. Nausea
   b. Vomiting
   c. Headaches
   d. Hypertension

10. How many years must an ex-smoker be smoke-free to expect to live out his/her normal life span?
    a. 2 years
    b. 5 years
    c. 10 years
    d. 15 years

11. A special target for marketing by tobacco companies is(are):
    a. Young people
    b. Poor minority groups
    c. Young women
    d. All of the above

12. A condition characterized by leathery white patches inside the mouth produced by contact with the irritants in tobacco juice is known as:
    a. Leukoplakia
    b. Neoplasm
    c. Dental fissures
    d. Oral cancer

13. A derivative of the chemical family of stimulants called xanthines is found in:
   a. Snuff
   b. Nicotine
   c. Tobacco
   d. Coffee

14. Which of the following products contains the most caffeine?
   a. Jolt cola
   b. Mountain dew
   c. One-ounce chocolate candy bar
   d. Hot steeped tea

15. Which of the following is(are) a symptom(s) of caffeinism?
   a. Chronic insomnia
   b. Irritability
   c. Involuntary muscle twitches
   d. All of the above

Practice Test #2

1. The thick brownish substance condensed from particulate matter in cigarette smoke is:
   a. Tar
   b. Nicotine
   c. Chewing tobacco
   d. Carbon monoxide

2. A powdered form of tobacco that is sniffed and absorbed through the mucous membranes in the nose or placed inside the cheek and sucked is called:
   a. Chewing tobacco
   b. Snuff
   c. Smoking
   d. All of the above

3. Which of the following is *not* a physical effect of nicotine stimulation?
   a. Constriction of blood vessels
   b. Decrease in stomach contractions
   c. Increase sensation in the taste buds
   d. Increased blood pressure

4. The leading cause of cancer death from smoking is:
   a. Throat cancer
   b. Colon cancer
   c. Lung cancer
   d. Stomach cancer

5. Stickiness of red blood cells associated with blood clots is called:
   a. Clumping
   b. Platelet adhesiveness
   c. Elevated HDLs
   d. Stroke

6. Which of the following respiratory diseases are primarily associated with smoking?
   a. Chronic bronchitis
   b. Emphysema
   c. Legionnaires disease
   d. Both a and b

7. Daily smoking of one cigar:
   a. Is a safe practice that does not increase a person's risk for health problems
   b. Increases a person's risk for cancer of the lip, tongue, mouth, larynx and lungs
   c. Is safe for others who may be exposed to the smoke
   d. Is safe because cigars do not have the harmful ingredients contained in cigarettes

8. Babies born to women who smoke during pregnancy are more likely to die from:
   a. Congenital heart failure
   b. Pneumonia
   c. Sudden infant death syndrome
   d. Infantile paralysis

9. Smoking has been associated with which of the following health effects?
   a. Gum disease
   b. Increased medication usage
   c. Impotence
   d. All of the above

10. Smoking has been shown to affect women by:
   a. Causing women to begin menopause one to two years earlier
   b. Contributing to the development of osteoporosis
   c. Increasing the risk of death from emphysema or chronic bronchitis
   d. All of the above

11. The age group with the highest percentage of smokers is:
   a. 15-24 year olds
   b. 25-44 year olds
   c. 44-55 year olds
   d. 55 year olds and older

12. The financial costs for smoking in the workplace include all of the following, *except*:
    a. Absenteeism
    b. Loss of productivity
    c. Training to replace employees who die prematurely
    d. Loss of time due to excessive breaks

13. Children, especially those under the age of 5, who are exposed to environmental tobacco smoke:
    a. Miss more school days
    b. Have more colds and respiratory infections
    c. Have a greater risk of pneumonia and bronchitis
    d. All of the above

14. Caffeine acts as a(n) _____ on the central nervous system.
    a. Stimulant
    b. Analgesic
    c. Depressant
    d. Hallucinogenic

15. Sensory disturbance from caffeine may be experienced after ___ cups of coffee within a 24-hour period.
    a. 3
    b. 5
    c. 7
    d. 10

13 Illicit Drugs

General Review Questions

1. What are the reasons for using drugs?
2. What are the health problems found in cocaine-affected babies?
3. List the physiological effects of LSD.
4. Who are the primary users of anabolic steroids?
5. What is the best approach to drug education?

Practice Test #1

1. The agency that administers the Controlled Substances Act of 1970 is:
   a. Food and Drug Administration
   b. Federal Trade Commission
   c. Drug Enforcement Agency
   d. Centers for Drug Control

2. According to the "schedule" of drugs, cocaine is categorized as a:
   a. Schedule I drug
   b. Schedule II drug
   c. Schedule III drug
   d. Schedule IV drug

3. A powerful stimulant drug made from the leaves of the South American coca shrub is:
   a. LSD
   b. Cocaine
   c. Marijuana
   d. Amphetamines

4. The most powerful distillate of cocaine is:
   a. Powdered cocaine
   b. Freebase cocaine
   c. Crack
   d. Rock cocaine

5. Which of the following is *not* an effect of amphetamines?
   a. Decreased heart rate, blood pressure, and respiration
   b. Appetite suppression
   c. Insomnia
   d. Restlessness

6. The active ingredient in marijuana is:
   a. PCP
   b. MDMA
   c. LSD
   d. THC

7. The primary drug action of opiates is:
   a. To depress the nervous system
   b. To stimulate the nervous system
   c. To relieve pain
   d. To elevate mood

8. A dark, brown sticky substance made from morphine is:
   a. Codeine
   b. Black tar heroin
   c. Morphine
   d. Opium

9. A major health concern for intravenous injection drug users is:
   a. AIDS
   b. Pneumonia
   c. Tetanus
   d. Hemophilia

10. A synthetic opiod that is used in the treatment of people addicted to heroin is called:
    a. Codeine
    b. Morphine
    c. Methadone
    d. Methamphetamine

11. An image (auditory or visual) that is perceived but is not real is called a:
    a. Blackout
    b. Flashback
    c. Synesthesia
    d. Hallucination

12. Ecstasy is categorized as a:
    a. Narcotic
    b. Depressant
    c. Hallucinogenic
    d. Designer drug

13. Rubber cement, model glue, spot removers, and gasoline are examples of:
    a. Depressants
    b. Inhalants
    c. Stimulants
    d. Psychedelics

14. Artificial forms of the hormone testosterone that promote muscle growth and strength are called:
    a. Aerobic steriods
    b. Anabolic steriods
    c. Anaerobic steroids
    d. Erogenic drugs

15. Which of the following is *not* a narcotic?
    a. Morphine
    b. Methamphetamine
    c. Codeine
    d. Heroin

Practice Test #2

1. Drugs with a high potential for abuse and addiction and have no medical use are categorized as:
   a. Schedule I drugs
   b. Schedule II drugs
   c. Schedule III drugs
   d. Schedule IV drugs

2. A potent, inexpensive stimulant that has long-lasting effects is:
   a. Caffeine
   b. Nicotine
   c. Cocaine
   d. "Ice"

3. "Snorting" cocaine through the nose can cause all of the following physical effects, *except*:
   a. Damage to the nucous membranes in the nose and sinusitis
   b. Severely damaged liver disease
   c. Destroy the user's sense of smell
   d. Creates a hole in the septum

4. A derivative of opium that is sometimes used to relieve pain is:
   a. Morphine
   b. Heroin
   c. Codeine
   d. Methadone

5. The sticky resin of the marijuana plant is called:
   a. Ghanja
   b. Hashish
   c. Black tar
   d. Cannabis sativa

6. Marijuana has been used in the medical treatment of:
   a. Glaucoma
   b. Cancer chemotherapy
   c. Diabetes
   d. Both a and b

7. The narcotic used in cough syrups and certain painkillers is:
   a. Morphine
   b. Cocaine
   c. Codeine
   d. Heroin

8. The most common route of administration for heroin addicts is:
   a. Inhalation
   b. Intravenous injection
   c. Ingestion
   d. Transdermal

9. Opiatelike hormones that are manufactured in the human brain and contribute to feelings of well-being are:
   a. Endorphins
   b. Acetaminaphine
   c. Adrenaline
   d. Acetylcholine

10. The group of drugs whose primary pharmacological effect is characterized by confusion and dis-orientation in the user is:
    a. Narcotics
    b. Deliriants
    c. Stimulants
    d. Depressants

11. The fastest growing illicit drug among the under-22 age group is:
    a. Black tar heroin
    b. Crack cocaine
    c. LSD
    d. Ecstasy

12. A hallucinogenic drug derived from the peyote cactus is:
    a. Mescaline
    b. Methamphetamine
    c. LSD
    d. Psilocybin

13. An example of a deliriant drug is:
    a. Tetrahydrocannabinol (THC)
    b. Phencyclidine (PCP)
    c. Ecstasy (MDMA)
    d. Lysergic Acid Diethylamide (LSD)

14. MPTP, a street analog of heroin, has been known to cause an irreversible brain syndrome similar to:
    a. Alzheimer's disease
    b. Huntington's disease
    c. Parkinson's disease
    d. Korsakoff's syndrome

15. The effects of nitrous oxide include all of the following *except*:
    a. Pain relief
    b. Giggling
    c. Skin flushing
    d. Euphoria

14 Nutrition

General Review Questions

1. What factors influence when, what, and how much a person will eat?
2. List the six basic nutrients and the recommended U.S. dietary guidelines for each nutrient.
3. Describe the types of vegetarian diets?
4. What are the symptoms of food-borne illness?
5. List four steps students can take to maintain a nutritious diet within the confines of a restrictive budget.

Practice Test #1

1. The science that investigates the relationship between physiological function and the essential elements of foods we eat is:
   a. Nutrition
   b. Dietology
   c. Metabolic studies
   d. Home economics

2. The feeling associated with physiological need to eat is called:
   a. Appetite
   b. Nutrition
   c. Hunger
   d. Nutritional survival

3. The nutrient that aids in fluid and electrolyte balance, maintains pH balance, and transports molecules and cells throughout the body is:
   a. Water
   b. Minerals
   c. Vitamins
   d. Fat

4. Substances that are made up of amino acids that are major components of cells are:
   a. Water
   b. Carbohydrates
   c. Proteins
   d. Minerals

5. Complete proteins are obtained from:
   a. Red meats
   b. Poultry
   c. Fish
   d. All of the above

6. The type of carbohydrates that are primarily found in grains, cereals, dark green leafy vegetables and cruciferous vegetables is:
   a. Simple carbohydrates
   b. Complex carbohydrates
   c. Glucose
   d. Dextrose

7. The nutrient that supplies us with the energy needed to sustain normal daily activity is:
   a. Protein
   b. Vitamins
   c. Carbohydrates
   d. Fiber

8. The best way to increase dietary fiber in a diet is to:
   a. Eat more meat
   b. Eat more complex carbohydrates
   c. Decrease the amount of water to 3-4 glasses per day
   d. Decrease the amount of fruit while increasing beans and nuts

9. Fiber found to be a factor in lowering blood cholesterol and thereby reducing the risk of cardiovascular disease is called:
   a. Alpha cellulose
   b. Triglycerides
   c. Soluble fiber
   d. Insoluble fiber

10. Compounds that facilitate the transportation of cholesterol in the blood to the liver for metabolism and elimination from the body are called:
    a. Plaque
    b. High-density lipoproteins
    c. Low-density lipoproteins
    d. Very low-density lipoproteins

11. When too many calories are consumed:
   a. The excess is excreted from the body
   b. The body works harder to "burn" the calories
   c. The excess are converted into triglycerides in the liver, which are stored throughout our bodies
   d. The excess is circulated until it is burned as energy

12. Calcium is vital to the body because:
   a. It builds strong bones and teeth
   b. It regulates heartbeat
   c. It is vital to nerve impulse transmission
   d. All of the above

13. The mineral folate has been shown to:
   a. Reduce the risk for colon cancer
   b. Decrease spina bifida and other neural tube defects in infants
   c. Decrease hypertension and diabetes
   d. Increase the risk for breast cancer

14. To prevent the chance of food-borne illness at home, a person should:
   a. Wash their hands with soap and water before working with food or eating
   b. Eat leftovers within three days
   c. When shopping, put meats in separate plastic bags to prevent meat juices from dripping onto other foods
   d. All of the above

15. While eating, Jenny begins to have difficulty breathing and her face begins to swell. This may indicate that:
   a. She is having food that is very spicy and may need to avoid foods with chili peppers
   b. She may be experiencing an anaphylactic reaction to her food and may require a shot of epinephrine
   c. She may have a food-borne illness
   d. All of the above

Practice Test #2

1. Fats that generally come from animals are called:
   a. Polyunsaturated fats
   b. Monounsaturated fats
   c. Saturated fats
   d. Low density lipoproteins

2. The recommended number of servings each day from the bread, cereals, rice, and pasta group is:
   a. 2-4 servings
   b. 3-5 servings
   c. 4-5 servings
   d. 6-11 servings

3. The process by which foods are broken down and either absorbed or excreted by the body is known as the:
   a. Digestive process
   b. Elimination process
   c. Metabolism process
   d. Nutritional process

4. A major factor in the tendency to be overweight is:
   a. A diet containing 48% of the total calories from complex carbohydrates
   b. Insufficient dietary intake of Vitamin A and C
   c. Excess calorie consumption
   d. A diet containing less than 30% of the calories from protein

5. If the body does not have sufficient water and becomes depleted of fluids:
   a. Serious problems can result within a matter of hours and after a few days death is likely
   b. Malnutrition will result due to lack of sufficient vitamins
   c. The body's defense system will increase antibody production
   d. The body will release hormones to increase metabolism

6. Amino acids that must be obtained from food are referred to as:
   a. Nonessential amino acids
   b. Essential amino acids
   c. Complete amino acids
   d. Incomplete amino acids

7. The type of simple sugar that is found in corn syrup, honey, molasses, vegetables, and fruit is:
   a. Simple carbohydrates
   b. Complex carbohydrates
   c. Glucose
   d. Dextrose

8. Oat bran and dried beans, especially kidney beans) are major sources of:
   a. Alpha cellulose
   b. Triglycerides
   c. Soluble fiber
   d. Insoluble fiber

9. The most common form of fat circulating in the blood is:
   a. Cholesterol
   b. Triglyceride
   c. Saturated fat
   d. Unsaturated fat

10. The nutrient that is vital for the maintenance of healthy skin and hair, insulates the body organs against shock and maintains body temperature is:
    a. Carbohydrates
    b. Water
    c. Protein
    d. Fat

11. A major cause of atherosclerosis is:
    a. Plaque
    b. High density lipoproteins
    c. Unsaturated fats
    d. Monounsaturated fats

12. Fatty acids that have unusual shapes and are produced when polyunsaturated oils are hydrogenated are called:
    a. Saturated fats
    b. Unsaturated fats
    c. Cholesterol
    d. Trans-fatty acids

13. Which of the following is *not* a fat-soluble vitamin?
    a. Vitamin A
    b. Vitamin B
    c. Vitamin D
    d. Vitamin K

14. Inorganic, indestructible elements that aid physiological processes within the body are:
    a. Vitamins
    b. Amino acids
    c. Minerals
    d. High density lipoproteins

15. For every three servings of fruits or vegetables per day, men can expect:
    a. Improved regulation of blood and body fluids
    b. A 50% reduction the risk of colon cancer
    c. A 14% reduction in pancreatic cancer
    d. A 22% lower risk of stroke

15 Managing Your Weight

General Review Questions

1. What are the factors associated with the desire to be thin and attractive?
2. What factors affect basal metabolic rate?
3. What is the importance of the endocrine influence in most obesity?
4. List the factors that determine the number of calories spent during physical activity.
5. What strategies can be used to change your eating habits and to select a nutritional plan that is right for you?

Practice Test #1

1. In general, a person is classified "obese" when they are:
   a. 5%-10% above their ideal weight
   b. 10%-20% above their ideal weight
   c. 20%-30% above their ideal weight
   d. 40%-50% above their ideal weight

2. An accumulation of fat beyond what is considered normal for a person's age, sex, and body type is called:
   a. Body composition
   b. Obesity
   c. Overweight
   d. Body fat

3. The ratio of lean body mass to fat body mass is:
   a. Obesity
   b. Body composition
   c. Overweight mass ratio
   d. Obesity ratio

4. The technique of body fat assessment that utilizes electrical currents that are passed through fat and lean tissue is called:
   a. Body Mass Index
   b. Hydrostatic weight technique
   c. Bioelectrical impedance analysis
   d. Soft-tissue roentgenogram

5. The ideal total body fat for women is:
   a. 11-15%
   b. 18-22%
   c. 23-29%
   d. 27-35%

6. Essential fat makes up approximately _____ percent of total body weight in men and approximately _____ percent of total body weight in women.
   a. 3 to 5; 18
   b. 3 to 7; 15
   c. 5 to 25; 13
   d. 3 to 5; 7

7. The part of the brain that regulates appetite and closely monitors levels of certain nutrients in the blood is the:
   a. Pituitary gland
   b. Hypothalamus
   c. Cerebral cortex
   d. Cerebellum

8. The theory of weight loss that proposes that a person's body has a set amount of weight at which it is programmed to be comfortable is called:
   a. Thermostatic maintenance theory
   b. Setpoint theory
   c. Plateau theory
   d. Endocrine balance theory

9. Most authorities argue that only ___ percent of the obese population have a thyroid problem that is attributed to obesity.
   a. 3-5
   b. 10-17
   c. 23-27
   d. 35-37

10. What percentage of all the calories you consume on a given day go to support your basal metabolism (i.e. heartbeat, breathing, maintaining body temperature, etc.)?
    a. 20-30%
    b. 40-60%
    c. 60-70%
    d. 75-85%

11. One pound of body fat contains approximately:
    a. 35 kilocalories
    b. 350 kilocalories
    c. 3,500 kilocalories
    d. 5,000 kilocalories

12. An acute form of self-starvation motivated by a fear of gaining weight and a severe disturbance in the perception of one's body is called:
    a. Anorexia nervosa
    b. Bulimia
    c. Binge/purge syndrome
    d. Compulsive eating disorder

13. A condition in which the body adapts to prolonged fasting or carbohydrate deprivation by converting body fat to ketones, which can be used as fuel for some brain activity is called:
    a. Caloric adaptation
    b. Carbohydrate synthesis
    c. Acidosis
    d. Ketones

14. Fat that is necessary for normal physiological functioning is called:
    a. Body fat
    b. Essential fat
    c. Brown fat
    d. Storage fat

15. An inborn physiological response to nutritional needs is:
    a. Hunger
    b. Appetite
    c. Satiety
    d. Adaptive thermogenesis

Practice Test #2

1. The ideal total body fat for men is:
   a. 5-10%
   b. 11-15%
   c. 16-20%
   d. 25-35%

2. The method of determining body fat by measuring the amount of water displaced when a person is completely submerged is called:
   a. Skin-fold caliper test
   b. Body mass index
   c. Hydrostatic weighing technique
   d. Bioelectrical impedance analysis

3. A medical standard used to define obesity using an index of the relationship of height and weight is the:
   a. Body composition index
   b. Body mass index
   c. Hydrostatic weight
   d. Waist-to-hip ratio

4. The mechanism in which the brain regulates metabolic activity according to caloric intake is called:
   a. Adaptive thermogenesis
   b. Hunger
   c. Satiety
   d. Appetite

5. Appetite is:
   a. Controlled by specialized fat cells known as brown cells
   b. An inborn physiological response to nutritional needs
   c. A learned response to food that is tied to an emotional or psychological craving for food that is often unrelated to nutritional needs
   d. None of the above

6. The gland that is located in the throat that produces a hormone that regulates metabolism is the:
   a. Lymph gland
   b. Thyroid gland
   c. Adrenal gland
   d. Pancreas

7. Eating food from fast-food restaurants is a problem because:
   a. Fast food is high in calories
   b. Fast food is eaten quickly so that there is not enough time for the "I'm full" signal
   c. Proportions tend to be bigger than they should be and tend to get eaten
   d. All of the above

8. The desire to "look good" that has a destructive and sometimes disabling affect on one's ability to function effectively in relationships and interactions with others is called:
   a. Appearance anxiety
   b. Obesity anxiety
   c. Social physique anxiety
   d. Anorexia nervosa

9. The best way to lose weight is:
   a. To lower calories
   b. To increase exercise
   c. To stagger calorie intake low or high calories on alternating days
   d. Both a and b

10. Approximately 90 percent of the daily calorie expenditures of most people occur as a result of:
    a. Basal metabolic rate
    b. Resting metabolic rate
    c. Exercise metabolic rate
    d. Sedentary metabolic rate

11. The major cause of low activity levels is:
    a. Vacuum cleaners
    b. Automobiles
    c. TV remote controls
    d. All of the above

12. The best way to improve one's chance for long-term success with weight loss is:
    a. Plan for nutrient-dense foods
    b. Plan for plateaus
    c. Chart your progress
    d. All of the above

13. An eating disorder among clinically obese individuals who binge eat much more often than the typical obese person is called:
    a. Anorexia nervosa
    b. Bulimia nervosa
    c. Binge/purge syndrome
    d. Binge eating disorder

14. Diets with caloric intake of 400 to 700 calories are called:
    a. Cambridge diet
    b. Liquid diets
    c. Jenny Craig
    d. Very low calorie diets

15. A man would be considered obese if his body fat exceeds ___ percent of his total body mass while a woman is considered obese if her body fat is ___ percent of her total body mass.
    a. 15; 20
    b. 20; 30
    c. 35; 45
    d. 40; 50

16 Personal Fitness

General Review Questions

1. What is physical activity?
2. List the four interdependent components of physical fitness.
3. What is your target heart rate?
4. Why is flexibility important for fitness?
5. What first-aid treatment can be used for virtually all personal fitness injuries?

Practice Test #1

1. The leading cause of death in the United States for both men and women is:
   a. Cancer
   b. Strokes
   c. Coronary heart disease
   d. Liver disease

2. The ability of the heart, lungs, and blood vessels to function efficiently is called:
   a. Cardiovascular output
   b. Cardiovascular status
   c. Cardiovascular fitness
   d. Cardiovascular endurance

3. A test of aerobic capacity administered by a physician, exercise physiologist, or other trained person is called:
   a. A graded exercise test
   b. A maximum aerobic capacity test
   c. An aerobic endurance test
   d. A cardiac output test

4. The length of a daily physical activity of exercise period to improve aerobic capacity is:
   a. No more than 10 minutes
   b. 10-15 minutes
   c. 15-20 minutes
   d. 20-60 minutes

5. A regular program of exercise designed to improve muscular strength and endurance in the major muscle groups is:
   a. Flexibility training program
   b. Aerobic exercise program
   c. Repetition maximum program
   d. Resistance exercise program

6. An Indian form of exercise widely practiced in the West today that promotes balance, coordination, flexibility and meditation is:
   a. Flexibility
   b. Tai chi
   c. Yoga
   d. Zen

7. The greatest amount of force in the muscles is produced during:
   a. Muscle overload
   b. Isometric muscle action
   c. Concentric muscle action
   d. Eccentric muscle actions

8. The primary category of physical activity known to improve cardiovascular fitness is:
   a. Aerobic exercise
   b. Anaerobic exercise
   c. Flexibility
   d. Body building

9. The type of muscle action in which force is produced while the muscle shortens is called:
   a. Dynamic
   b. Static
   c. Concentric
   d. Eccentric

10. The resistance provided by exercises that require your muscles to lift your body weight off the floor (i.e. situps, pushups, pullups) is called:
    a. Fixed resistance
    b. Variable resistance
    c. Accommodating resistance
    d. Body weight resistance

11. The general term for any pain that occurs below the knee and above the ankle is:
    a. Shin splints
    b. Tendinitis
    c. Muscle cramps
    d. Muscle strain

12. Superior stretching techniques that are best performed with a certified athletic trainer or physical therapist are called:
    a. Static stretching techniques
    b. Proprioceptive neuromuscular facilitation
    c. Ballistic stretching techniques
    d. Tandem stretching techniques

13. The amount of force a muscle is capable of exerting is:
    a. Muscular efficiency
    b. Muscular strength
    c. Muscular endurance
    d. Muscular overload

14. The use of free-weight barbells and dumbbells that offer a resistance to your exertion is an example of:
    a. Body weight resistance
    b. Fixed resistance
    c. Variable resistance
    d. Static resistance

15. A condition in which the body's rate of heat production exceeds its ability to cool itself is known as:
    a. Hypothermia
    b. Heat stress
    c. Compression
    d. Muscle strain

Practice Test #2

1. People who exercise regularly often report:
    a. An increased ability to cope with stress
    b. An increased self-esteem
    c. Feeling good about personal appearance
    d. All of the above

2. Muscle endurance is:
    a. The force exerted by a muscle that is less than or equal to the resistance
    b. A muscle's ability to exert force repeatedly without fatiguing
    c. The length of time a particular movement can be sustained by a muscle or muscle group
    d. A withering of muscle tissue that can result from injury or disease

3. The strongest predisposing factor for non-insulin dependent diabetes is(are):
    a. Obesity
    b. Increasing age
    c. Family history of diabetes
    d. All of the above

4. The systematic performance of exercise at a specified frequency, intensity, and duration to achieve a desired level of physical fitness is called:
    a. Fitness training
    b. Physical fitness
    c. Exercise training
    d. Physical endurance

5. Force produced while lengthening the muscle is called:
    a. Eccentric muscle action
    b. Isotonic muscle action
    c. Concentric muscle action
    d. Endurance muscle action

6. The recommended minimum number of times per week that a physical activity and/or exercise should be done to reach aerobic fitness is:
    a. 1 time per week
    b. 3 times per week
    c. 5 times per week
    d. 7 times per week

7. Increased levels of high density lipoproteins can diminish the risk of:
    a. Diabetes
    b. Osteoarthritis
    c. Osteoporosis
    d. Cardiovascular disease

8. Which of the following is(are) warning signs of overuse injury?
    a. Muscle stiffness
    b. Whole body fatigue
    c. Joint pain
    d. All of the above

9. The type of resistance that provides a "constant load" on the muscle throughout the entire range of motion is called:
   a. Body weight resistance
   b. Static resistance
   c. Fixed resistance
   d. Accommodating resistance

10. The use of resistance that is altered throughout the range of motion so that the effort by the muscle is more consistent throughout the full range of motion is called:
    a. Static resistance
    b. Muscular function resistance
    c. Variable resistance
    d. Isometric resistance

11. The maximal volume of oxygen consumed by muscles during exercise is:
    a. Flexibility
    b. Muscle endurance
    c. Aerobic capacity
    d. Maximum oxygen capacity

12. To lose weight, how many workouts a week will you need to do in order to see reductions in your total body mass and fat mass?
    a. At least 2 workouts per week
    b. At least 3 workouts per week
    c. At least 4 workouts per week
    d. At least 5 workouts per week

13. Injuries that result from the cumulative effects of day-after-day stress placed on tendons, muscles, and joints are called:
    a. Overuse injuries
    b. Traumatic injuries
    c. Overtraining injuries
    d. Repetitive injuries

14. Joel enjoys various types of fitness exercises. He alternates his training days with jogging, cycling, and step aerobics. This type of training is called:
    a. Cardiac fitness training
    b. Static training
    c. Cross training
    d. Multisport training

15. Techniques to gradually lengthen a muscle to an elongated position (to the point of discomfort) and hold that position for 10 to 30 seconds is called:
    a. Dynamic stretching
    b. Static stretching
    c. Variable stretching
    d. Concentric stretching

17 Cardiovascular Disease

General Review Questions

1. List the risk factors for cardiovascular disease.
2. What are the risk factors for cardiovascular disease that we cannot prevent or control?
3. Discuss the common treatments for angina pectoris.
4. List the specific factors that cause secondary hypertension?
5. What are the reasons for the widespread neglect of the signs of heart disease in women?

Practice Test #1

1. The leading cause of death in the United States is:
   a. Strokes
   b. Transient Ischemic Attacks
   c. Cardiovascular Diseases
   d. Cancer

2. The part of the cardiovascular system that takes blood away from the heart is(are) the:
   a. Atrium
   b. Veins
   c. Capillaries
   d. Arteries

3. A blockage of the normal blood supply to an area of the heart is called:
   a. A stroke
   b. A coronary thrombosis
   c. A heart attack
   d. Angina pectoris

4. An irregularity in heartbeat is called:
   a. Fibrillation
   b. Bradycardia
   c. Tachycardia
   d. Arrhythmia

5. The drug used to dilate veins and reduce the amount of blood returning to the heart and thus lessening its workload is:
   a. Nitroglycerin
   b. Inderal
   c. Prinivil
   d. Lopressor

6. When the blood supply to the brain is cut off, the result may be:
   a. A myocardial infarction
   b. A thrombosis
   c. A stroke
   d. An aneurysm

7. Nonessential hypertension is caused by:
   a. Smoking
   b. Obesity
   c. Kidney disease
   d. No specific cause

8. A surgical technique whereby a blood vessel is implanted to bypass a blocked artery is called:
   a. Angioplasty
   b. Coronary by-pass surgery
   c. Electrocardiogram
   d. Pacemaker implantation

9. The organ that is a muscular, four-chambered pump that is roughly the size of a man's fist is:
   a. The heart
   b. The capillaries
   c. The lungs
   d. The atria

10. The mitral valve is located:
    a. Between the right ventricle and the pulmonary artery
    b. Between the left atrium and the left ventricle
    c. Between the right atrium and the right ventricle
    d. Between the left ventricle and the aorta

11. An abnormally fast heartbeat is known as:
    a. Arrhythmia
    b. Tachycardia
    c. Vasodilation
    d. Aneurysm

12. What are the underlying causes of congenital heart disease?
    a. Maternal diseases
    b. Chemical intake by the mother during pregnancy
    c. Streptococcal infection
    d. All of the above

13. Which of the following is(are) the symptom(s) of a transient ischemic attack?
    a. Sudden weakness or numbness of the face, arm, or leg on one side of the body
    b. Loss of speech, or trouble talking or understanding speech
    c. Sudden, severe headaches with no known cause
    d. All of the above

14. The variety of cholesterol that is associated with cardiovascular risks is:
    a. High-density lipoproteins
    b. Very high-density lipoproteins
    c. Low-density lipoproteins
    d. Omega-3 transfatty acids

15. The diagnostic technique that uses powerful magnets to look inside the body is called:
    a. Radionuclide imaging
    b. Magnetic resonance imaging
    c. Digital cardiac angiography
    d. Cardiomagnetic angioplasty

Practice Test #2

1. The development of new, small blood vessels that reroute needed blood through other areas as a result of minor heart blockage is called:
    a. Coronary circulation
    b. Collateral circulation
    c. Converse circulation
    d. Coronary thrombosis

2. Severe chest pain occurring as a result of reduced oxygen flow to the heart is called:
    a. Angina pectoris
    b. Arrhythmias
    c. Myocardial infarction
    d. Congestive heart failure

3. A type of heart disease caused by untreated streptococcal infection of the throat is:
    a. Congestive heart failure
    b. Congenital heart disease
    c. Rheumatic heart disease
    d. Coronary thrombosis

4. The greatest alterable risk factor for CVD is:
    a. Smoking
    b. Diet
    c. Exercise
    d. Hypertension

5. The blood pressure value that refers to the pressure being applied to the walls of the arteries when the heart contracts is called:
    a. Diastolic pressure
    b. Systolic pressure
    c. Normal pressure
    d. Contraction pressure

6. The diagnostic technique in which a needle-thin catheter is threaded through blocked arteries of the heart, a dye injected, and an X-ray is taken to find the blocked areas is called:
    a. Angiography
    b. Angioplasty
    c. Electrocardiogram
    d. Positron Emission Tomography

7. Under normal circumstances, the body contains ___ quarts of blood.
    a. 4
    b. 6
    c. 8
    d. 10

8. A general term for the thickening or hardening of the arteries is:
    a. Myocardial infarction
    b. Cerebrovascular accident
    c. Atherosclerosis
    d. Arrhythmia

9. Medications that are used for the relief of fluid accumulation are called:
    a. Diuretics
    b. Vasodilators
    c. Calcium channel blockers
    d. Beta blockers

10. A weakening in a blood vessel that causes it to bulge and, in severe cases, burst is called:
    a. Congestive heart failure
    b. Angina pectoris
    c. An aneurysm
    d. An arrhythmia

11. Which of the following is(are) effective in improving a stroke victim's chances of survival?
    a. Surgery
    b. Drugs
    c. Acute hospital care
    d. All of the above

12. Reperfusion therapy for a heart attack is called:
    a. Nitroglycerin
    b. Thrombolysis
    c. Angioplasty
    d. Angiogram

13. The blood vessels through which blood flows as it returns to the heart and lungs are called:
    a. Arteries
    b. Capillaries
    c. Veins
    d. Arterioles

14. The average adult heart at rest beats _____ times per minute.
    a. 45 to 55
    b. 50 to 60
    c. 60 to 70
    d. 70 to 80

15. Drugs that expand the blood vessels and decrease resistance thereby allowing blood to flow more easily and ease the heart's workload are called:
    a. Diuretics
    b. Vasodilators
    c. Anorexics
    d. Calcium channel blockers

18 Cancer

General Review Questions

1. What factors influence a person's decision to seek care, participate in screenings, or follow treatment options?
2. List the symptoms of lung cancer.
3. What is the ABCD rule for malignant melanoma?
4. List the high-tech diagnostic techniques that are used to detect cancer.
5. Describe the preventive actions an individual can take to prevent cancer.

Practice Test #1

1. When a neoplasmic mass forms a clumping of cells it is called:
   a. Cancer
   b. Neoplasm
   c. A tumor
   d. Carcinogen

2. Which of the following is a source (are sources) of ionizing radiation?
   a. Radon
   b. Microwaves
   c. Computer screens
   d. Electric blankets

3. Human Papilloma virus has been linked to:
   a. Testicular cancer
   b. Breast cancer
   c. Cervical cancer
   d. Ovarian cancer

4. Cancer of the blood-forming parts of the body, particularly the bone marrow and spleen, is called:
   a. Lymphoma
   b. Leukemia
   c. Carcinoma
   d. Sarcoma

5. The second leading cause of cancer death in males is:
   a. Lung cancer
   b. Breast cancer
   c. Testicular cancer
   d. Prostate cancer

6. The treatment of skin cancer that involves tissue destruction by freezing is called:
   a. Surgery
   b. Cryosurgery
   c. Electrodesication
   d. Radiation therapy

7. Cancers that occur in the mesodermal layers of tissue (i.e., bones, muscles, and general connective tissues) are called:
   a. Carcinomas
   b. Lymphomas
   c. Leukemia
   d. Sarcomas

8. A yearly Pap test and pelvic exam should be performed if:
   a. A woman is sexually active
   b. A woman is over the age of 18
   c. Only if a woman has a history of cervical cancer
   d. Both a and b

9. A large group of diseases characterized by uncontrolled growth and spread of abnormal cells is called:
   a. Mutant cells
   b. Neoplasms
   c. Carcinogens
   d. Cancer

10. The most common and most dangerous carcinogen is:
    a. Coal tar
    b. Tar in cigarettes
    c. Asbestos
    d. Pesticides

11. Physicians who specialize in the treatment of malignancies are called:
    a. Oncologists
    b. Internalists
    c. Cancerologists
    d. Epidemiologists

12. According to the American Cancer Society, which of the following is(are) a recommended dietary guideline for cancer prevention?
   a. Maintain desirable weight
   b. Include cruciferous vegetables in your diet
   c. Cut down on fat intake
   d. All of the above

13. Cancer of the epithelial tissues, in particular the breast, lungs, intestines, skin and mouth, are classified as:
   a. Carcinomas
   b. Sarcomas
   c. Lymphomas
   d. Leukemia

14. Risk factors for breast cancer include all of the following, *except*:
   a. Female, under the age of 20
   b. Family history, in particular a grandmother, mother, or sister
   c. Female, never had children
   d. Female, first child after the age of 30

15. One of the most common types of cancer, characterized by solid tumors, found in males between the ages of 17 and 34 is:
   a. Testicular cancer
   b. Prostate cancer
   c. Liver cancer
   d. Stomach cancer

Practice Test #2

1. Carcinomas are:
   a. Antigens found in the prostate of cancer patients
   b. Cancer-causing agents
   c. Harmless, noncancerous tumors
   d. Suspected cancer causing genes

2. Which of the following types of cancer is related to alcohol consumption?
   a. Liver cancer
   b. Lymphoma
   c. Carcinoma
   d. Sarcoma

3. Hodgkin's disease is a type of:
   a. Leukemia
   b. Lymphoma
   c. Carcinoma

d. Sarcoma

4. The second leading cause of cancer death for women is:
   a. Breast cancer
   b. Lung cancer
   c. Cervical cancer
   d. Ovarian cancer

5. The deadly form of skin cancer that is the most frequent cancer in women ages 24 to 29 is:
   a. Basal cell skin cancer
   b. Malignant melanoma
   c. Squamous cell skin cancer
   d. Epithelial cell cancer

6. A food additive suspected of causing cancer is:
   a. Sodium
   b. Diethylstilbestrol
   c. Nitrosamines
   d. Asbestos

7. The process by which cancer spreads from one area to different areas in the body is called:
   a. Metastasis
   b. Biopsy
   c. Virulence
   d. Mutation

8. In general, ordinary-looking cells enclosed in a fibrous shell or capsule that prevents their spreading to other body areas are called:
   a. Mutant cells
   b. Malignant tumors
   c. Benign tumors
   d. Metastatic tumors

9. Suspected cancer-causing genes present on chromosomes are called:
   a. Mutations
   b. Familial genes
   c. Oncogenes
   d. Prototype genes

10. The most common occupational carcinogens are:
   a. Asbestos
   b. Pesticides
   c. Coal tars
   d. Lead

11. A virulent cancer of the melanin portion of the skin that can be fatal and results from radiation from the sun is:
    a. Multiple myelomas
    b. Malignant melanoma
    c. Kaposi's sarcoma
    d. Basal cell carcinoma

12. Those at highest risk for lung cancer are:
    a. Smokers who have smoked for over 20 years
    b. People who have been exposed to asbestos
    c. People who have been exposed to radiation
    d. All of the above

13. The second leading cause of cancer death in the United States is:
    a. Uterine cancer
    b. Prostate cancer
    c. Colon and rectal cancer
    d. Malignant melanoma

14. The leading cause of cancer death among white females (particularly young teens) and black males is:
    a. Stomach cancer
    b. Colon and rectal cancer
    c. Lung cancer
    d. Leukemia

15. The use of radiation to kill cancerous cells is called:
    a. Radiotherapy
    b. Chemotherapy
    c. Immunotherapy
    d. Interferon

19 Infectious Diseases and Sexually Transmitted Infections

General Review Questions

1. What factors influence your susceptibility to diseases?
2. What are the routes that pathogens enter the body?
3. List and give an example of the major types of pathogens.
4. What are the body linings that provide protection against pathogens?
5. Who is the fastest-growing segment of the HIV population in the United States?

Practice Test #1

1. Organisms that normally live in coexistence with human hosts and are usually harmless are called:
   a. Pathogens
   b. Exogenous microorganisms
   c. Endogenous microorganisms
   d. Infections microorganisms

2. Staphylococcal infection is a form of:
   a. Rickettsia infection
   b. Fungi infection
   c. Viral infection
   d. Bacterial infection

3. The smallest of the pathogens is:
   a. Rickettsia
   b. Virus
   c. Parasitic worms
   d. Bacteria

4. For whom can the flu be very serious?
   a. The elderly
   b. Those with respiratory or heart disease
   c. Very young children
   d. All of the above

5. The body's single most critical early defense system to infection is:
   a. Cilia
   b. T-lymphocytes
   c. Tears
   d. Skin

6. White blood cells that aid in the antigen-antibody response are known as:
   a. Antigens
   b. Lymphocytes
   c. Phagocytes
   d. Erythrocytes

7. The early symptom(s) of HIV infection is(are):
   a. Night sweats
   b. Fever
   c. Sore throat
   d. All of the above

8. The most commonly reported sexually transmitted infection (STI) in the United States is:
   a. Human papilloma virus
   b. Urinary tract infections
   c. Syphilis
   d. Genital herpes

9. An inherited blood disease that affects African Americans that results in organ damage and premature death is:
   a. AIDS
   b. Sickle cell anemia
   c. Diabetes
   d. Muscular dystrophy

10. Sexual relations, kissing, or touching are examples of which type of disease transmission?
    a. Direct contact
    b. Indirect contact
    c. Food-borne infection
    d. Airborne infection

11. Benny prefers his beef cooked very rare. What type of food-borne infection should he be concerned about?
    a. Lyme disease
    b. Rabies
    c. E. coli
    d. Botulism

12. The person(s) at greatest risk for tuberculosis is(are):
   a. Persons residing in overcrowded prisons
   b. Persons residing in homeless shelters
   c. The poor
   d. All of the above

13. The sexually transmitted infection that is characterized in males by a white milky discharge from the penis, along with painful, burning urination two to nine days after contact is:
   a. Syphilis
   b. Gonorrhea
   c. Candidiasis
   d. Genital warts

14. The slow-acting virus that causes AIDS is:
   a. Herpes simplex
   b. Human papilloma virus
   c. Human immunodeficiency virus
   d. Neisseria gonorrhea

15. Which of the following is not a major body fluid of concern for HIV?
   a. Blood
   b. Semen
   c. Saliva
   d. Vaginal secretions

Practice Test #2

1. Touching the handle of a towel dispenser that has just been touched by a person whose hands were contaminated by a sneeze is an example of:
   a. Direct contact
   b. Indirect contact
   c. Food-borne transmission
   d. Airborne transmission

2. Microorganisms that are disease-causing agents are called:
   a. Endogenous microorganisms
   b. Virulent organisms
   c. Pathogens
   d. All of the above

3. Which of the following is a (are) controllable risk factor(s) for infectious diseases?
   a. Too much stress
   b. Inadequate diet
   c. Lack of sleep
   d. All of the above

4. Which of the following is(are) a major type of bacteria?
   a. Cocci
   b. Bacilli
   c. Spirilla
   d. All of the above

5. The time between when an agent breaks through the body's defenses and the first appearance of symptoms is called the:
   a. Infection period
   b. Incubation period
   c. Antibody period
   d. Immune period

6. A viral disease that causes inflammation of the liver is:
   a. Hepatitis
   b. Herpes simplex
   c. AIDS
   d. Measles

7. Single-celled organisms that cause diseases such as trichomoniasis and giardiasis are called:
   a. Fungi
   b. Bacteria
   c. Rickettsia
   d. Protozoa

8. Which of the following infections is caused by fungi?
   a. Ringworm
   b. Trichomoniasis
   c. Rabies
   d. Pneumonia

9. Treatments that are administered orally or by injection for the purpose of forming an artificial immunity are called:
   a. Vaccinations
   b. Acquired immunity
   c. Natural immunity
   d. Passive immunity

10. The most common mode of transmission for sexually transmitted infections is(are):
   a. Sexual intercourse
   b. Hand-genital contact
   c. Oral-genital contact
   d. All of the above

11. The stage of syphilis that is often characterized by the development of a sore known as a chancre is:
    a. Primary syphilis
    b. Secondary syphilis
    c. Latent syphilis
    d. Late syphilis

12. Human papilloma viruses have been associated with increased risk of:
    a. Chancres
    b. Blistering sores or eruptions on the skin
    c. Cervical cancer
    d. Pelvic inflammatory disease

13. In adults, the average length of time it takes HIV to cause slow, degenerative changes in the immune system is:
    a. 4-6 years
    b. 8-10 years
    c. 11-13 years
    d. 15 years or longer

14. The blood test used to detect the presence of HIV antibodies is the:
    a. ELISA
    b. HIV antibody test
    c. HIV-1 immunoassay
    d. Colposcopy

15. One of the most widespread sexually transmitted infections in the world is:
    a. HIV infection
    b. Genital herpes
    c. Genital warts
    d. Trichomoniasis

20 Noninfectious Conditions

General Review Questions

1. What are the most common environmental antigens that cause responses for allergy-induced problems?
2. List the "five f's" of gallbladder disease risk.
3. List the risk factors for low back pain.
4. What are the criteria for diagnosing Chronic Fatigue Syndrome?
5. What injuries can result from repetitive stress injury?

Practice Test #1

1. A respiratory disease in which the alveoli of the lungs are gradually destroyed is known as:
   a. Asthma
   b. Hay fever
   c. Emphysema
   d. Chronic Bronchitis

2. Epilepsy is:
   a. Localized headaches on only one side of the head
   b. A neurological disorder caused by abnormal electrical brain activity
   c. Characterized by excruciating pain that lasts for minutes or hours
   d. A hereditary disease that is more common in women than men

3. Migraine headaches are characterized by all of the following *except*:
   a. Primarily treated with relaxation training and biofeedback
   b. Are more common among women than men
   c. Occur when blood vessels in the membrane that surrounds the brain dilate
   d. Often are accompanied by nausea and sensitivity to light and sounds

4. Symptoms for diabetes include all of the following *except*:
   a. Excessive thirst
   b. Hypoglycemia
   c. Frequent urination
   d. Skin eruptions

5. Type-2 Diabetes is:
   a. Adult-onset diabetes
   b. Non-insulin dependent
   c. Tends to develop later in life
   d. All of the above

6. When the gallbladder has been repeatedly irritated and reduces its ability to release bile, a disease that can result is:
   a. Diverticulosis
   b. Colitis
   c. Cholecystitis
   d. Appendicitis

7. Rheumatoid arthritis is:
   a. A progressive deterioration of the bones and joints
   b. Affected by weather changes, excessive strain and injury
   c. An autoimmune disorder that attacks the synovial membrane which produces the lubricating fluids of the joint
   d. Caused by abnormal use of the joint and abnormalities in joint structure

8. The risk of low back pain can be reduced by all of the following *except*:
   a. Exercises that strengthen stomach muscles
   b. Maintaining good posture
   c. Sleeping on your stomach
   d. Stretching the back muscles

9. A syndrome describing a series of characteristic symptoms that occur prior to menstruation in some women is:
   a. Endometriosis
   b. Fibrocystic breast condition
   c. Premenstrual syndrome
   d. Diabetes

10. A common occupational injury associated with video display terminals is:
    a. Carpal tunnel syndrome
    b. Chronic Fatigue Syndrome
    c. Chronic Epstein Barr disease
    d. Seasonal affective disorder

11. Chemical substances that dilate blood vessels, increase mucous secretions, cause tissues to swell, and produce other allergy-like symptoms are called:
   a. Allergens
   b. Antibodies
   c. Histamines
   d. Antigens

12. A major cause(s) of exercise-induced asthma is(are):
   a. Cold, dry air
   b. Ragweed and flower blooms
   c. Animal dander
   d. Mold

13. A seizure disorder that is characterized by no convulsions, minor loss of consciousness that may go unnoticed, and a minor twitching of muscles is called:
   a. Jacksonian seizure
   b. Grand mal seizure
   c. Petit mal seizure
   d. Psychomotor seizure

14. Diverticulosis occurs when:
   a. The intestinal walls become inflamed
   b. The intestinal walls become weakened for undetermined reasons and small pea-shaped bulges develop
   c. The pancreas fails to produce enough insulin
   d. Endometrial tissue develops abnormally outside the uterus

15. All of the following are common treatments for PMS, *except*:
   a. Aspirin
   b. Stress relaxation techniques
   c. Exercise
   d. Decreased intake of complex carbohydrates

Practice Test #2

1. Noninfectious and chronic diseases are characterized as:
   a. Not being transmitted by any pathogen or by any form of personal contact
   b. Usually developing over a long period of time
   c. Appearing to be the result of lifestyle and personal health habits
   d. All of the above

2. Which of the following is *not* a characteristic of hay fever?
   a. Sneezing
   b. Itchy, watery eyes and nose
   c. Lifestyle behaviors are a significant risk factor
   d. Appears to run in families

3. A chronic respiratory disease characterized by attacks of wheezing, shortness of breath and coughing spasms is called:
   a. Allergies
   b. Asthma
   c. Emphysema
   d. Chronic bronchitis

4. A major risk factor for chronic bronchitis is:
   a. Ragweed and pollen
   b. Use of cigarettes
   c. Animal dander
   d. Dust

5. The majority of all headaches are caused by:
   a. Excessive physical or psychological tension
   b. Dilated blood vessels within the brain
   c. Underlying organic problems
   d. All of the above

6. A common noncancerous problem among women in the United States is:
   a. Fibrocystic breast condition
   b. Petit mal seizures
   c. Colitis
   d. Diverticulosis

7. Endometriosis is characterized by:
   a. Painful bowel movements with periods
   b. Constipation
   c. Unusually heavy or light menstrual flow
   d. All of the above

8. Hyperglycemia is:
   a. Excessive thirst
   b. Increased appetite
   c. Elevated blood sugars
   d. Increased urinary output

9. Ulcerative colitis is characterized by:
   a. Nausea
   b. Bloody diarrhea
   c. Severe stomach cramps
   d. All of the above

10. Some peptic ulcers are caused by:
    a. Inflammation of the intestinal walls
    b. The weakening of intestinal walls for undetermined reasons and the development of small pea-shaped bulges
    c. The inability of the pancreas to produce enough insulin
    d. The erosive effect of digestive juices on the lining of the stomach or the duodenum

11. A condition of repetitive cessation of breathing during sleep that can lead to dramatic rises in blood pressure is called:
    a. Sleep apnea
    c. Systemic lupus erythematosus
    d. Rheumatoid arthritis

12. People suffering from Raynaud's Syndrome may experience:
    a. Numbing of fingers and toes
    b. Fingers and toes turning white, then deep purple
    c. An overexaggerated vasoconstriction of the small arteries in the extremities
    d. All of the above

13. Uterine fibroids:
    a. Are commonly found in women ages 20 to 30
    b. Can cause miscarriages and infertility
    c. Rarely affect surrounding organs
    d. Occur in nearly 50 percent of all women

14. An illness characterized by debilitating fatigue in the absence of a pathogen and affects many adults in their 30s is:
    a. Epstein-Barr disease
    b. Carpal tunnel syndrome
    c. Chronic fatigue syndrome
    d. Grave's disease

15. A butterfly-shaped rash covering the bridge of the nose and both cheeks is a common symptom of:
    a. Chronic fatigue syndrome
    b. Raynaud's syndrome
    c. Scleroderma
    d. Systemic lupus erythematosus

21 Healthy Aging

General Review Questions

1. Describe the two psychosocial theories of personality development that encompass the human life span.
2. What are the estimated health care costs of the elderly?
3. List the risk factors for osteoporosis.
4. How is intelligence affected by age?
3. Describe the reasons why the elderly are at greater risk of dangerous drug interaction and the symptoms of drug induced interactions.

Practice Test #1

1. The study of the individual and collective aging process is:
   a. Ageology
   b. Gerontology
   c. Genealogy
   d. Archeology

2. A person's habits and roles relative to society's expectations refers to his or her:
   a. Functional age
   b. Psychological age
   c. Legal age
   d. Social age

3. A term used to describe loss of memory and judgment and orientation problems occurring in a small percentage of the elderly is:
   a. Senility
   b. Depression
   c. Psychosis
   d. Schizophrenia

4. One of the most common forms of dementia for the elderly is:
   a. Alzheimer's disease
   b. Incontinence
   c. Depression
   d. Psychosis

5. The "young-old" are people who are:
   a. 55-64 years of age
   b. 65-74 years of age
   c. 75-84 years of age
   d. 85 years or older

6. According to the cellular theory:
   a. Aging is caused by the human body wearing out
   b. Aging is caused by the body's cells having reached the end of their reproductive cycle
   c. Aging is caused by the decline of the body's immunological system
   d. Aging is caused by an increased number of cells exhibiting unusual or different characteristics with increased age

7. As the mind ages:
   a. Short-term memory fluctuates on a daily basis
   b. The ability to remember events from past decades remains unchanged
   c. The elderly are extremely heterogeneous
   d. All of the above

8. To reduce age-related risks, it is important to:
   a. Keep active mentally
   b. Learn to accept help when needed
   c. Have regular medical checkups
   d. All of the above

9. Art is now in his 70s and has noticed that his hearing seems to have changed. What change(s) may have occurred?
   a. His ability to hear high-frequency consonants may have diminished
   b. His ability to distinguish extreme ranges of sound
   c. His ability to distinguish normal conversational tones
   d. Both a and b

10. With age, all of the following occur *except*:
    a. Earlobes get fatter and grow longer
    b. Overall head circumference increases
    c. Brain size increases
    d. The skull becomes thicker

11. A clouding of the eye lens is called:
   a. Cataracts
   b. Glaucoma
   c. Colorblindness
   d. Astigmatism

12. During menopause, women may experience:
   a. Hot flashes
   b. Weight gain
   c. The development of facial hair
   d. All of the above

13. Your grandmother has suddenly been acting strange. She has been disoriented, erratic, and cannot make a cup of coffee. What may be causing her to behave so strangely?
   a. She may be developing an age-related disorder (i.e., dementia)
   b. She may be having an adverse reaction to OTC drugs
   c. She may be having an adverse reaction to a prescription medication
   d. All of the above

14. The inability to control urination is called:
   a. Osteoporosis
   b. Vital capacity
   c. Urinary incontinence
   d. None of the above

15. A chronic condition involving changes in nerve fibers of the brain that results in mental deterioration is called:
   a. Alzheimer's disease
   b. Presenile dementia
   c. Parkinson's disease
   d. Senility

Practice Test #2

1. The patterns of life changes that occur in members of all species as they grow older is called:
   a. Aging
   b. Gerontology
   c. Maturity
   d. Maturation

2. The most common definition of age in the United States is:
   a. Biological age
   b. Social age

   c. Legal age
   d. Functional age

3. What percent of all people between the ages of 65 and 74 are forced to seek nursing-home care?
   a. 1%
   b. 15%
   c. 20%
   d. 40%

4. According to the autoimmune theory:
   a. Aging is caused by the human body wearing out
   b. Aging is caused by the body's cells having reached the end of their reproductive cycle
   c. Aging is caused by the decline of the body's immunological system
   d. Aging is caused by an increased number of cells exhibiting unusual or different characteristics with increased age

5. As a person ages, s/he can expect:
   a. Her/his resting heart rate to stay about the same as it was in younger years
   b. The stroke volume of her/his heart to increase
   c. Her/his vital cpaacity to increase
   d. Exercise to have little impact on her/his heart and lung function

6. By the age of 70, changes in the urinary tract may include:
   a. Kidneys filter waste from the blood only half as fast as at age 30
   b. The need to urinate becomes more frequent
   c. Bladder capacity declines
   d. All of the above

7. The elevation of pressure within the eyeball that can lead to blindness is called:
   a. Cataracts
   b. Glaucoma
   c. Far-sightedness
   d. Near-sightedness

8. As a man ages, he may experience all of the following changes *except*:
   a. An increased ability to maintain an erection
   b. Orgasms that are shorter in duration
   c. Reduced ability to an obtain erection
   d. A greater amount of time required for the refractory period between orgasms

9. Elderly people are at increased risk of hypothermia, heat stroke, and heat exhaustion because:
   a. Pain receptors are more sensitive
   b. Loss of body fat
   c. Tactile senses improve
   d. Skin becomes thicker

10. Prevention of osteoporosis focuses on:
    a. Maintaining muscular strength and flexibility
    b. Daily weight bearing exercise
    c. Adequate calcium intake
    d. All of the above

11. Based on a recent study by the National Council on Aging:
    a. Most older American males cannot have sexual intercourse
    b. Nearly half of Americans over the age of 60 engage in sexual activity at least once a month
    c. Most older American women do not want to have sexual intercourse
    d. Most older American females cannot have sexual intercourse due to the physical changes from menopause

12. Which of the following factors tends to have an impact on increased skin pigment production?
    a. Smoking
    b. The sun
    c. Skin deterioration
    d. All of the above

13. Elderly women are more likely to need assistance from their children, other relatives, friends, and neighbors than men because:
    a. There are more elderly women than men
    b. Women do not age as well as men
    c. Women have more serious health problems (i.e. osteoporosis) than men
    d. Men are the primary caregivers

14. The most commonly used over-the-counter drug(s) among the elderly is(are):
    a. Aspirin and laxatives
    b. Vitamin supplements
    c. Geritol and One-a-Day Vitamins
    d. Antacids and laxatives

15. What country has the highest percentage of their population that is 60 years of age and over?
    a. Uruguay
    b. United States
    c. France
    d. Italy

22 Dying and Death

General Review Questions

1. How is death determined by the Uniform Determination of Death Act?
2. What factors influence our attitudes about death?
3. List the five stages of dying.
4. Describe the common methods of body disposal.
5. What artificial life support techniques may be legally refused by competent patients in some states?

Practice Test #1

1. Dying is:
   a. The final cessation of the vital functions of the body
   b. An irreversible situation in which a person is laid to rest
   c. The process of decline in body functions resulting in the death of an organism
   d. The cessation of electrical activity in the brain

2. Brain death occurs when:
   a. There is no response even to painful stimuli
   b. There is no movement for a continuous hour after observation by a physician and no breathing after three minutes off a respirator
   c. The pupils are fixed and dilated
   d. All of the above

3. Angela's grandmother is dying but she keeps assuring her sisters that their grandmother will be and will be coming home soon. Angela is most likely experiencing:
   a. Grief
   b. Mourning
   c. Death denial
   d. Bereavement

4. The stage of grief that is characterized by the dying person resolving to be a better person in return for an extension of life is called:
   a. Denial
   b. Anger
   c. Bargaining
   d. Depression

5. An irreversible situation in which a person is not treated like an active member of society is called:
   a. Local death
   b. Functional death
   c. Social death
   d. Somatic death

6. Bereavement is:
   a. Mental distress caused by a loss that cannot be openly acknowledged, publicly mourned, or socially supported
   b. Loss or deprivation experienced by a survivor when a loved one dies
   c. A culturally sanctioned display of grief
   d. Mental distress that occurs in reaction to the loss of a loved one

7. Extramarital lovers who find it difficult to mourn the death of their lover because of societal stigmas may experience:
   a. Bereavement
   b. Bereavement displacement
   c. Disenfranchised grief
   d. Denial

8. Saul has experienced many losses in his life, including the loss of his wife, friends, and children. His gloomy outlook and disturbing behavior patterns may be symptomatic of:
   a. An age-associated dementia
   b. Self-pity
   c. Bereavement overload
   d. Depression

9. The death of a child:
   a. Is considered a major tragedy
   b. May cause surviving children to be emotionally abandoned by their parents
   c. May cause surviving children to feel uncomfortable talking about death
   d. All of the above

10. May has not dated anyone for the past year since her fiancée died and has visited his grave every week. Her actions may be described as:
    a. Mourning
    b. Grief
    c. Death affiliation
    d. Death expectations

11. Funerals serve the purpose of:
    a. Maximizing the quality of life of the survivors
    b. Relieving a dying person' pain
    c. Assisting survivors of the deceased in coping with their loss
    d. Keeping the memory of the deceased alive to the family and friends

12. Burial vaults are:
    a. Concrete or metal containers that hold the casket
    b. The actual container for the body or remains
    c. A funeral ritual in which the embalmed body is viewed
    d. Above ground burial sites

13. Without a legal will:
    a. Everything you have will go to a charity chosen by the state
    b. Everything you have will go to your parents if
    c. Only your children will be able to have everything you had
    d. While laws vary from state-to-state, the courts will make up a will for you

14. The type of "mercy-killing" which is accomplished by administering large doses of painkillers that depress the central nervous system to the extent that basic life-sustaining regulatory centers cease to function is called:
    a. Suicide
    b. Active euthanasia
    c. Passive euthanasia
    d. Dyathanasia

15. An abduction or kidnapping, a divorce, a move to a distant place, and the loss of a romance are examples of:
    a. Quasi-death experiences
    b. Grief
    c. Disenfranchised grief
    d. Mourning

Practice Test #2

1. The view that death as the "mortal enemy of mankind" reflects:
   a. Death acceptance
   b. Death denial
   c. Death procrastination
   d. Death avoidance

2. In making funeral arrangements, you:
   a. Have the right to choose the funeral goods and services you want and any exceptions must be disclosed in writing on the general price list
   b. Have the right to have the funeral provider disclose the specific state law that requires you to purchase any particular item
   c. Have the right to have the funeral provider handle a casket you bought elsewhere without refusal or a fee charged
   d. All of the above

3. The funeral visitation provides:
   a. A chance for the family to visit with friends and loved ones
   b. A time and place for friends to offer their expression of sorrow and sympathy
   c. An opportunity for friends and loved ones to see the flowers and cards sent to the family
   d. An opportunity for friends and loved ones to specify what charitable organization they sent a donation to in the deceased's name

4. The form of "mercy killing" in which life-prolonging treatments or interventions are not offered or withheld, thereby allowing a terminally ill person to die naturally is called:
   a. Self-deliverance
   b. Euthanasia
   c. Dyathanasia
   d. Suicide

5. The study of death and dying is called:
   a. Thanatology
   b. Gerontology
   c. Kublerology
   d. Social death

6. The stage of grief in which vitality diminishes and the patient begins to experience distress symptoms with increasing frequency is called:
   a. Denial
   b. Bargaining
   c. Depression
   d. Acceptance

7. Mourning is:
   a. The loss or deprivation experienced by a survivor when a loved one dies
   b. The effects of multiple losses and the accumulation of sorrow in the lives of some elderly people
   c. Culturally prescribed and accepted time periods and behavior patterns for the expression of grief
   d. When a person experiences a loss that cannot be openly acknowledged, publicly acknowledged, or socially supported

8. Bereavement overload occurs when:
   a. There is the loss of a loved one that cannot be openly acknowledged or publicly mourned
   b. The loss is a significant loved one
   c. There are multiple losses and the accumulating sorrow in the lives of some elderly people
   d. The survivor experiences significant physical and mental distress

9. After her husband died, Sue began to experience a loss of appetite, an inability to sleep at night, and was unable to concentrate. She may be experiencing:
   a. Bereavement
   b. Mourning
   c. Denial
   d. Grief

10. Grief work is:
   a. The process of integrating the reality of the loss with everyday life and learning to feel better
   b. The total acceptance that a loved one has died
   c. Assigning feelings to the loss of a loved one
   d. Completing the cultural rituals that are required to express one's grief

11. To help children cope, it is important to:
   a. Give children the opportunity to attend the funeral
   b. Encourage the expression of feelings
   c. Provide convincing assurance that there will be somebody to love and look after the child
   d. All of the above

12. All of the following are characteristics of hospice programs, *except*:
   a. Services are provided by only specially trained nurses
   b. Emphasis is placed on symptom control, primarily the alleviation of pain
   c. Coverage is provided 24 hours a day, seven days per week
   d. Care of the family extends through the bereavement period

13. Prior to disposition of the body, the part of the funeral ritual in which the deceased may be displayed to formalize last respects and increase social support to the bereaved is called:
   a. A wake
   b. A viewing
   c. A memorial service
   d. Both a and b

14. While people react differently to losses:
   a. Most people experience a release of joy when a loved one dies
   b. Few people have physical symptoms in response to their loss
   c. People who have a stronger social support system tend to progress through the progression of grief more smoothly
   d. Most people recall all of the good and bad things that the deceased did to them

15. Kerri's grandmother is been very sick and wants to die. Her family has agreed to withhold treatment that may prolong her life. This is called:
   a. Rational suicide
   b. Self-deliverance
   c. Passive euthanasia
   d. Active euthanasia

23 Environmental Health

General Review Questions

1. What environmental concerns arise as global population continues to expand?
2. List the six primary sources of indoor air pollution.
3. What are the global environmental consequences of rapid deforestation in Central and South America, Africa, and Southeast Asia?
4. What are the sources of nonpoint pollution?
5. List three ways that our society can manage solid waste.

Practice Test #1

1. The United Nations projects that the world population will grow to _____ in the year 2000:
   a. 5.7 billion
   b. 6.1 billion
   c. 7.5 billion
   d. 10 billion

2. What course(s) of action for controlling population growth are advocated by proponents?
   a. Zero population growth
   b. Limit family size to only one offspring per couple
   c. Limit family size to only two offspring per couple
   d. Both a and c

3. Sulfur dioxide, a yellowish-brown gas, can:
   a. Aggravate heart and lung disease
   b. Corrode metals
   c. Impair visibility
   d. All of the above

4. The principle source of hydrocarbons is(are):
   a. Automobile engines
   b. Industrial paints
   c. Coal-burning plants
   d. All of the above

5. A weather condition occurring when a layer of cool air is trapped under a layer of warmer air and prevents the air from circulating, is called:
   a. Greenhouse effect
   b. Ozone
   c. Temperature inversion
   d. Photochemical smog

6. Precipitation that has fallen through acidic air pollutants, particularly those containing sulfur dioxides and nitrogen dioxides is known as:
   a. Ozone
   b. Acid rain
   c. Photochemical smog
   d. Temperature inversion

7. A substance that separates into stringy fibers, lodges in lungs and can cause lung cancer is:
   a. Asbestos
   b. Particulate matter
   c. Radon
   d. Formaldehyde

8. Chlorofluorocarbons, chemicals that contribute to the depletion of the ozone layer, are found in:
   a. Refrigerators
   b. Air conditioners
   c. Various foam products
   d. All of the above

9. How much of the earth is covered with water?
   a. 15%
   b. 45%
   c. 60%
   d. 75%

10. Industrial chemicals that can cause cancer and are used in high voltage electrical equipment, such as transformers, are known as:
    a. Dioxins
    b. Polychlorinated biphenyls (PCBs)
    c. Pesticides
    d. Trichlorethylene (TCE)

11. Municipal solid waste contains:
    a. Containers and packaging
    b. Durable goods
    c. Industrial wastes
    d. All of the above

12. The only way to reduce air pollution significantly is:
    a. Increase reliance on alternative energy sources such as windmills
    b. To ban the use of chlorofluorocarbons
    c. To require that all automobiles be converted to electricity
    d. Shift away from automobiles as the primary source of transportation

13. The recommended maximum "safe" dosage of radiation is:
    a. 0.5 rads to 5 rads per year
    b. 2.5 rads to 35 rads per year
    c. 50 rads to 60 rads per year
    d. 100 rads to 200 rads per year

14. Radiation produced by photons having energy high enough to ionize atoms is called:
    a. Radioactive emissions
    b. Nuclear energy
    c. Fission
    d. Ionizing radiation

15. The most predominant greenhouse gas is:
    a. Lead
    b. Formaldehyde
    c. Carbon dioxide
    d. Chlorofluorocarbons

Practice Test #2

1. The bulk of population growth is in:
    a. Eastern Europe
    b. Developing countries in urban areas
    c. The South American rain forests
    d. The United States

2. The reason large families are desired in many developing countries is:
    a. High infant mortality rates
    b. Children are viewed as "social security"
    c. The low economic status of women
    d. All of the above

3. The single biggest contributor towards zero population growth is:
    a. Institutionalized birth control with methods such as Depo-provera and Norplant
    b. Mass sterilization
    c. Education
    d. Abortion

4. The single greatest source of acid rain in the United States is:
    a. Coal-fired power plants
    b. Motor vehicle exhaust
    c. Chemical pollutants
    d. Wood stove smoke

5. Exposure to formaldehyde can cause which of the following health problems?
    a. Respiratory problems
    b. Fatigue
    c. Cancer
    d. All of the above

6. The most noticeable adverse effect(s) of exposure to smog is(are):
    a. Difficulty breathing
    b. Burning eyes
    c. Nausea
    d. All of the above

7. Chemicals that are designed to kill insects, rodents, plants, and fungi are called:
    a. Pesticides
    b. Polychlorinated biphenyls
    c. Dioxins
    d. Benzene

8. Chemicals that contribute to the depletion of the ozone layer are called:
    a. Ozone
    b. Chlorofluorocarbons
    c. Hydrocarbons
    d. Carbon monoxide

9. Which of the following is *not* a greenhouse gas?
    a. Carbon dioxide
    b. Radon
    c. Ground level ozone
    d. Methane

10. The two major categories of point source pollutants are:
    a. Sewage treatment plants and landfills
    b. Sewage treatment plants and industrial facilities
    c. Acid mine leakage and landfills
    d. Industrial facilities and landfills

11. The most common way to detect the presence of petroleum products in the water supply is:
    a. To test for benzene
    b. To test for leaching in groundwater
    c. To calculate the number of miscarriages and cancer cases in the community
    d. To test for carbon monoxide

12. Long-term exposure to pesticides has been linked to:
    a. Birth defects
    b. Liver and kidney damage
    c. Nervous system disorders
    d. All of the above

13. A symptom of noise-related distress is:
    a. Decreased blood pressure
    b. Increased productivity
    c. Decreased cholesterol levels
    d. Increased secretion of adrenaline

14. Solid waste that, due to its toxic properties, poses a health hazard to humans or to the environment is called:
    a. Municipal waste
    b. Environmental waste
    c. Hazardous waste
    d. Toxic waste

15. The most dangerous type of radiation is:
    a. Alpha particles
    b. Beta particles
    c. Gamma rays
    d. All of the above are equally dangerous

24 Consumerism

General Review Questions

1. Differentiate between nonprofit and proprietary hospitals.
2. What are examples of common ambulatory facilities?
3. List the major problems with the health care system that have lead to change.
4. What is the impact associated with the lack of health insurance?
5. Describe the three major types of HMOs.

Practice Test #1

1. What is the single greatest difficulty that we face as health care consumers?
   a. The limited number of physicians who will accept new patients
   b. Being reimbursed by insurance companies and limited coverage
   c. The sheer magnitude of choices available to consumers
   d. Not knowing the adverse and often unforeseeable effects of medical treatments

2. It is important to seek medical care if experiencing:
   a. Any serious accident or injury
   b. Tingling sensation in the arm accompanied by slurring speech or impaired thought processes
   c. Unexplained sudden weight loss
   d. All of the above

3. A medical practitioner who treats routine ailments, advises on preventive care, gives general medical advice, and makes appropriate referrals when necessary is called a(n):
   a. General practitioner
   b. Family primary provider
   c. Primary care practitioner
   d. Primary family physician

4. Medical alternatives to traditional medicine are called:
   a. Allopathic medicine
   b. Nonallopathic medicine
   c. Managed medicine
   d. Allied medicine

5. A midlevel practitioner trained to handle most standard cases of care is called a:
   a. Physician's assistant
   b. Nurse practitioner
   c. Licensed practical nurse
   d. Physician's Assistant

6. Medical alternatives to traditional medicine are known as:
   a. Allopathic medicine
   b. Primary medicine
   c. Nonallopathic medicine
   d. Chiropractic medicine

7. The type of medical practice in which a physician renders care to patients independently of other practitioners is called:
   a. Group practice
   b. Single specialty group practice
   c. Solo practitioner
   d. Both a and b

8. Treatments or services that do not require an overnight stay in a hospital are called:
   a. Ambulatory care
   b. Proprietary services
   c. Outpatient care
   d. Both a and c

9. When a private hospital (for-profit) hospital transfers a patient who is unable to pay to a public hospital, this is called:
   a. Skimming
   b. Patient dumping
   c. GOMERS
   d. Bumping

10. Hospitals run by religious or other humanitarian groups that reinvest their earnings in the hospital to improve health care are called:
    a. Health maintenance organizations
    b. Outpatient care centers
    c. For-profit hospitals
    d. Nonprofit hospitals

11. Medicaid provides coverage for:
    a. Elderly over 65 years of age
    b. All people total and permanently disabled
    c. All people with end-stage renal failure
    d. All of the above

12. Physicians who belong to a Preferred Provider Organization are:
    a. Usually reimbursed on a discounted fee-for-service basis
    b. Do not need to participate in utilization reviews
    c. Must restrict their practice to only patients on the insurance plan
    d. Are only reimbursed at 50-60% of the cost of services

13. George has a suspicious growth on his back that his doctor wants to have biopsied. What type of ambulatory facility will he most likely go to for his biopsy?
    a. An emergency center
    b. A surgicenter
    c. A hospital
    d. A cancer treatment center

14. Health insurance is built on the concept of:
    a. Health care is the right of all people
    b. Spreading the risk among a large, diverse group of people
    c. Reducing the risk of catastrophic illness
    d. Providing quality health care coverage for a reasonable cost

15. Rosa is a college student who works part-time and has limited health insurance through her student fees. She only makes about $13,000 a year. If she has to have her appendix removed, it could cost about $7,000. At this point in her life, Rosa is:
    a. Not insured
    b. Underinsured
    c. Overinsured
    d. Doesn't need insurance

Practice Test #2

1. Amanda is having trouble seeing and needs to have new glasses. She would most likely visit an:
   a. Orthodontist
   b. Optometrist
   c. Ophthalmologist
   d. Orthopedist

2. As a result of an automobile accident, Huang had a broken jaw that will require extensive surgical procedures. He will most likely need to see a(n)
   a. Dentist
   b. Orthodontist
   c. Orthopedic surgeon
   d. Oral surgeon

3. Informed consent is the right to have understandable information about:
   a. Side effects of the medical treatment
   b. Benefits of the medical treatment
   c. Available options to the medical treatment
   d. All of the above

4. A medical practice based on scientifically validated methods and procedures whose objective is to heal by countering the patient's symptoms is considered:
   a. Allopathic medicine
   b. Nonallopathic medicine
   c. Osteopathic medicine
   d. Chiropractic medicine

5. A nonallopathic practice that is based on the medicinal qualities of plants or herbs and is based on the theory that the administration of extremely diluted doses of potent natural agents that produce disease symptoms in healthy persons will cure the disease in the sick is called:
   a. Osteopathic medicine
   b. Homeopathic medicine
   c. Chiropractic medicine
   d. Orthopedic medicine

6. Herbal medicine, massage, megavitamins, and energy healing are all types of:
   a. Allopathic medicine
   b. Placebos
   c. Complimentary medicine
   d. Chiropractic medicine

7. All of the following are true about nonprofit hospitals, *except*:
   a. They are traditionally run by religious or other humanitarian groups
   b. They routinely transfer indigent or uninsured patients to public hospitals
   c. They generally reinvest their earnings in the hospital for the purpose of improving health care
   d. They have often cared for patients whether or not they could pay

8. Hospitals that provide a return on earnings to the investors who own them are called:
   a. Group practices
   b. Nonprofit hospitals
   c. For-profit hospitals
   d. Ambulatory care centers

9. In recent years, how much of the gross domestic produce (GDP) has been spent on health care?
   a. 5%
   b. 15%
   c. 20%
   d. 35%

10. A Chinese medical treatment that has been shown to improve quality of life and improve or cure certain health conditions is:
    a. Massage
    b. Accupressure
    c. Homeopathy
    d. Herbal medicine

11. To be sure that you will have a high likelihood of obtaining quality care, you should use a hospital that is:
    a. Registered with the American Medical Association
    b. Accredited by the Joint Commission on the Accreditation of Healthcare Organizations
    c. Uses only Registered Nurses to care for their patients
    d. Provides a wide array of medical services, including a 24-hour anesthesiologist

12. A type of health insurance that provides a wide range of covered health benefits for a fixed amount prepaid by the employee, employer, or Medicare is called:
    a. A prepaid group practice
    b. A health maintenance organization
    c. A preferred provider organization
    d. A public plan insurance

13. Ophthalmologists specialize in the medical and surgical care of:
    a. The eyes
    b. The heart and blood vessels
    c. The female reproductive system
    d. Cancerous growths and tumors

14. Cost-control procedures used by health insurers to coordinate treatment are called:
    a. Managed care
    b. Deductibles
    c. Copayments
    d. Coinsurance

15. The type of medical practice in which a group of physicians combine resources, sharing offices, equipment, and staff costs is called:
    a. Solo practice
    b. Group practice
    c. Fee-for-service practice
    d. For-profit practice

Appendix A Injury Prevention and Emergency Care

General Review Questions

1. What is the "Good Samaritan Law?"
2. What are the symptoms of internal bleeding?
3. What population is at greatest risk of poisoning?
4. When does frostbite generally occur?
5. List the symptoms of hypothermia.

Practice Test #1

1. Which of the following questions should you be prepared to answer when calling for emergency assistance?
   a. Where are you and the victim located?
   b. Do you know the victim's name?
   c. What is the victim's apparent condition?
   d. All of the above

2. If a victim is unconscious:
   a. You must obtain the victim's consent in writing before administering first aid
   b. You must make every reasonable effort to persuade the victim to accept your help
   c. In emergency situations, consent is implied
   d. You should wait until the victim regains consciousness to obtain consent

3. Unintentional injuries are the leading cause of death for Americans:
   a. Over the age of 65
   b. Between the ages of 55-65
   c. Between the ages of 45-55
   d. Under the age of 45

4. Failure to expel an obstructed object and restore breathing can lead to death in:
   a. 30 seconds
   b. 2 minutes
   c. 6 minutes
   d. 12 minutes

5. The most effective method for assisting a choking victim is:
   a. Abdominal thrusts
   b. Heimlich maneuver
   c. Rescue breathing
   d. Cardiopulmonary resuscitation

6. If you suspect that someone is suffering from internal bleeding, which of the following steps should you take?
   a. Have the person lie on a flat surface with knees bent
   b. Keep the victim warm
   c. Do not give the victim any medications or fluids
   d. All of the above

7. Victims of shock display all of the following symptoms, except:
   a. Dilated pupils
   b. Dry, hot skin
   c. Vomiting
   d. Delayed or unrelated responses to questions

8. The majority of poisonings reported in the United States each year are caused by:
   a. Household products
   b. Gasoline
   c. Swimming pool chemicals
   d. Prescription drugs

9. Injuries that result when ligaments and others tissues around a joint are stretched or torn are called:
   a. Fractures
   b. Strains
   c. Sprains
   d. Ruptures

10. A head injury can result from:
    a. An auto accident
    b. A fall
    c. An assault
    d. All of the above

11. A significant factors in many drowning cases is:
    a. Alcohol
    b. Exhaustion
    c. Sun exposure
    d. Hypothermia

12. Victims of heatstroke may have all of the following symptoms, except:
    a. Hot, dry, flushed skin
    b. Disorientation
    c. High body temperature
    d. Low blood pressure

13. The heat related injury that results from excessive loss of salt and water is:
    a. Hyperthermia
    b. Heat exhaustion
    c. Heat stroke
    d. Hyperexhaustion

14. The most painful heat-related injury is:
    a. Hyperthermia
    b. Heat stroke
    c. Heat cramps
    d. Heat exhaustion

15. If you provide first aid to a victim of hypothermia, you should do all of the following, except:
    a. Make sure the person is evenly warmed using blankets, heating pads or hot water bottles
    b. Give the victim alcohol or caffeinated beverages
       to warm them
    c. Replace wet clothing
    d. Do not allow the victim to exercise

Practice Test #2

1. The risk of dying in an auto crash is highest among:
   a. Drivers 16-24 years of age
   b. Drivers 25-34 years of age
   c. Drivers 45-54 years of age
   d. Drivers 55 years of age and older

2. When someone stops breathing, you should:
   a. Perform mouth-to-mouth resuscitation
   b. Begin cardiopulmonary resuscitation
   c. Proceed with the Heimlich maneuver
   d. Apply pressure to the abdominal area

3. The number of breaths given in rescue breathing to a child is to :
   a. Two breaths every three seconds
   b. Two breaths every five seconds
   c. One breath every four seconds
   d. One breath every ten seconds

4. The universal sign of distress related to choking is:
   a. Pain in the left arm
   b. Clasping of the throat with one or both hands
   c. Being unable to talk
   d. Clutching the chest over the heart

5. The method to control external bleeding that involves applying firm pressure by covering the wound with sterile dressing, bandage, or clean cloth is called:
   a. Direct pressure
   b. Indirect pressure
   c. Use of pressure points
   d. Elevation

6. For minor burns caused by fire or scalding water, the best treatment is to:
   a. Apply running water or cold compresses for 20-30 minutes
   b. Put butter or grease on the burn
   c. Apply typical burn ointments to the burned areas
   d. Apply aloe vera to the burn

7. A condition in which the cardiovascular system fails to provide sufficient blood circulation to all parts of the body is called:
   a. Heart attack
   b. Stroke
   c. Shock
   d. Cardiovascular obstruction

8. When your car breaks down, you should:
   a. Try to get off the road as far as possible
   b. Set out flares or reflective triangles
   c. Stay in your car until a law enforcement officer arrives
   d. All of the above

9. A break in the bone, including chips, cracks, splinters, and complete breaks, are called:
   a. Fractures
   b. Sprains
   c. Strains
   d. Compound breaks

10. All head injuries can potentially lead to:
    a. Brain damage
    b. Cessation of breathing
    c. Cessation of pulse
    d. All of the above

11. For severe head injuries, it is important to:
    a. Check the airway for breathing
    b. Check for fluid flowing from the ears or nose
    c. Remove any objects imbedded in the person's skull
    d. Both a and b

12. A condition of generalized cooling of the body resulting from exposure to cold temperatures or immersion in cold water is called:
    a. Hyperthermia
    b. Hypothermia
    c. Frostbite
    d. Shock

13. Alcohol overdose is considered a medical emegency when:
    a. A person has an irregular heartbeat
    b. A person is in a coma
    c. A person has warm, moist skin
    d. Either a or b

14. To treat a victim of heat exhaustion, you should:
    a. Get the victim out of the sun
    b. Have the victim lie down flat with their feet elevated
    c. Replace lost fluids slowly and steadily
    d. All of the above

15. To relieve the symptoms of heat cramps, the victim should:
    a. Be immersed in cool water
    b. Drink electrolyte-rich beverages
    c. Be placed by a fan
    d. Drink alcohol or caffeinated beverages

Answers

CHAPTER 1

Answers to General Review Questions

1. Physical, Social, Mental, Emotional, Environmental, and Spiritual Health.
2. Prevention is taking positive actions now to avoid even becoming sick; primary, secondary, and tertiary prevention
3. Predisposing, enabling, and reinforcing factors.
4. Perceived seriousness of the health problem; perceived susceptibility to the health problem; cues to action.
5. Frequency, duration, seriousness, basis for problem behavior, antecedents.

Answers to Practice Test #1

1. C	6. A	11. A
2. B	7. C	12. B
3. B	8. A	13. D
4. D	9. D	14. A
5. D	10. C	15. A

Answers to Practice Test #2

1. A	6. C	11. B
2. D	7. D	12. B
3. B	8. D	13. D
4. B	9. A	14. A
5. C	10. D	15. D

CHAPTER 2

Answers to General Review Questions

1. They feel good about themselves, feel comfortable with other people, control tension and anxiety, able to meet the demands of life, curb hate and guilt, maintain a positive outlook, enrich the lives of others, cherish the things that make them smile, value diversity, and appreciate nature.
2. Violence; sexual, physical, or emotional abuse; negative behaviors; distrust; anger; dietary deprivation; drug abuse; parental discord; and, other negative characteristics are present; and love security, and unconditional trust are lacking.
3. Hereditary traits, hormonal functioning, physical health status, physical fitness level, and selected elements of mental and emotional health.
4. Family history of suicide, previous suicide attempts, excessive drug and alcohol use, prolonged depression, financial difficulties, serious illness in contemplator or loved ones.
5. Find a support group, complete required tasks, form realistic expectations, take/make time for self, maintain physical health, examine problems and seek help.

Answers to Practice Test #1

1. A	6. B	11. D
2. B	7. B	12. D
3. C	8. B	13. A
4. D	9. A	14. B
5. B	10. D	15. D

Answers to Practice Test #2

1. B	6. A	11. D
2. C	7. B	12. C
3. A	8. D	13. A
4. A	9. A	14. D
5. D	10. C	15. C

CHAPTER 3

Answers to General Review Questions

1. Alarm, Resistance, and Exhaustion.

2. Psychosocial factors such as changes, hassles, pressure, inconsistent goals and objectives, conflict, overload and burnout, environmental stressors (i.e., natural and man-made disasters), and self-imposed stress.
3. Hard-driving, competitive, anxious, time-driven, extremely impatient, angry, and perfectionistic.
4. Control, commitment, and challenge.
5. Increases the predictability of stressful events, fosters coping skills, generates self-talking, encourages confidence about successful outcomes, builds a commitment to personal action and responsibility for an adaptive course of action.

Answers to Practice Test #1

1. D	6. D	11. A
2. C	7. A	12. A
3. C	8. A	13. C
4. D	9. D	14. A
5. B	10. D	15. D

Answers to Practice Test #2

1. A	6. D	11. A
2. C	7. D	12. A
3. A	8. D	13. D
4. B	9. C	14. B
5. B	10. A	15. C

CHAPTER 4

Answers to General Review Questions

1. Tension building, Acute battering, Remorse/reconciliation.
2. Poverty, unemployment, hopelessness, lack of education, inadequate housing, poor parental role models, cultural beliefs that objectify women and empower men to act as aggressors, lack of social support systems, discrimination, ignorance about people who are different, religious self-righteousness, breakdowns in the criminal justice system, stress and economic uncertainty.
3. Minimization, trivialization, blaming the victim, and "boys will be boys."

4. Gangs provide sense of belonging to a "family" and economic security.
5. Ask harasser to stop, document harassment, complain to a higher. (Remember that you have not done anything wrong.)

Answers to Practice Test #1

1. D	6. D	11. A
2. D	7. D	12. D
3. D	8. D	13. D
4. D	9. D	14. A
5. C	10. B	15. C

Answers to Practice Test #2

1. B	6. D	11. A
2. B	7. D	12. C
3. D	8. A	13. D
4. D	9. A	14. B
5. A	10. B	15. D

CHAPTER 5

Answers to General Review Questions

1. The sender has an idea, sender encodes the message, channel carries the message, receiver decodes the message, and the receiver sends feedback.
2. Differences in backgrounds; alcohol and drugs.
3. Language specialization, sociocultural differences, patient anxiety, and patient misinterpretation.
4. Mental barriers: inattention, prejudgment, frame of reference, closed-mindedness, faking listening. Physical and other barriers: hearing impairment, noisy surroundings, speaker's appearance, speaker's mannerisms, lag time.
5. Stop talking, work hard at listening, maintain an open mind, provide verbal and nonverbal feedback, paraphrase the speaker's ideas, take selective notes.

Answers to Practice Test #1

1. D	6. D	11. D
2. C	7. D	12. B

3. D	8. C	13. A
4. A	9. C	14. B
5. D	10. D	15. D

Answers to Practice Test #2

1. D	6. D	11. A
2. D	7. B	12. B
3. D	8. A	13. A
4. C	9. D	14. C
5. C	10. C	15. B

CHAPTER 6

Answers to General Review Questions

1. Approval and a sense of purpose in life, intimacy, social integration, nurturant; assistance reassurance or affirmation of our own worth.
2. All the characteristics of friendship (enjoyment, acceptance, trust, respect, mutual assistance, confiding, understanding, spontaneity) as well as fascination, exclusiveness, sexual desire, giving the utmost, being a champion, advocate.
3. Inhibited psychological growth rather than encouraging self-love, emotional expression, and individual growth.
4. Overdependence on the relationship, high value on sexual exclusivity, severity of the threat, low self-esteem, and fear of losing control.
5. While the reasons are numerous, such reasons include: tragedies such as the death of a child, serious illness of one's partner, severe financial reverses, career failure, breakdown in communication and cooperation between partners, unmet expectations regarding marriage itself or personal roles within the marriage.

Answers to Practice Test #1

1. C	6. B	11. B
2. B	7. D	12. A
3. A	8. D	13. D
4. A	9. D	14. D

5. A	10. B	15. B

Answers to Practice Test #2

1. D	6. A	11. A
2. B	7. B	12. B
3. D	8. D	13. B
4. D	9. D	14. B
5. C	10. B	15. B

CHAPTER 7

Answers to General Review Questions

1. Females: breast development, enlargement of external genitalia, growth of pubic hair, deposits of fat on hips and buttocks, and fine-textured skin and body hair. Males: growth of facial and body hair, deepening of voice, broadening of shoulders, and harrowing of hips.
2. Excitement/arousal, plateau, orgasm, and resolution. In males: refractory.
3. Areas in the body that, when touched, lead to sexual arousal. Includes: genital and nongenital areas, such as earlobes, mouth, breasts, and inner thighs.
4. Any behavior is normal which (1) you both enjoy, (2) hurts nobody, (3) is not associated with anxiety, (4) does not cut down your scope.
5. Can reduce inhibitions to make sexual behaviors less stressful. As a depressant in quantity it can impair erection ability, arousal, and orgasm.

Answers to Practice Test #1

1. D	6. D	11. A
2. A	7. C	12. A
3. C	8. D	13. B
4. B	9. C	14. B
5. B	10. C	15. B

Answers to Practice Test #2

1. A	6. B	11. D
2. B	7. D	12. D

3. B	8. B	13. D
4. D	9. B	14. C
5. B	10. A	15. D

CHAPTER 8

Answers to General Review Questions

1. A viable egg, a viable sperm, and possible access to the egg by the sperm.
2. For early detection of fetal abnormalities and the identification of high-risk mothers and infants.
3. Missed period, breast tenderness, extreme fatigue, sleeplessness, emotional upset, nausea, and vomiting.
4. Suppresses ovulation, prevents growth of uterine lining, and thickens the cervical mucus.
5. Infection, incomplete abortion, excessive bleeding, and cervical and uterine trauma. Also, in second trimester abortions: increased risk of uterine perforation, bleeding, infection, and incomplete abortion because the uterine wall becomes thinner as the pregnancy progresses.

Answers to Practice Test #1

1. B	6. C	11. A
2. D	7. D	12. B
3. D	8. C	13. B
4. A	9. D	14. B
5. B	10. D	15. B

Answers to Practice Test #2

1. B	6. D	11. C
2. C	7. D	12. D
3. C	8. A	13. C
4. A	9. D	14. A
5. B	10. B	15. D

CHAPTER 9

Answers to General Review Questions

1. (1) The presence of an abstinence syndrome--withdrawal; (2) an association pattern of pathological behavior; (3) relapse.
2. Compulsion characterized by obsession; loss of control; negative consequences; and denial.
3. Biological, psychological, sociocultural, and environmental.
4. The need of self-value and fulfillment.
5. Highly structured programs that include wellness programs to teach self-care skills, educational programs to formulate a deep understanding of the addiction, self-help groups to provide a foundation of self-help after treatment and several forms (i.e., individual, family, and group) of therapy.

Answers to Practice Test #1

1. A	6. A	11. C
2. C	7. D	12. B
3. B	8. B	13. C
4. C	9. D	14. C
5. A	10. C	15. B

Answers to Practice Test #2

1. B	6. D	11. D
2. B	7. D	12. D
3. A	8. C	13. A
4. C	9. D	14. C
5. B	10. B	15. D

CHAPTER 10

Answers to General Review Questions

1. Receptor site theory: Drugs attach themselves to specific receptor sites in the body.
2. Set and Setting.
3. Drugs that restrain the production and release of prostaglandin hormones associated with arthritis or menstrual pain. Examples: ibuprofen (Motrin) and sodium naprosyn (Anaprox).

4. Severe withdrawal effects experienced by users of stimulants. Withdrawal symptoms include depression, nausea, irritability, violent behavior, headaches, nausea, and deep fatigue.
5. Know the product, read the label, follow the instructions precisely.

Answers to Practice Test #1

1. B	6. A	11. A
2. A	7. C	12. D
3. B	8. C	13. A
4. B	9. D	14. B
5. A	10. C	15. C

Answers to Practice Test #2

1. A	6. C	11. A
2. B	7. C	12. D
3. A	8. C	13. D
4. C	9. D	14. C
5. B	10. D	15. A

CHAPTER 11

Answers to General Review Questions

1. The alcohol concentration in the drink, the amount of alcohol consumed, the amount of food in the stomach, pylorospasm, and the person's mood.
2. Impairs the body's ability to recognize and fight foreign bodies such as bacteria and viruses.
3. An inability to develop social attachments, a need to be in control of all emotions and situations, low self-esteem, and depression.
4. $117 billion
5. When they have a turning point or dramatic occurrence: a spouse walks out, taking children and possessions; the boss issues an ultimatum; a courtroom judge offers the alternatives or prison or a treatment; when confronted by a friend or colleague.

Answers to Practice Test #1

1. C	6. C	11. A
2. B	7. C	12. C
3. A	8. C	13. A
4. A	9. C	14. B
5. D	10. D	15. C

Answers to Practice Test #2

1. A	6. D	11. A
2. A	7. D	12. B
3. D	8. C	13. D
4. C	9. D	14. D
5. B	10. D	15. C

CHAPTER 12

Answers to General Review Questions

1. Particulate matter, tar, benzopyrene, phenol, carbon monoxide, hydrogen cyanide, and hydrocarbons.
2. Increased heart and respiratory rate, constriction of blood vessels, increased blood pressure, decreased stomach contractions, decreased blood sugar levels, decreased sensation of the taste buds, reduction in appetite.
3. Color changes or lumps inside the lips; white, smooth or scaly patches in the mouth or on the neck, lips, or tongue; a red spot or sore on the lips or gums or inside the mouth that does not heal in two weeks; repeatedly bleeding in the mouth, difficulty or abnormality in speaking or swallowing.
4. Aversion therapy (pairs the act of smoking with some sort of noxious stimulus so that smoking itself is perceived as unpleasant); operant strategies (Pairs the act of smoking with an external stimulus); Self-control (identifies specific situations and teaching smokers the skills necessary to resist smoking).
5. It does not appear to be linked to high blood pressure, strokes, or heart disease. However, people who suffer from irregular heartbeat should be cautions. Coffee can contribute to ulcers and has been linked with fibrocystic breast cancer.

Answers to Practice Test #1

1. C	6. D	11. D
2. C	7. C	12. A
3. B	8. D	13. D
4. A	9. D	14. A
5. A	10. C	15. D

Answers to Practice Test #2

1. A	6. D	11. B
2. B	7. B	12. D
3. C	8. C	13. D
4. C	9. D	14. A
5. B	10. D	15. D

CHAPTER 13

Answers to General Review Questions

1. A person's age, gender, genetic background, physiology, personality, experiences, and expectations are all factors.
2. Brain damage, heart defects, kidney problems, and malformed heads, arms and fingers. They seem to be unable to respond or relate to people the way normal babies do, they are difficult to console and comfort. They have a significant increase in the risk of crib death.
3. Slightly increased heart rate, elevated blood pressure and temperature, goose flesh, increased reflex speeds, muscle tremors and twitches, perspiration, increased salivation, chills, headaches, and mild nausea. Can cause uterine muscle contractions and lead to premature labor and miscarriage in pregnant women.
4. Young men to increase their strength, power, bulk, and speed.
5. Multimodal approach.

Answers to Practice Test #1

1. C	6. D	11. D
2. B	7. C	12. D
3. B	8. B	13. B

4. B	9. A	14. B
5. A	10. C	15. B

Answers to Practice Test #2

1. A	6. D	11. C
2. D	7. C	12. A
3. B	8. B	13. B
4. A	9. A	14. C
5. B	10. B	15. A

CHAPTER 14

Answers to General Review Questions

1. Sensory stimulation (i.e., smelling, seeing, tasting), social pressures (i.e., family traditions, social events), economic status, and cultural factors.
2. Proteins (12% of total calories), carbohydrates (48% of total calories from complex carbohydrates; 10% of total calories from simple carbohydrates), fats (no more than 30% of total calories), water, vitamins, minerals.
3. Vegans: avoid all food of animal origin; lacto-vegetarians: avoid flesh foods but eat dairy products; ovo-vegetarians: avoid flesh foods but eat eggs; lacto-ovo-vegetarians: avoid flesh foods but eat both dairy products and eggs; pesco-vegetarians: avoid meat but eat fish, diary products, and eggs; semivegetarians eat chicken, fish, dairy products, and eggs.
4. Depending on the contaminant eaten, symptoms vary tremendously. Symptoms may appear as early as a half hour after eating or they may take several days or weeks to develop. In most people, they come on 5-8 hours after eating and last only a day or two.
5. Buy fruits and vegetables in season; use coupons and specials; shop at discount warehouse food chains; plan ahead to avoid extra trips to store; purchase meats and other products in volume; cook large meals and freeze smaller portions; drain off fat.

Answers to Practice Test #1

1. A	6. B	11. C
2. C	7. C	12. A
3. A	8. B	13. D
4. C	9. C	14. D
5. D	10. B	15. D

Answers to Practice Test #2

1. C	6. B	11. A
2. D	7. C	12. D
3. A	8. D	13. B
4. C	9. B	14. C
5. B	10. D	15. D

CHAPTER 15

Answers to General Review Questions

1. Television, movies, magazines, beautiful models, athletic male superstars, warnings of the dangers of obesity from legitimate health organizations.
2. Ectomorphic: tall, slender frames, generally experience few difficulties with weight control; Endomorphic: rounded, soft appearance, often with a large abdomen and typically a history of weight problems beginning in childhood; Mesomorphic: shorter, more muscular, athletic-looking, tendency to gain weight later in life.
3. The thyroid gland produces a hormone that regulates metabolism. While many people feel that an underactive thyroid impeded their ability to burn calories, most authorities agree that only 3-5% of the obese population have a thyroid problem.
4. The amount of muscle mass moved, the amount of weight being moved, and the amount of time the activity takes.
5. Determine what triggers your eating behavior, change your triggers, set realistic goals, seek assistance from reputable sources in selecting a dietary plan that is easy to follow and includes adequate amounts of the basic nutrients.

Answers to Practice Test #1

1. B	6. B	11. C

2. B	7. B	12. A
3. C	8. B	13. D
4. C	9. A	14. B
5. B	10. C	15. A

Answers to Practice Test #2

1. B	6. B	11. D
2. C	7. B	12. A
3. B	8. C	13. B
4. A	9. B	14. D
5. B	10. B	15. B

CHAPTER 16

Answers to General Review Questions

1. Physical activity is any force exerted by skeletal muscles that results in energy usage above the level used when the body's systems are at rest.
2. Cardiorespiratory endurance, flexibility, muscular strength and endurance, body composition.
3. Calculated as the percentage of maximum heart rate (220) minus age; heart rate (pulse) taken during aerobic exercise to check of exercise intensity is at the desired level (i.e., 70 percent of maximum heart rate).
4. Tai chi and yoga.
5. RICE: Rest, ice, compression, and elevation.

Answers to Practice Test #1

1. C	6. C	11. A
2. C	7. D	12. B
3. B	8. A	13. B
4. D	9. C	14. A
5. D	10. D	15. B

1. D	6. B	11. C
2. B	7. D	12. B
3. D	8. D	13. A
4. C	9. C	14. C
5. A	10. C	15. B

CHAPTER 17

Answers to General Review Questions

1. Heredity, age, obesity, smoking, exercise, cholesterol levels, gender, systolic and diastolic blood pressure, stress, present heart disease symptoms, past personal history, diabetes.
2. Heredity, age, gender, and race.
3. Rest, drugs that affect: 1) the blood supply to the heart muscle and 2) the heart's demand for oxygen.
4. Kidney disease, obesity, or tumors of the adrenal glands.
5. Physicians may often be gender-biased in their delivery of health care, physicians tend to view male heart disease as a more severe problem, and women decline major procedures more often than men do.

Answers to Practice Test #1

1. C	6. C	11. B
2. D	7. D	12. D
3. C	8. B	13. D
4. D	9. A	14. C
5. A	10. B	15. B

Answers to Practice Test #2

1. B	6. A	11. D
2. A	7. B	12. B
3. C	8. C	13. C
4. A	9. A	14. D
5. B	10. C	15. B

CHAPTER 18

Answers to General Review Questions

1. Culturally influenced values and belief systems, socioeconomic status, lack of health insurance or lack of transportation.
2. Persistent cough, blood streaked sputum, chest pain, and recurrent attacks of pneumonia or bronchitis.
3. A: Asymmetry, half of the mole does not match the other half; B: Border irregularity, the edges are ragged, notched, or blurred; C: Color, pigmentation is not uniform; D: Diameter greater than six millimeters.
4. Magnetic resonance imagery uses magnetic fields, radio waves, and computers; computerized axial tomography uses radiation to view internal organs not normally visible by x-rays.
5. Stop smoking; avoid excessive sunlight; avoid excessive alcohol consumption, do not use smokeless tobacco; properly monitor estrogen use; avoid excessive radiation exposure; avoid occupational exposures to carcinogens; control your diet.

Answers to Practice Test #1

1. B	6. B	11. A
2. A	7. D	12. D
3. C	8. D	13. A
4. B	9. D	14. A
5. D	10. B	15. A

Answers to Practice Test #2

1. B	6. C	11. B
2. D	7. A	12. D
3. B	8. C	13. C
4. A	9. C	14. C
5. B	10. A	15. A

CHAPTER 19

Answers to General Review Questions

1. Susceptible host, disease agent, and environment. In addition, heredity, age, environmental conditions, and lifestyle.
2. Direct contact, indirect contact, food-borne infection, animal-borne infection, and water-borne infection.
3. Bacteria - Toxic shock syndrome, strep throat, tuberculosis; Viruses - common cold, influenza, hepatitis; Rickettsia - Rocky Mountain spotted fever, typhus; Fungi - Candidiasis, athlete's foot, ringworm; Protozoa - Trichomoniasis, giardiasis; Parasitic Worms - tapeworms, pinworms.
4. Skin; mucous membranes in the respiratory track and other linings of the body; cilia; tears, nasal secretions, ear wax, and other secretions found at the body's entrances.
5. Women, especially African-American women, followed by white and then Latina women.

Answers to Practice Test #1

1. C	6. B	11. C
2. D	7. D	12. D
3. B	8. A	13. B
4. D	9. B	14. C
5. D	10. A	15. C

Answers to Practice Test #2

1. B	6. A	11. A
2. C	7. D	12. C
3. D	8. A	13. B
4. D	9. B	14. A
5. B	10. D	15. B

CHAPTER 20

Answers to General Review Questions

1. Molds, animal dander (hair and dead skin), pollen, ragweed, or dust.

2. Female, fat, fair, forty, and flatulent.
3. Between ages 20 and 45; women lifting heavy objects quickly; very tall and overweight or lanky body types; poor posture; lower overall trunk strength and total level of fitness and conditioning; psychological factors including depression, apathy, inattentiveness, boredom, emotional upsets, drug abuse, and family and financial problems; occupations such as truck drivers and materials handlers; smokers or persons with chronic coughs.
4. Major criteria: debilitating fatigue that persists for at least six months, ad the absence of diagnosis of other illnesses that could cause the symptoms; minor criteria: headaches, fever, sore throat, painful lymph nodes, weakness, fatigue after exercise, sleep problems, and rapid onset of these symptoms.
5. Eyestrain and discomfort in the low back, neck, shoulders, and wrists; possible radiation exposure, especially for pregnant women and their fetuses; carpal tunnel syndrome.

Answers to Practice Test #1

1. C	6. C	11. C
2. B	7. C	12. A
3. A	8. C	13. C
4. B	9. C	14. B
5. D	10. A	15. D

Answers to Practice Test #2

1. D	6. A	11. A
2. C	7. D	12. D
3. B	8. C	13. B
4. B	9. D	14. C
5. D	10. D	15. D

CHAPTER 21

Answers to General Review Questions

1. Erik Erikson and Robert Peck emphasized adaptation and adjustment as related to self-development. Erikson stated that people must progress through eight critical stages during their

life-times. Peck focuses on the critical issues of middle and old age. Key to both theories is the age-related factors of lifelong behavior patterns.

2. Taste declines; salivary glands secrete less fluid; and the ability to distinguish sweet, sour, bitter, and salty tastes diminishes.

3. Gender, age, low bone mass, early menopause, thin, small-framed body, race, lack of calcium, lack of physical activity, cigarette smoking, alcohol and/or caffeine abuse, and heredity.

4. Given an appropriate length of time, elderly people may learn and develop skills in a similar manner to younger people. What elderly people may lack in speed of learning, they make up for in practical knowledge.

5. The elderly tend to take an increased number of drugs a day (est. 4-6 prescriptions/OTCs). The risk of adverse effects are greater for people with circulatory impairments and declining kidney and liver functions. Symptoms: bizarre behavior patterns or an appearance of being out of touch.

Answers to Practice Test #1

1. B	6. B	11. A
2. D	7. D	12. D
3. A	8. D	13. D
4. A	9. D	14. C
5. B	10. C	15. A

Answers to Practice Test #2

1. A	6. D	11. B
2. C	7. B	12. B
3. A	8. A	13. A
4. C	9. B	14. A
5. A	10. D	15. D

CHAPTER 22

Answers to General Review Questions

1. Irreversible cessation of circulatory and respiratory functions, or irreversible cessation of all functions of the entire brain, including the brainstem.

2. Resistance, life review, and transcendence.

3. Denial, anger, bargaining, depression, and acceptance.

4. Burial in the ground, entombment above the ground in a mausoleum, cremation, and anatomical donation.

5. Electrical or mechanical resuscitation of the heart, mechanical respiration by machine, nasogastric tube feedings, intravenous nutrition, gastrostomy, medications to treat life-threatening infections.

Answers to Practice Test #1

1. C	6. B	11. C
2. D	7. C	12. A
3. C	8. C	13. D
4. C	9. D	14. B
5. C	10. A	15. A

Answers to Practice Test #2

1. B	6. C	11. C
2. D	7. C	12. A
3. B	8. C	13. D
4. C	9. D	14. C
5. A	10. A	15. C

CHAPTER 23

Answers to General Review Questions

1. Environmental degradation caused by loss of top-soil, pesticides, toxic residues, deforestation, global warming, air pollution, and acid rain.

2. Woodstoves, furnaces, asbestos, passive smoke, formaldehyde, and radon.

3. A rapid rise in the production of greenhouse gases. Trees transform carbon dioxide into oxygen.

4. Soil erosion and sedimentation, construction wastes, pesticide and fertilizer runoff, urban street runoff, wastes from engineering projects, acid mine drainage, leakage from septic tanks, and sewage sludge.

5. Recycle, reuse, and reduce.

Answers to Practice Test #1

1. B	6. B	11. D
2. D	7. A	12. D
3. D	8. D	13. A
4. A	9. D	14. D
5. C	10. B	15. C

Answers to Practice Test #2

1. B	6. D	11. A
2. A	7. A	12. D
3. C	8. B	13. D
4. A	9. B	14. C
5. D	10. B	15. C

CHAPTER 24

Answers to General Review Questions

1. Nonprofit hospitals generally reinvest their earnings in the hospital for improving health care and often care for patients whether they could pay or not. Proprietary hospitals do not receive tax breaks and provide far less charity care.
2. Surgicenters, freestanding emergency centers, urgicenters, freestanding imaging and diagnostic laboratory centers, trauma centers, and health clinics.
3. Cost, access, malpractice, unnecessary procedures, complicated and cumber-some insurance, and dramatic ranges in quality.
4. Delayed health care and increased mortality.
5. Reduced consumer administrative requirements; reduced utilization, especially of inpatient services; broader benefit structure, especially for preventive services; enhanced provider risk-sharing; and greater management control over providers and consumers.

Answers to Practice Test #1

1. C	6. C	11. D
2. D	7. C	12. A
3. C	8. D	13. B

4. D	9. B	14. B
5. A	10. D	15. B

Answers to Practice Test #2

1. B	6. C	11. D
2. C	7. B	12. B
3. D	8. B	13. B
4. A	9. B	14. A
5. B	10. B	15. B

APPENDIX A

Answers to General Review Questions

1. Laws that grant immunity (protection from civil liability if you act in good faith to provide care to the best of your ability, according to your level of training.
2. Symptoms of shock; coughing up or vomiting blood; blood in urine; black, tarlike stools; and, abdominal discomfort or pain (rigidity or spasms).
3. Children under the age of 5.
4. Temperatures below 32 degrees F.
5. Shivering; vague, slow, slurred speech; poor judgment; lethargy, or extreme exhaustion; slowed breathing and heartbeat; and, numbness and loss of feeling in extremities.

Answers to Practice Test #1

1. D	6. D	11. A
2. C	7. B	12. D
3. D	8. A	13. B
4. C	9. C	14. C
5. B	10. D	15. B

Answers to Practice Test #2

1. A	6. A	11. D
2. A	7. C	12. B
3. C	8. D	13. D
4. B	9. A	14. D
5. A	10. D	15. B